Uprooting Sexua
in Higher Education

With national conversation turned toward sexual assault on college campuses, knowing how to identify, prevent, and address these incidents in a safe and productive way is essential for administrators and faculty. *Uprooting Sexual Violence in Higher Education* provides colleges and universities with a foundational understanding of 12 risk factors related to sexual assault, stalking, and intimate partner violence. By presenting a blend of theory, research, and the personal reflections of professionals 'on the front lines,' this book provides insights into the motivations, attitudes, and behaviors behind sexual assault on campus, as well as strategies for mitigating these risk factors in an effort to tailor prevention efforts. Whether you are seeking a way to navigate the recent regulations on sexual violence from the federal government or wish to safeguard the welfare of students on your campus, this book will provide the necessary and invaluable foundation you need to empower, respect, and support all students.

Amy Murphy is Assistant Professor of Student Development and Leadership in Higher Education at Angelo State University and formerly the Dean of Students at Texas Tech University, USA.

Brian Van Brunt is Senior Vice President for Professional Program Development at the National Center for Higher Education Risk Management (NCHERM), USA.

Uprooting Sexual Violence in Higher Education

A Guide for Practitioners and Faculty

Amy Murphy and
Brian Van Brunt

Routledge
Taylor & Francis Group

NEW YORK AND LONDON

First published 2017
by Routledge
711 Third Avenue, New York, NY 10017

and by Routledge
2 Park Square, Milton Park, Abingdon, Oxon, OX14 4RN

Routledge is an imprint of the Taylor & Francis Group, an informa business

Library of Congress Cataloging-in-Publication Data
Names: Murphy, Amy (Amy L.), author. | Van Brunt, Brian, author.
Title: Uprooting sexual violence in higher education : a guide for practitioners and faculty / by Amy Murphy and Brian Van Brunt.
Description: New York : Routledge, 2017. | Includes bibliographical references.
Identifiers: LCCN 2016014447 (print) | LCCN 2016026310 (ebook) | ISBN 9781138960602 (hardback) | ISBN 9781138960626 (pbk.) | ISBN 9781315660240 (ebk.) | ISBN 9781315660240 (Ebook)
Subjects: LCSH: Rape in universities and colleges—United States—Prevention.
Classification: LCC LB2345.3.R37 M87 2017 (print) | LCC LB2345.3.R37 (ebook) | DDC 371.7/82—dc23
LC record available at https://lccn.loc.gov/2016014447

ISBN: 978-1-138-96060-2 (hbk)
ISBN: 978-1-138-96062-6 (pbk)
ISBN: 978-1-315-66024-0 (ebk)

Typeset in Sabon
by Apex CoVantage, LLC

Printed and bound in the United States of America by Publishers Graphics, LLC on sustainably sourced paper.

"I believe in bold and shattering commitment
to the problems of our times."
—Ignatius P. Reily,
A Confederacy of Dunces

"I wish we could turn back time to the good
old days when the mama sang us to sleep but
now we are stressed out."
—twenty-Øne pilØts, "Stressed Out"

"Push the envelope. Watch it bend."
—Maynard James Keenan,
Tool, "Lateralus"

Contents

Preface

A tree lives on its roots. If you change the root, you change the tree.
—*Jane Hirshfield*

A GUIDE FOR HIGHER EDUCATION PRACTITIONERS, ADMINISTRATORS, AND FACULTY

This book is written as a primer on the prevention of sexual violence for higher education practitioners, administrators, and faculty. We recognize many of you did not spend a great deal of time exploring the elements of sexual violence on college campuses in your bachelor's or master's programs. Whether you choose this book in response to the recent regulations on sexual violence from the federal government or merely wish to safeguard the welfare of students on your campus, the content is designed to provide you with a framework to approach this work. Our approach integrates research and theory from a variety of disciplines into a summarized set of 12 risk factors. These risk factors may then be infused in your education, prevention, and intervention efforts.

WHY UPROOTING SEXUAL VIOLENCE?

- Sexual violence is not only a series of incidents perpetrated by individuals but also an epidemic within our society that can be better prevented by addressing systemic attitudes and characteristics that support the reoccurrence of sexual violence.
- Primary prevention efforts are most effective when they focus on the root causes of sexual violence.

- Education and training must address actual, evidence-based risk factors for sexual violence and not those that instead shift the blame to victims or place the responsibility for prevention disproportionately on women.
- Sexual violence exists on college campuses because it manifests in part with other intermingled issues of concern often buried deep in the history and traditions of our institutions and organizations, eventually creeping to the surface in the behaviors and attitudes of both individuals and groups in our communities.
- Colleges and universities have a critical role in the prevention of sexual violence and the opportunity to impact the continued perpetuation of violence on our campuses. *Colleges and universities are required to be part of the prevention solution (see Title IX & Violence Against Women Act [VAWA] requirements ahead).*

TITLE IX AND SEXUAL VIOLENCE

If there was ever any doubt, it is now clear: sexual assault is a form of gender-based discrimination. Students experiencing incidents of sexual violence, particularly when the perpetrator is another student, are no longer able to access the educational environment in the same way. Title IX reminds us:

> No person in the United States shall, on the basis of sex, be excluded from participation in, be denied the benefits of, or be subjected to discrimination under any education program or activity receiving Federal financial assistance.

Title IX is a federal law that prohibits gender-based discrimination and harassment, including all forms of sexual violence, such as sexual assault, stalking, and interpersonal violence. Colleges and universities are required to be in compliance with Title IX and must do so regardless of the involvement of law enforcement or other criminal proceedings.

The enforcement body for Title IX is the Office of Civil Rights (OCR) in the Department of Education. According to OCR guidance, if the college or university knows or reasonably should know about harassment that creates a hostile environment involving a student or employee, it must take immediate corrective action stop the harassment, prevent its reoccurrence, and remedy the harm caused to individuals or the community.

Recent efforts have focused on how institutions respond to incidents of sexual violence. Title IX also requires the elimination and prevention of hostile environments for students, which means even after responding and assisting an individual victim, there is still work to do for the rest of campus. This book approaches sexual violence with a primary prevention framework and asks practitioners to consider instead the root factors of sexual violence and how to cultivate healthier attitudes and behaviors before incidents occur.

Think about a tree for a minute. How difficult it is to remove an unwanted tree? You can cut down the tree. You can add new landscaping and plant around where the tree was, but often the tree roots continue to grow beneath the surface and make their way into other areas. To kill the tree, the roots have to be eliminated.

For sexual violence to be prevented, campuses must identify where the root factors related to sexual violence are growing and work to eliminate those attitudes and behaviors. By planting new seeds to empower, respect, and support all students, the campus can become healthier even beyond incidents of sex and gender.

WHAT TO EXPECT IN THIS BOOK

We have divided this book into three parts. The first offers an introduction to the federal requirements under the Violence Against Women Act, a look at prevention and developmental theory, and a summation and rationalization for the creation of the 12 risk factors. The second part offers an in-depth review of the 12 risk factors, along with detailed suggestions on how to reduce the risk through education and prevention for each of these risk factors. The final section provides some deeper reflections from the authors related to assessing campus climate and understanding and teaching consent, and some concluding thoughts to aid readers moving forward with bringing these concepts back to their campus to better address the problem of sexual violence.

The following chapter will take a moment to ground our work in the VAWA Reauthorization Act as well as establishing a common language for the terminology we will use throughout the text. Chapter 3 offers an overview of prevention theories and methodologies, borrowing from the public health model as well as student development theory in order to ground our prevention work in the literature and research to improve its efficacy and effectiveness.

Starting in chapter 4, we describe each risk factor and provide examples for individuals and groups to get you thinking about how the risk factor might present on your campus. Then we follow with a section called "Reducing the Risk," which provides examples of how consideration of the factor can be integrated into various types of prevention initiatives on a college campus. Colleagues and experts from around the country also joined us to share information in "From the Front Lines" about each of the factors. These accounts give a subjective and personal reflection on the concepts discussed in each chapter. Chapters 15 and 16 focus on areas we felt were particularly important to comprehensive prevention plans—consent education and campus climate. We end the book with perspectives on the future directions of prevention work and the 12 risk factors.

Part I

Introduction

Chapter 1

Violence Against Women Act

Long after cutting down an unwanted tree and modifying your landscape, the tree roots can stay alive beneath the soil surface, sending suckers into unwanted garden areas. In order to prevent the tree suckers, you must first kill the tree's root system. After killing the root system, the roots begin to decompose in the soil, making it easier to dig and maintain flower beds in the surrounding area.

—*Amelia Allonsy,* How to Kill a Tree Root System

KEY TAKE-AWAYS

1. Title IX requires that colleges and universities work to prevent and eliminate hostile environments resulting from gender-based harassment and remedy the impact of harm to individuals and the community through education, prevention, and accountability initiatives.

2. The Violence Against Women Reauthorization Act of 2013 modified the Clery Act to require college and universities to implement strategies for students and employees related to the prevention of sexual assault, stalking, dating violence, and domestic violence.

3. Primary prevention requires the identification of root factors related to sexual violence and initiatives targeted toward associated attitudes and behaviors.

In the past few years, colleges and institutions have seen a rapid and intense focus on how to prevent sexual assault and violence on our campuses. It is important to recognize that counselors and psychologists, student conduct officers, health educators, and sexual assault advocates have long been working to reduce these problems on campus and serve those who struggle with the burden of recovery. Discussions of consent, the dangers of high-risk drinking, and negative attitudes toward women have been areas of attention and emphasis for many frontline staff and administrators.

Following the reauthorization of the Violence Against Women Act, increased federal and cultural attention has served as a springboard to bring these concerns to the forefront of higher education discussions. Schools panicked as they watched a number of their procedures and practices come under the microscope of OCR and the court of public opinion. Administrators redoubled efforts focused on prevention and looked to improve existing investigation processes for Title IX offenses.

The benefit of this increased attention has been a national investment in the intense review and development of better systems of awareness, education, and investigation of sexual assault on college campuses. As schools rush to comply with the educational requirements of VAWA and find ways to reduce sexual violence on their campuses, it would be reasonable to pause and better understand the contributing factors to this violence on our campuses. Before beginning on that journey, we wanted to take an opportunity to explain the impetus for the recent attention on these issues and build a foundation as we look to explore the root causes of this violence.

WHAT IS THE VIOLENCE AGAINST WOMEN ACT (VAWA)?

The Violence Against Women Reauthorization Act of 2013 (34 CFR § 668.46 [VAWA]) outlines obligations for colleges and universities in regard to the prevention of sexual violence through modification of the requirements of the Higher Education Act of 1965 (HEA) and the Jeanne Clery Disclosure of Campus Security Policy and Campus Crime Statistics Act (20 USC x 1092(f) [Clery Act]).

The major provisions of the new VAWA regulations include:

- increased reporting requirements related to incidents of dating violence, domestic violence, sexual assault, and stalking;
- procedural requirements for responding to incidents of sexual violence; and
- prevention programming for students and employees.

A section of VAWA called the Campus Sexual Violence Elimination Act (Campus SaVE Act) modified the Clery Act. The Clery Act, adopted in 1990, requires that colleges and universities collect and report crimes that occur on or adjacent to campus and disseminate an annual security report each October, as well as other requirements related to notifying the campus community of threats to the campus. Since its inception, the Clery Act required the collection of crime statistics, including rape, fondling, incest, and statutory rape. VAWA expanded the requirements for Clery crime reporting to include domestic violence, dating violence, and stalking. In addition, it added gender identity to the category of types of prejudice that can be reported as hate crimes. The annual security report requirements were further modified to require that institutions report on how they provide prevention programming for students and employees annually. Violations of the Clery and VAWA provisions can be penalized by fines of $35,000 per violation.

WHAT ARE THE PREVENTION PROGRAMMING REQUIREMENTS UNDER VAWA FOR COLLEGE AND UNIVERSITIES?

VAWA requires the development of primary prevention and awareness programs for incoming students and new employees and ongoing prevention and awareness campaigns for all students and employees to stop domestic violence, dating violence, sexual assault, and stalking. VAWA also outlines requirements for the programs to include statements of prohibition, definitions of "consent" in reference to sexual activity, other definitions based on local jurisdiction, descriptions of options for bystander intervention, information on risk reduction, and policies and procedures following an incident of sexual violence. Institutions must include program descriptions to meet this mandate in the Clery Annual Security Report, beginning with the reports published October 1, 2014.

While VAWA provides some definition and discussion around the types of programs and initiatives for institutions to implement, it was noted during the final rule making that research on effective prevention of sexual violence is limited. Schools are directed broadly that these efforts should be

comprehensive, intentional, and integrated programming, initiatives, strategies, and campaigns intended to end dating violence, domestic violence, sexual assault, and stalking that are culturally relevant, inclusive of diverse communities and identities, sustainable, responsive to community needs, and informed by research or assessed for value, effectiveness, or outcome.

(668.46(a))

VAWA specifically mentions an ecological model and prevention approach that considers environmental risk and protective factors for individuals, relationships, institutions, communities, and society, and identifies goals of decreasing perpetration and bystander inaction. We discuss prevention models in detail in chapter 3.

VAWA also outlines that prevention programs, initiatives, and strategies should include the following elements:

- Statement that the institution prohibits domestic violence, dating violence, sexual assault, and stalking;
- Definitions of domestic violence, dating violence, sexual assault, and stalking in the applicable jurisdiction;
- Definition of consent with regard to sexual activity, in the applicable jurisdiction;
- Safe and positive options for bystander intervention that may be carried out by an individual to prevent harm or intervene when there is a risk of domestic violence, dating violence, sexual assault, or stalking against a person other than such individual;
- Information on risk reduction to recognize warning signs of abusive behavior and how to avoid potential attacks;
- Possible sanctions and protective measures after a final determination regarding rape, acquaintance rape, domestic violence, dating violence, sexual assault, or stalking;
- Procedures for victims after a sex offense, including preservations of evidence, resources for protection orders, reporting options, options regarding notifying police and campus authorities, and rights of victims;
- Resources available to students such as counseling, health, victim advocacy, legal assistance, and other services, on campus and in the community;
- Options for remedies related to academics, living, transportation, and work, regardless of willingness to report;
- Confidentiality options and processes;
- Information on the prevention of retaliation.

It is our hope that this text will provide a tool for institutions to outline strategies to meet the VAWA mandates and, more importantly, to identify root factors of sexual violence and bystander attitudes in the college community.

WHY IS UNDERSTANDING RISK FACTORS FOR SEXUAL ASSAULT, STALKING, AND IPV IMPORTANT?

As a tool for the primary prevention of sexual violence, this text offers specific root factors associated with perpetration and promotes the development of healthy attitudes and behaviors for campus communities. VAWA requires the use of risk reduction in prevention programming. Risk reduction includes programming and options designed "to decrease perpetration and bystander inaction, and to increase empowerment for victims in order to promote safety and to help individuals and communities address conditions that facilitate violence" (34 CFR § 668.46(j)(2)(v)).

The root factors provide a framework for staff to use for early alert and intervention with individuals who demonstrate high-risk behaviors. In addition, each factor can be used educationally to empower community members with information to recognize and respond to high-risk attitudes and behaviors of concern. For staff working with organizations or other institutional groups, the root factors can be helpful in identifying organizations that are sustaining environments that condone and encourage attitudes supportive of sexual violence or educationally for leaders in those organizations.

TERMS AND DEFINITIONS

The prevention of sexual violence begins with continued conversations among college administrators, faculty, and students about sexual violence on the college campus. Open and engaging dialogue cannot occur with strict and formal rules related to terminology and language. With that, ahead we provide what we mean by some of the terms used throughout the book, but we also recognize that definitions vary from campus to campus. We want to be respectful to those who have experienced violence, and we want to create an environment where communication about these issues is encouraged.

Sometimes when we argue as a community about terminology, we only discourage the conversation. With that, it is important to recognize that if a person does not recognize behavior as sexual violence, it is problematic to prevention and accountability efforts, so definitions and terms are critical especially in policy and prevention programs. For the purposes of our book, we will use these terms and definitions—use what is appropriate for your campus, but mainly just keep the conversation going.

Sexual violence: The American College Health Association describes sexual violence as "a continuum of behaviors instead of an isolated, deviant act" (2008). We consider this a comprehensive term that includes all acts of unwelcome sexual touching, intercourse, and harassment. The continuum is used as a descriptor that accounts for the social norms and belief systems as the foundation on which other sexual violence is built.

Intimate partner violence (IPV): a term inclusive of dating violence and domestic violence that is committed by a person who is or has been in a social relationship of an intimate nature with the victim.

Dating violence: violence committed by a person who is or has been in a social relationship of a romantic or intimate nature with the victim; and where the existence of such a relationship shall be determined based on a consideration of the following factors: length of the relationship, type of relationship, and frequency of interaction between the persons involved in the relationship.

Domestic violence: felony or misdemeanor crimes of violence committed by a current or former spouse of the victim, a person with whom the victim shares a child in common, a person who is cohabitating with or has cohabitated with the victim as a spouse, a person similarly situated to a spouse of the victim under the domestic or family violence laws of the jurisdiction receiving grant monies or any other person against an adult or youth victim who is protected from that person's acts under the domestic or family violence laws of the jurisdiction.

Stalking: engaging in a course of conduct directed at a specific person that would cause a reasonable person to fear for the person's safety or the safety of others, or suffer substantial emotional distress (VAWA 2013).

Nonconsensual sexual contact: any intentional sexual touching, however slight, with any object, by a man or a woman upon a man or a woman, that is without consent and/or by force.

Victim/survivor/reporting party/complainant: the person or persons bringing forward the complaint to student conduct, law enforcement, or the Title IX office. *Victim* tends to be more of a legal term, while *survivor* is often used in counseling and advocacy work. *Reporting party* and *complainant* are more neutral terms preferred in student conduct and Title IX work.

Perpetrator/accused/responding party: the person or persons who are the subject of the complaint brought to student conduct, law enforcement, or the Title IX office. *Perpetrator* tends to be a more law enforcement– and counseling-based term, while the *accused* is more legal in nature. *Responding party* is a more neutral term preferred in student conduct and Title IX work.

FROM THE FRONT LINES

VAWA/Title IX Challenge

Just when those individuals responsible for addressing sex/gender discrimination and conduct on our campuses thought they may have had a handle on the compliance mandates under Title IX, the Violence Against Women Reauthorization Act (VAWA) of 2013 passed. The reauthorization of this law incorporated language from the Campus Sexual Violence Elimination Act in Section 304 of VAWA. The Campus SaVE Act provisions amended the Clery Act and added new requirements involving training, prevention, and new accountability categories. Since the Title IX administrators already addressed sexual harassment and misconduct on campuses, the evolution of training, prevention, and new conduct categories naturally moved under the Title IX umbrella—or, as I frequently say, "If not them, then who?"

A brief overview of Title IX and VAWA is necessary to create the context for the discussion of the challenges. Title IX was passed in 1972 and is a federal nondiscrimination law prohibiting discrimination based on sex in education entities that accept federal funding (applies to K–12 and higher education). This law is overseen by the U.S. Department of Education's Office of Civil Rights. It is a civil rights law and provides for civil rights remedies. The Violence Against Women Act originally passed in 1994 (applies only to institutions of higher education [IHE]). This act was the first comprehensive federal law to address sexual violence on our college and university campuses and is overseen by the U.S. Justice Department. This law provides funding for prevention of sexual assault by providing institutional grants for victim services. Because VAWA is a funding-based law it requires reauthorization every five to seven years. Of course, when a law is up for reauthorization it is also subject to redefinitions. The VAWA Act of 2013 incorporated dating violence, domestic violence, and stalking categories in addition to the original category of sexual assault. But what created a sea change for campuses across the United States was the adoption of the provisions of a bill titled the Sexual Assault Violence Elimination Act into the VAWA Reauthorization (Section 304). This act amended an existing law called the Jeanne Clery Disclosure of Campus Security

Policy and Campus Crime Statistics Act (Clery Act) (again, this law applies only to IHE).

Why is this so important? Because the VAWA, Sec. 304, incorporated the new categories of dating violence, domestic violence, stalking, and sexual assault as mandates for both reporting and prevention. The VAWA, Sec. 304, imposed new crime reporting categories, along with mandatory training and required prevention programming and policy elements, previously incorporated into Title IX guidance from OCR. Thus, those individuals on our campuses originally charged with oversight of Title IX compliance and the many compliance mandates included with that guidance are now faced with not only providing a "prompt and effective" response to sexual discrimination or violence, but also implementing prevention programming and training. Additionally, the response protocol of "prompt and effective" applied to reports of sexual assault is wholly inappropriate when the reported conduct includes intimate partner violence (IPV) or stalking. IPV and stalking issues require a response that is implemented by individuals with specialized training in order to prevent further or continuing harm to the victim.

Here's an example: Erin and Bob, third-year students at NMU, have been together for two years. Early in their relationship Erin reported to her resident assistant (RA) that Bob engaged in anal sex with her despite her protests. Erin shared that she was very conflicted about what to do. She wanted Bob to understand that it wasn't acceptable, that she felt violated, but she didn't want to ruin his life by getting him kicked out of school. Her RA informed her of all the resources available and that she must report to the Title IX coordinator, who will contact her to reinforce her rights and resources. Erin subsequently met with the Title IX coordinator, and because Bob persisted in texting her and hanging outside her classes, she asked the Title IX coordinator to impose a no-contact order, but that she would not participate in an investigation or hearing. The Title IX coordinator agreed to provide remedial support but encouraged Erin to come back in any time to discuss or to engage in a more formal action.

Six months later Erin again visited the Title IX coordinator's Office and asked that the no-contact order be lifted. She shared that she and Bob talked everything out and decided to resume their relationship. Now (a year later), the Title IX coordinator received an e-mail from Erin's advisor. She shared that Erin seems withdrawn, often misses class, has bruises on her arms and face, and that Erin's boyfriend waits for her outside her class every day. The Title IX coordinator contacted Erin to "check in" and suggested a meeting. Erin agreed to talk with her on condition of confidentiality. Erin shared that Bob is very controlling with her, he constantly accuses her of hooking up with someone else, he won't let her hang out with her friends, and he tries to always be with her when she's not in class. She has become afraid of him. Erin has dropped out of all campus activities because of Bob's anger when she's gone. She fearfully shared that he has become physically aggressive and sexually demanding, especially when he thinks she's talking with or hanging out with someone else.

The Title IX coordinator knows that her mandate under Title IX is to (1) investigate or otherwise determine what's occurring, (2) take action to stop the abuse/misconduct, (3) engage in action to reasonably prevent the abuse from recurring, and (4) provide remedial support for Erin. However, in cases of IPV, intervening immediately can place a victim of IPV in increased danger of harm. Conduct involving IPV or stalking necessitates a different approach. These behaviors require a comprehensive risk assessment of the risks that Erin is facing and a subsequent safety plan to be implemented to ensure that Erin can be protected while the institution moves forward to address the IPV.

This scenario demonstrates how a Title IX–based conduct can also become one involving the VAWA categories of prohibited conduct. This scenario is the least complicated of IPV because the institution has control over both of the parties. Institutional response becomes increasingly complex when one of the parties is not a member of the IHE community, yet schools (under VAWA) are required to address these circumstances.

Saundra K. Schuster, Esq.
Partner, The NCHERM Group, LLC

DISCUSSION QUESTIONS

1. What comes to mind when you think of root factors related to sexual violence? Anecdotally, what do you know about the incidents of sexual violence on college campuses and the attitudes and behaviors related to the occurrence of violence?

2. Title IX is almost 45 years old. Why do you think educational institutions are still struggling to maintain compliance?

3. What are the current programs, initiatives, or strategies on campus related to Title IX and VAWA requirements? Who are the stakeholders involved in the various efforts?

4. When you think of the term "hostile environment," what aspects of campus life come to mind?

5. Consider the VAWA requirements outlined in the chapter. Did lawmakers get it right? Do the prevention guidelines outlined adequately address sexual violence concerns on college campuses?

Chapter 2

Summary of the 12 Risk Factors

You can't hate the roots of a tree and not hate the tree.

—*Malcolm X*

KEY TAKE-AWAYS

1. In the past, sexual assault prevention was narrow in scope, often reinforced rape myths, and until recently, did not incorporate elements of college and university life.

2. While numerous studies exist related to sexual predation, there has not previously been a list of risk factors for sexual violence on a college or university campus. The risk factors in this book combine past work into a framework for higher education practitioners to use in prevention efforts.

3. Risk factors occur as both behaviors and attitudes at the individual level as well as the group level. Examples throughout the book will explore how to recognize the risk factors and how to reduce the associated risk.

Along with many professionals in higher education, we were thrilled at the increased focus sexual violence has drawn from the federal government and in popular media in the past year. It was gratifying to see Barack Obama educate on these issues through the *It's on Us* campaign. It was heartening to see Lady Gaga and Joe Biden bring the issue of sexual violence to the forefront at the Oscar ceremony in early 2016. Budget moneys on campuses across the country have been reallocated to support survivors, improve education efforts, and train Title IX investigators, law enforcement, and student conduct officers.

As we rush ahead and improve our programs for students, it is helpful to pause and review what the research tells us are the root causes for this violence. While action is needed and a noble pursuit, action driven by research and aimed at reducing the causal factors will be more effective at addressing this problem. To this end, we offer a summary of 12 risk factors called the DD-12, or dirty dozen, that should inform our prevention efforts moving forward. In this chapter, we offer some insight into how these factors were developed.

HISTORY OF PREVENTION EFFORTS

Consider for a moment how the movies, TV, and even schools have portrayed sexual assault. Sexual assault occurs in the darkness. Frequent images include women running at dusk and then being approached and dragged into the bushes by a stranger. Others show a woman entering her car and being grabbed from behind or by someone waiting in her backseat. Perpetrators are often portrayed as minorities. The female victim is rarely pictured drinking alcohol or engaging in "questionable" behaviors (McMahon 2011). Even as perspectives began to shift away from the idea of "stranger rape," most prevention efforts still utilized scenarios highlighting the use of physical force, indicating that evidence of a sexual assault must include a struggle or physical marks and injury.

It's interesting here to note the images presented in many early prevention efforts for sexual assault also rarely occurred on a college campus, so scenarios involving parties with friends and going out drinking were rare as well. Even as efforts began to address the relationship between alcohol and other drugs in sexual assault, women were still left to imagine that if they were victimized, there was an implication they must have done something wrong or inappropriate, such as leaving their drink unattended or partying too hard to be mindful of who poured their drinks. Women were told to go out only in groups or to drink less in order to reduce their likelihood of being assaulted. These efforts still disregarded information that assaults usually occur when we feel comfortable and safe, in environments with friends, and behind closed doors with individuals we thought liked us or cared for us. They shift the burden to go unharmed primarily to the woman.

The combination of these types of educational efforts often reinforces rape myths and other victim-blaming attitudes. Images of male victims or same-sex violence were nonexistent, and there was little information about domestic violence or stalking until recent years. Domestic violence and dating violence was often not recognized as a form of sexual violence or as impacting the educational environment of a student because it was not seen as something that occurred on campus. Stalking was seen through the lens of flirtation and a boys-will-be-boys attitude, where women were just being too sensitive and should see this attention as flattery.

In recent years, college and university administrators have started to gain a better understanding of the dynamics of sexual assault and how they relate to responding to and investigating campus incidents. Universities have begun hiring specialized investigators for Title IX–related incidents and participating in intensive trainings to learn to gather information related to issues of consent, including understanding coercion, intimidation, and other threats. Investigators are increasingly knowledgeable about making determinations about incapacitation from alcohol or other drugs, gathering relevant statements related to the credibility of the involved parties, completing thorough investigations with little to no available physical evidence, and recognizing and managing the effects of trauma on the reporting party. Unfortunately, this is only secondary prevention; much of this same learning has not translated to improved primary prevention and education programs on college campuses. In fact, the interrelationship between the response to incidents and the prevention of incidents is still often not recognized by colleges and universities, when in fact poor reporting, response, and accountability mechanisms contribute to the cycle of sexual violence.

Comprehensive prevention efforts must include education and training information for campus communities based on accurate information about the root causes of sexual violence and be deployed in long-term and sustainable ways for diverse populations. Importantly, prevention of sexual assault requires effective and equitable response processes for incidents that occur. These processes must include an infrastructure that encourages reporting, support systems for reporting and responding parties, and transparent accountability structures that leave no doubt that sexual violence is not tolerated in the educational environment. Chapter 3 will explore prevention models and comprehensive prevention strategies in more detail.

WHAT ARE THE 12 RISK FACTORS?

The 12 factors identified throughout this book provide a new prevention framework for higher education practitioners and faculty. Primary prevention strategies include the need to consider root factors associated with sexual violence. This prevention framework incorporates root factors for sexual violence and considers the unique aspects of the college environment while acknowledging both individual and social group influences. The risk factors are described in Table 2.1.

The history of research on sexual violence is a long one, with involvement from the Department of Justice, Federal Bureau of Investigation, and the Center for Disease Control. While there have been numerous studies addressing sexual predation, addiction, pedophilia, and paraphilia, there is not a clear summary for practitioners of the risk factors for sexual violence perpetration on college campuses.

Commonly cited characteristics of sexual violence on campuses are as follows:

- Men make up the majority of perpetrators (Jewkes et al. 2002; Zapp 2014).
- At least 50% of sexual assaults are associated with alcohol use (Abbey et al. 2001; Krebs et al. 2007; American College Health Association 2008; Zapp 2014).
- Feminist and social justice frameworks have often included societal norms, gender roles, and issues related to power and oppression as root factors of sexual violence (Davis et al. 2006).

This book will expand on these more commonly cited characteristics and incorporate other high-risk attitudes, behaviors, and experiences into 12 risk factors for sexual violence on college campus. In addition, this book provides practitioners with descriptive examples of how the risk factors may be observed in both individual and group behaviors and attitudes. By bringing together different motivations and contributing factors to sexual violence—including predation, addiction, paraphilia, social factors, and crimes of ease—we aim to construct a starting place for those engaging in prevention in order to help identify and/or create programming that will aid in reducing these 12 risk factors.

Let us be clear at the outset of this book: gender-based and sexual violence on college campuses is not singularly the result of a few "bad apples" whose worldview and behaviors shape an otherwise healthy and enlightened population of young adults. Instead, we suggest that the problem lies in the subtle encroachment of negative and unhealthy ideas about sexuality (degrading and/or nonconsensual), objectification, obsessive and possessive desires, and depersonalization and dehumanizing thoughts and behaviors that have become

Table 2.1 Overview of DD-12 Risk Factors

	Risk Factor	Description
Chapter 4	Objectification and depersonalization	Focus on self and seeing others as objects for pleasure without their own sense of agency
Chapter 5	Obsessive and/or addictive pornography/sex focus	Frequent viewing of pornography to a point where it impacts ability to attend class, maintain social connections, or maintain relationships; consumption of rape pornography
Chapter 6	Threats and ultimatums	An individual or group who makes threats and demands to meet their needs; a common way they address conflict is to set up "if then" ultimatums and demand compliance
Chapter 7	Misogynistic ideology	A pervasive belief that the female gender is less worthy or deserving of respect or consideration when compared to males
Chapter 8	Grooming behaviors	These behaviors are varied and are focused on lessening victims' ability to advocate for their safety
Chapter 9	Using substances to obtain sex	Making use of alcohol or other drugs to lower resistance and defenses of those targeted and to lower their resistance to give consent to sexual behavior
Chapter 10	Hardened or inflexible point of view	There is a steadfast and intractable point of view or belief system that is highly defended against change or further rational debate
Chapter 11	Pattern of escalating threat strategies	There is a series of increasingly dangerous practices and testing behaviors designed to move toward a higher level of violence
Chapter 12	Lack of empathy	The needs of the individual or group are narcissistic in nature and lack awareness of the societal, community, or personal harm they may cause others
Chapter 13	Sensation-seeking behaviors	The individual or group is focused on achieving pleasure and sensation as a central goal; their outlook resists discussion and change and their central desire is experiencing something pleasurable in the here and now
Chapter 14	Obsessive and/or addictive thoughts or behaviors	A tendency to focus fanatically on a particular goal at the cost of other reasonable alternative behaviors
Chapter 15	Past experiences	This includes a variety of past behaviors and experiences that may contribute to a predisposition for sexual assault; this also includes mitigating items that decrease inhibition, making the individual or group more likely to act out in the future

pervasive in our culture. The 12 factors incorporate both psychological conditions and societal conditions that relate to the perpetration of sexual violence on college campuses.

It is also important to note that the list of factors is not meant to indicate the ability to predict that a person or group will be sexually violent. The factors are provided to outline behaviors and attitudes that are related to sexual violence and can be observed in individuals and groups as behaviors of concern to be addressed. The list also provides a framework that can be described and taught to others in order to increase awareness of these concerns and to assist with problem identification in the campus community. This book is a first step to cutting back some of these invading influences by first calling attention to the risk factors that contribute to an escalation in gender-based sexual violence.

DD-12 RISK FACTORS: A MULTIDISCIPLINARY APPROACH

There are some exceptional tests, assessments, and measures available to law enforcement, psychologists, and clinicians in the arena of sexual predation and addressing recidivism. These assessments and checklists are often normed on criminal or probationary populations and have not specifically addressed the needs of those charged with reducing sexual violence on college campuses. However, these assessments provide some helpful research and a useful starting point to understand some facets of sexual violence. Several of these measures are discussed here.

The *Spousal Assault Risk Assessment (SARA)* was created in 1994 by Kropp et al. (1994, 1995, 1998) to help criminal justice professionals predict the likelihood of domestic violence. It was normed on adult male offenders who had probationary or inmate status following their offense.

The 20-item scale looks at past assaults, relationship or employment problems, victim or witness of family violence, substance abuse, suicidal or homicidal ideation/intent, mental health history, sexual assault history, jealousy, use of weapons in threats, escalation in frequency or severity of assault, attitudes that support or condone spousal assault, extreme minimization or denial of spousal assault history, and violations of no-contact orders.

The *Static-99* score is used to predict risk of sexual reoffense, based on the offender's score category. It is designed to be used with adult male offenders and is one of the most common assessments used in the world. There are ten items on the Static-99, which includes age of release from a facility, history of living with an intimate partner, past nonsexual and sexual convictions, convictions from no-contact sex offenses, unrelated victims, stranger victims, or male victims (Harris et al. 2003; Helmus and Hanson 2007).

In 2003, Hare revised the *Psychopathy Checklist (PCL-R)* that he developed after years of research (Hare 1985, 1991, 2003). While not directly related to sexual violence, the lack of empathy and connection to others is present in an individual with a significant PCL-R. This provides critical insight in understanding how objectification, lack of empathy, and aggression toward others can contribute to violence.

The checklist includes questions related to glib and superficial charm, cunning and manipulation, lack of remorse or guilt, superficial emotional responsiveness, callousness and lack of empathy, sexual promiscuity, early problem behaviors, impulsivity, irresponsibility, and failure to accept responsibility for one's own actions.

There are additional stalking and IPV assessments and checklists that provide insight into understanding risk factors and motivations for these behaviors (Kropp et al. 1998, 2002, 2008; Belfrage and Strand 2008). These include assessing escalation of physical or sexual violence threats, negative attitudes about women in relationships, stressors such as employment or financial problems, mental health or substance abuse problems, and shifts in power and control dynamics.

Identifying patterns or constellations of behaviors in a person's background is critical in order to understand his or her personality and tendency to act violently. The manifestation of a single behavior on one day is meaningless. However, patterns of behavior that involve inappropriate or out-of-control anger, repeated rule breaking, poor coping skills, equal opportunity hating, prior use of violence, and so forth should be considered in any risk assessment for sexual violence. Prior patterns of aggressive and inappropriate behavior are more predictive of future behavior than a single behavior taken out of context (O'Toole and Bowman 2011).

These measures provide useful tools for experts assessing sexual violence risk and a useful research-based framework to assist in the development of this text. However, they leave a gap for those who are more interested in addressing the broader issue of sexual assault violence in a more preventive and less clinical or law enforcement capacity.

While the issue of sexual violence, particularly as it relates to recidivism, is well explored in the criminal justice system, colleges and universities are more specifically interested in answering these questions related to sexual violence:

- What factors should be addressed on college campuses in terms of risk mitigation through our prevention education programs?
- How should audience characteristics inform or change our approach to prevention programming?
- After numerous cases of sexual violence involving fraternities and athletes, how should our college proceed with prevention efforts to reduce this risk?
- When adjudicating conduct cases and Title IX investigations regarding sexual assault, are there additional risk factors that should be examined to improve the sanctioning process beyond a punitive suspension? What behaviors should we attempt to address to reduce future incidents?
- What factors should be considered in safety planning, threat assessment, and behavioral intervention teamwork related to risks for future incidents?
- What factors would indicate potential campus climate concerns or hostile environments within the institution?

ADDRESSING BOTH THE INDIVIDUAL AND GROUPS

The presence of risk factors in groups and organizations is highlighted throughout this book for a number of reasons. Specifically, we know that members of all-male organizations, such as fraternities and athletics, have less healthy attitudes and behaviors related to sexual assault (Jewkes et al. 2002; Bleeker and Murnen 2005; Forbes et al. 2006; Sanday 2007; Zapp 2014). The members can be less likely to recognize behaviors as sexual violence and more accepting of rape myths.

DeKeseredy's male peer-support model explains that the support men receive from their male peers "may under certain conditions encourage and justify the physical, psychological, and sexual abuse of women." He gives the example of a man seeking guidance related to a situation with a woman where he is angered or hurt and where his male peers may suggest that he should not "put up with this behavior by women and should strike back" (Schwartz and DeKeseredy 1997, p. 45). This is by no means always the case, but it is possible to see how, particularly in a collegiate environment during a time of a stressful transition to college, these male peer-support mechanisms become even more significant in influencing behaviors and attitudes.

The research also indicates that the effect of male peer support (Schwartz and DeKeseredy 1997) results in abusive men often having attachments to other abusive men and attempting to maintain a certain image for those other men. Further, abusive male friends may reinforce negative attitudes and behaviors through verbal and emotional support and encouragement. Organizational considerations become critical for prevention of sexual violence on the college campus because not only can membership in a group bolster member behavior that exists on the continuum of sexual violence, but also some organizational cultures may be prone to members with similar negative behaviors and attitudes.

The influence of group development shifts the effectiveness of some prevention strategies. Bystander intervention, for example, can work only when it accounts for the powerful desire for membership and acceptance within the social organization. With each of the 12 factors, we consider how to reduce the risk associated with that concept from both an individual and group perspective.

FROM THE FRONT LINES

What Causes Sexual Violence?

Rape is an act that is about power and control, not about sex. Sex is the weapon, but not the goal of the perpetrator. Sort of.

I know that challenging this idea will be controversial, but I've worked on well more than 1,000 campus sexual violence cases in the last 18 years, and I think this explanation is part of the story, but not the entire story.

Let me start by stating that I agree with this widely held feminist belief about the etiology of sexual violence. I agree that many sex offenders (male and female) engage in sexually and physically abusive behaviors as a way to show dominance, to excise inner feelings of powerlessness through outwardly violent and ultimately cowardly acts, in an effort to establish power and/or control over others. I believe we live in a rape culture that tolerates and condones male violence against women, and other forms of interpersonal violence. Hegemonic masculinity makes it possible to normalize this violence, and even hide it. Male (and other) privilege makes it difficult to hold men accountable for violent acts when they occur, which in turn emboldens men who expect they can and will get away with it.

That said, the power and control paradigm applies only to some offenders and perpetrations I have investigated. I don't need to debate if they are the majority of such acts, but they are prevalent. I don't need to establish that another paradigm occurs more or less often, only that it occurs. What is the other paradigm? Some men weaponize sex to get sex. So do some women.

Some sexual assault is caused by ignorance, lack of respect, peer pressure and placing one's sexual needs over someone else's right to autonomy, and isn't really power/control motivated at all. Men still know and expect they will get away with such acts through the reassurance that the hegemonic masculinity of our society affords, and thus power and control are never far from the analysis, but I think it is too simplistic to deny that sex is sometimes exactly the goal.

Sex on college campuses today is messy. Students deliberately obfuscate sexual agency via vague terms and operate within artificial social constructs associated with popularity and peer group expectations, often fueled by overdoses of alcohol. What is a boundary today may not be tomorrow. What is not okay sober may well be welcomed when drunk. I don't think consent is a gray area, but I think that young men and women can lack the skills to negotiate and communicate effectively around sexual desire and boundaries. Abstinence-only education didn't create this problem, but it has exacerbated it. A man may push his partner's sexual boundaries to derive power from the exchange, or because he has not been taught how to find those boundaries respectfully, but only by crossing them. He may be pressured by what he believes his peers are doing or expecting, or he may be too motivated to ignore ambiguous signals because he wants to get laid, not just because society tells him he's not a real man unless he does. Sometimes, power and sex are both the goals.

This does not excuse any form of sexual violence, or minimize it. It is also important to realize that power and control do not always manifest themselves obviously as the motivation for sexual violence, and it may not even be the conscious motivator of the perpetrator, at least looking at the behaviors in retrospect as an investigator.

But work with enough perpetrators, and you can begin to see daylight between power/control offenders and "sex offenders," as I'll call them based on their motivation. Those who exercise their male privilege as a function of power/control are entitled. They see no wrongdoing on their part. They've been led on or are deserving, or their partner was sending mixed signals or was a "cocktease." They ply their targets with alcohol, and often reveal predatory tendencies.

And then there are guys who are timid, remorseful, contrite, and sincerely concerned that they have harmed another human being. They still deserve the same consequences for causing harm as a power/control offender, in my book, but they seem to be coming from a different place. Ultimately, harm caused is the problem, for whatever motivation, but as we look to improve our tools for prevention, we can't solve the problem without better understanding its cause.

Brett Sokolow, JD
Executive Director and Founder of ATIXA

DISCUSSION QUESTIONS

1. What do you remember being taught about sexual assault and sexual violence in school? What were the common ideas or themes of the prevention programs that you remember?

2. How do you think media, television, and advertising convey sexual violence?

3. What do you think some of the risk factors for sexual violence are in your campus community for individuals and for groups?

4. What do you think of the idea that sexual violence is about more than a small group of perpetrators and that it is about systemic attitudes and characteristics of the larger population? Is it both? One or the other? Something different?

5. This chapter explores ideas related to male peer support and the prevalence of risk factors for sexual violence in fraternities and athletic groups? What other organizations or groups need to be considered?

Chapter 3

The Seven C's and Doing Prevention Well

If I had eight hours to chop down a tree, I'd spend six sharpening my axe.

—Abraham Lincoln

KEY TAKE-AWAYS

1. Prevention strategies are most effective when based on a theoretical framework or model that considers the developmental stage and readiness of the learner and the context of the environment.

2. The seven C's provide an outline for comprehensive strategic prevention planning that can be modified for any college or university.

3. Theory has its limitations and is most effective when applied in practice to actual prevention planning and case scenarios.

Prevention of sexual assault and gender-based violence is a central theme of this book. While we will move on shortly to assist you in better understanding the underlying root causes of sexual violence on campus, we will first take some time to review some key concepts related to prevention programming to ensure the work we do in education and prevention is grounded in theory and reaches populations in the most effective way.

In this chapter we introduce you to a problem and corresponding outreach and prevention efforts that are put into place to address the problem. In the following sections, we will discuss several foundational prevention philosophies as well as the seven C's of prevention programming in the context of this example, a core element of

ATIXA's approach to prevention. Our sincere thanks to ATIXA and Brett Sokolow, Daniel Swinton, Michelle Issadore, and Marianne Price in their assistance with this overview chapter.

This overview is meant as an introduction, rather than a complete survey, of the prevention methodologies, curricular learning, and developmental theories.

A CASE EXAMPLE

A Title IX coordinator reviews his cases from the previous semester and notices several incidents related to nonconsensual sharing of nude pictures. Three incidents involved intimate partners and occurred in residence hall environments. Of those incidents, one involved a male posting pictures of a female on several websites with derogatory comments, one involved a male threatening to share pictures of another male involved in homosexual activity with his family if he did not stay with him in the relationship, and the last involved a male athlete allowing a friend to take pictures of him and his girlfriend having sex without her knowledge. An additional off-campus incident involved a male giving a picture of his ex-girlfriend to his new girlfriend, who is in a sorority. The new girlfriend posted the picture on her new member GroupMe account, where the ex-girlfriend was also a new member. An additional report involved a male student and a female faculty member in the College of Engineering where the male student threatened to share pictures of the female faculty member following a consensual relationship between the two. The Title IX coordinator wants to document a clear plan to respond to this trend of reports and prevent future incidents.

THE PUBLIC HEALTH MODEL

The public health approach focuses "on the safety and well-being of entire populations" (CDC 2016a, p. 1). A defining characteristic of public health is the goal toward providing services that benefit the most people. A multidisciplinary scientific basis draws from medicine, epidemiology, sociology, psychology, criminology, education, and economics (Dahlberg and Krug 2002). This allows for a broad application of the approach to various worldwide health conditions. Stakeholder input from health, education, social services, justice, and policy also influences collective action. The following is a four-step approach to applying the public health model on your campus:

1. **Define and monitor the problem:** understand the who, what, when, where, why, and how associated with a given issue. Analyze data from sources such as police reports,

medical examiner files, vital records, hospital charts, registries, population-based surveys, and more.

2. **Identify risk and protective factors:** pinpoint where to focus prevention efforts. Recognize that risk factors do not cause health conditions.

3. **Develop and test prevention strategies:** design prevention programs based on needs assessments, community surveys, stakeholder interviews, and focus groups. This type of informed approach is evidence-based and evaluated to determine effectiveness.

4. **Assure widespread adoption:** dissemination techniques include training, networking, technical assistance, and evaluation.

The Title IX coordinator begins by taking a closer look at the related incidents. He determines that several of the incidents are related to intimate partner violence and begins to consider risk and protective factors related to intimate partner violence. Since it seems that several of the incidents related to bad breakups, he considers how to utilize residence hall staff to promote healthy relationships within the residence hall community and targeted referrals to the social coaching group in the counseling center for individuals who may be struggling in social relationships. The Title IX coordinator decides that before implementing new initiatives, he should host a focus group with housing professional and student staff to see what information they have about dating violence in the residence halls.

GORDON'S OPERATIONAL CLASSIFICATION

Prevention curriculum should rely on the predominant classification for levels of prevention:

1. **Primary:** ensuring that a problem does not occur;
2. **Secondary:** reducing the prevalence of a problem or harm;
3. **Tertiary:** stopping or slowing the progress of a problem though the basic condition persists (Gordon 1963).

Gordon's Operational Classification, as put forward by Robert Gordon, Jr., MD, MPH, also divides the continuum of care into three parts: prevention, treatment, and maintenance. The curriculum targets the prevention category, whose subdivisions include:

1. **Universal:** address an entire population, such as at the national, community, school, or neighborhood level, with prevention programs, initiatives, and messages;

2. **Selective:** target subsets of a total population deemed to be at greater risk;
3. **Indicated:** look at individuals experiencing early signs of problem behaviors.

Gordon's typology is utilized by the National Institute on Drug Abuse and the United States Institute of Medicine as a system for understanding and organizing prevention and intervention. In conjunction with the social-ecological model we describe next, which takes into account environmental-level approaches, levels of prevention theory and Gordon's Operational Classification allow for the use of a common language when discussing prevention efforts. They also provide for a framework in which we can highlight primary prevention, a goal of this book.

The Title IX coordinator thinks that one factor that may be impacting the reoccurrence of sexual misconduct involving nonconsensual sharing of pictures is that the campus community may not be aware that it is a violation of school policy. The Title IX coordinator contacts the conduct office to discuss an effort to better disseminate information about the sexual misconduct policy to the campus community and to provide clear examples of "revenge porn" scenarios. They also discuss some additional policy changes to clarify this for the following semester.

The Title IX coordinator contacts liaisons within some of the special populations identified in the reports, specifically fraternities, sororities, and athletics, and updates them on the trends. He mentions the possibility of some targeted campaigns around the policies. The Title IX coordinator also reaches out to a staff member working with the Lesbian, Gay, Bisexual, Transgender and Queer Student Association to discuss what examples would be appropriate in the campaign to represent same-sex intimate partner violence.

Last, the Title IX coordinator places a call to the behavioral intervention team (BIT) chair and asks her to discuss at the next BIT meetings students who are coming onto their radar for having relationship issues and what types of interventions and referrals are being made for those students.

SOCIAL-ECOLOGICAL

The social-ecological model addresses the intricate interaction between individual, relationship, community, and societal factors (CDC 2016b). The curriculum targets each of these areas as strategic prevention efforts should include a range of activities that tap into more than one level of the model.

1. **Individual:** the first level identifies individual factors, such as age, education, income, substance use, and personal history.

Prevention efforts at the individual level often include elements to promote healthy attitudes, beliefs, and behaviors, such as education and life skills training.

2. **Relationship:** the second level looks at close relationships that may increase risk, such as peers, partners, and family members who may influence behavior and contribute to life experiences. Prevention efforts at the relationship level can include mentoring and peer programs.

3. **Community:** the third level addresses settings, such as schools, workplaces, and neighborhoods, in which social relationships occur and seeks out the characteristics of these settings that may be associated with health conditions. Prevention efforts at the community level aim to impact the climate, processes, and policies in a given system, such as social norm and social marketing campaigns.

4. **Societal:** the fourth level explores the broad societal factors that create a climate, such as social and cultural norms. Additional factors are the health, economic, educational, and social policies that serve to maintain economic or social inequalities between groups in society.

The Title IX coordinator noticed that the majority of the residence hall incidents occurred around midterms during the fall semester with new freshman students. The college already employs a number of educational initiatives for new freshmen related to sexual misconduct in orientation programming and in an online educational module during the first few weeks of school, but he makes a note to review the content related to intimate partner violence and dissemination of sexual pictures. The Title IX coordinator also notices that several of the students involved in the incidents did not complete the online educational module since the completion date was after midterms and decides that the timing of that content should be moved up in the semester.

After talking with the Greek Life and Athletics staff, he decides that incorporating similar scenarios into the current bystander intervention curriculum used in those areas could be helpful in order to try to shift some of the attitudes that it is acceptable to share pictures like this in the current social environments. The Greek Life staff also plan to utilize some upcoming sisterhood programming in the sororities to target some victim-blaming attitudes apparent in the organizations.

The Title IX coordinator also talks with Human Resources about updates to the consensual relationship policy for faculty and students and how to disseminate the policy to faculty. A meeting with the dean of the College of Engineering explores some climate concerns in the department related to female faculty

members and their treatment by their male colleagues as well as how this incident between the student and the female faculty member may exacerbate the
problems. They discuss several strategies, including some changes in resources
and opportunities available to junior faculty, especially women, and they plan to
conduct a departmental climate survey for the faculty.

BLOOM'S TAXONOMY OF CRITICAL THINKING

Bloom's Taxonomy of Critical Thinking refers to a classification of
the different objectives that educators set for students, also referred
to as learning objectives. It divides educational objectives into three
domains: cognitive, affective, and psychomotor. Within the domains,
learning at the higher levels is dependent on having attained pre-
requisite knowledge and skills at lower levels (Orlich et al. 2004).
A goal of Bloom's taxonomy is to motivate educators to focus on all
levels of learning, creating a more holistic form of education.

Domains of educational activities/learning:

- **Cognitive:** Mental skills (knowledge)
- **Affective:** Growth in feelings or emotional areas (attitude or
  self)
- **Psychomotor:** Manual or physical skills (skills)

The cognitive domain involves knowledge and the development of
intellectual skills, including the recall or recognition of specific facts,
procedural patterns, and concepts that serve in the development of
intellectual abilities and skills. There are six major categories, from
the simplest behavior to the most complex. The categories have
been referenced as degrees of difficulty; the earlier ones must nor-
mally be mastered before the next ones can take place.

Bloom's (1956) cognitive domains are as follows:

1. Knowledge involves the recall of specifics and universals, the
   recall of methods and processes, or the recall of a pattern,
   structure, or setting.
2. Comprehension refers to a type of understanding or appre-
   hension such that the individual knows what is being communicated and can make use of the material or idea being
   communicated without necessarily relating it to other material or seeing its fullest implications.
3. Application refers to the use of abstractions in particular and
   concrete situations.

29

4. Analysis represents the breakdown of a communication into its constituent elements or parts such that the relative hierarchy of ideas is made clear and/or the relations between ideas expressed are made explicit.
5. Synthesis involves the putting together of elements and parts so as to form a whole.
6. Evaluation engenders judgments about the value of material and methods for given purposes.

> The Title IX coordinator decides to review the online educational module for new freshmen related to sexual misconduct and intimate partner violence. The module was designed several years ago by the student activities office and primarily includes information about bystander intervention. The Title IX coordinator begins considering how to revise the content to include information for the students about what sexual misconduct is and what it may look like on the college campus because he knows that bystander intervention is effective only if the student can recognize problematic behaviors.

CHICKERING'S THEORY OF IDENTITY DEVELOPMENT

Chickering's theory of identity development remains arguably the most well-known, widely used, and comprehensive model available for understanding and describing the psychosocial development of college students. Chickering combined this research with some of his previous development studies to generate the seven vectors.

These vectors symbolize the direction and magnitude of college student development. Vectors were chosen as determinants of development, as opposed to stages, because college student development is too diverse and unique to be characterized by specific maps or pigeonholes. Rather, movement along any vector can occur at different rates and can interact with movement along the others (Chickering and Reisser 1993).

The seven vectors are as follows (Robinson 2013):

1. **Developing Competence**: An individual develops within intellectual, physical, and manual skills, and interpersonal competencies.
2. **Managing Emotions**: An individual becomes competent in his or her ability to recognize and manage emotions.
3. **Moving Through Autonomy Toward Interdependence**: An individual develops ability to have an independent outlook on life but understand successful relationships are based upon interdependence.

4. **Developing Mature Interpersonal Relationships:** An individual develops intercultural relations, appreciation for others, and tolerance for those around them.
5. **Establishing Identity:** An individual processes through his or her identity to emerge with a healthy self-concept in all facets of identity.
6. **Developing Purpose:** An individual has a strong outlook on professional life, makes meaning within his or her own interests, and establishes positive relationships with others.
7. **Developing Integrity:** An individual is able to articulate and emulate his or her own values affirmed as an individual through three stages: humanizing values, personalizing values, and developing congruence.

In addition, one or many of the following institutional controls can influence an individual's vectors (Robinson 2013):

- **Institutional objectives:** Consistency in policies, programs, and objects can lead individuals to challenge or acceptance.
- **Institutional size:** This influences the degree to which a student has the ability to participate in the larger community.
- **Student–faculty relationships:** Positive relationships facilitate a deeper intellectual and relationship identity for individuals.
- **Curriculum:** Individuals who can better relate to their curriculum have an increased ability to encounter situations and critically reason through situations.
- **Teaching:** Involvement of active learning helps students develop better interpersonal relationships and positive intercultural identity.
- **Friendships and student communities:** Individuals learn best from one another and other individuals' situations.
- **Student development programs and services:** The collaborative environment is necessary to provide programs to challenge and support students.

Other essentials in the learning environment can produce an increase in positive development for any student within the campus community. When considering prevention curriculum development, educators must be actively aware of differences, and be willing to create environments where students learn from each other. They should provide opportunities to challenge and stretch individuals' thought processes, while gaining a deeper understanding of themselves and others.

> The Title IX coordinator notices that two of the incidents involve students who have been involved in previous issues related to sexual misconduct. After reviewing the sanctioning guidelines utilized by the conduct office for sexual misconduct, the Title IX coordinator suggests revisions that include the development of an individualized, structured interview protocol and educational session for students involved in picture-sharing incidents before their reenrollment in the campus community.

SANFORD'S CHALLENGE AND SUPPORT THEORY

Sanford developed his theory for student development based on a balance of challenge and support (Sanford 1966). Too much support with too little challenge creates a comfortable environment for the student, where little development is possible. However, too little support with too much challenge makes development an impossible and negative experience. People grow best where they continuously experience an appropriate balance of support and challenge.

Environments that lean too heavily in the direction of challenge without adequate support can be toxic and promote anxiety. Those weighted too heavily toward support without the ability for challenge are boring and sterile. An imbalance in both can lead to withdrawal and the inability to maintain retention. The balance of support and challenge leads to engagement.

> The Title IX coordinator notices a note in one of the reports from an RA who took one of the initial reports from the woman whose picture was shared on the Internet. The RA's notes mention referring the student to the police department and referring her back to the website providers for assistance. The RA did not notify professional Housing staff until two days later, when the student returned to the RA in even greater distress over the lack of help received from the website providers. The Title IX coordinator adds an action item to update the reporting protocols for Housing student staff and to provide new printed materials to give to students reporting incidents.

KOHLBERG'S THEORY OF MORAL DEVELOPMENT

Kohlberg's theory of moral development is dependent on the thinking of both psychologists and philosophers before him, specifically the emphasis that human beings develop philosophically and psychologically in a progressive fashion. The theory holds that moral reasoning, the basis for ethical behavior, has six identifiable developmental stages, each more adequate at responding to moral dilemmas than its predecessor (Kohlberg 1973). Kohlberg determined that the process of moral development was principally concerned with justice.

Kohlberg's theory specifies six stages of moral development, arranged in three levels.

Level I: Preconventional Morality

Stage 1: Punishment Orientation: *Rules are obeyed so the individual may avoid punishment.*

Stage 2: Instrumental Orientation or Personal Gain: *Rules are obeyed because obeying rules creates the potential for personal gain.*

Level II: Conventional Morality

Stage 3: "Good Boy" or "Good Girl" Orientation: *Rules are obeyed to receive the approval of others.*

Stage 4: Maintenance of the Social Order: *Rules are obeyed to maintain the social order of things.*

Level III: Postconventional Morality

Stage 5: Morality of Contract and Individual Rights: *Rules are obeyed if they are impartial. Democratic rules are challenged if they infringe on the rights of others.*

Stage 6: Morality of Conscience: *The individual establishes his or her own rules in accordance with a personal set of ethical principles.*

These stages are not the product of socialization—that is, socializing agents (e.g., parents and teachers) do not directly teach new forms of thinking (Crain 1985). Indeed, it is difficult to imagine them systematically teaching each new stage structure in its particular place in the sequence. The stages emerge, instead, from our own thinking about moral problems.

Social experiences do promote development, but they do so by stimulating our mental processes. As we get into discussions and debates with others, we find our views questioned and challenged and are therefore motivated to come up with new, more comprehensive positions. New stages reflect these broader viewpoints.

The Title IX coordinator considers the various offenses from Kohlberg's stages of moral reasoning to better understand the thinking of those involved in the conduct code violations. For example, consider the man posting pictures of a woman on several websites with derogatory comments. In addressing the issue, it may be helpful to engage the student with questions addressing preconventional morality ("Have you considered that what you just did is going to result in a fine and you being placed on probation?"), conventional morality ("What would it be like if everyone did what you did?"), or postconventional morality ("How do you think this action infringed on the rights of the woman?").

CREATING A MULTIYEAR STRATEGIC PLAN

Many campuses use effective prevention practices, based on researched models, strong data, and proven methodologies. Some campuses have originated models that achieve admirable outcomes. These notable efforts are all too often applied piecemeal to addressing aspects of problem drinking, sexual violence, and other health and safety challenges. Very few campuses embrace prevention strategies that manifest the seven C's that encompass effective strategic initiatives across all health and violence risk issues for students, faculty, and staff. The seven C's are:

- Cogent,
- Community-wide,
- Collaborative,
- Consistent,
- Compliant,
- Comprehensive, and
- Centrally planned.

Colleges and universities need to transform prevention education by doing what they do best—education—real, pervasive, sustained, targeted, and informed education, infused with the seven C's. The ultimate question for strategic prevention education is this: Can you create a framework today for what your students will learn, teach, and model about prevention for the next four-plus years of their stakeholding in your campus community?

THE SEVEN C'S

1. **Cogent:** Cogent prevention programming aims to make the content and the curriculum persuasive, convincing, clear,

coherent, and sound. Cogent prevention programming relies on researched models, strong data, and proven methodologies. It relies on best practices, harnesses and employs assessment efforts, and has primary prevention as its foundation, rather than an afterthought. Cogent prevention programming is well thought-out, targeted, and tailored to the specific campus community and often to specific constituencies.

> *In the foregoing case study, you can see the Title IX coordinator exploring each element of his prevention strategy related to the trend of concerns on his campus and applying formal and informal sources of information to improve the program. He considered what the research indicated as root factors of intimate partner violence, but he paired that with a qualitative focus group of students in the residence halls to add depth to his understanding. He also sought to align his different prevention strategies with similar messages but oriented for different audiences or purposes.*

2. **Community-wide**: Community-wide prevention programming aims to reach all students and acknowledges the spectrum of types of community members on a campus. Prevention efforts at the community level are intended to impact the climate, processes, and even policies in a given system. Through community education, we are reaching groups of people with information and resources to promote a given mission, statement, or initiative. These programmatic efforts should be targeted to ensure that every student has the opportunity to participate. We need to ensure that our educational efforts are more than just preaching to the converted. We need to make sure every student is present for the educational opportunities we work so hard to provide, and that every student takes away at least some benefit from our intended learning outcomes.

   > *Institutions should develop programs and educational events for students in each year. When designing our primary prevention efforts, our programming should be focused on more than just first-year students. Too many times we create our programming to fit the needs of those new to our campus or new to the collegiate environment. We have to build opportunities for prevention education for all of our students, and focus our efforts on a curriculum designed to reach our entire campus community.*

The prevention strategies identified by the Title IX coordinator went far beyond the elements of one programmatic strategy. He considered the impact of institutional policy and the dissemination of that policy on the trend of concerns. He also looked at accountability mechanisms that might impact the reoccurrence of offenses. His strategies also considered multiple populations in the campus community, including faculty and an academic department, which resulted in an additional climate survey to gather more information.

3. **Collaborative:** Collaboration is fundamental in both the development of your multiyear strategic plan and in your prevention-based programmatic efforts. It provides educators with the opportunity to bring together a multitude of students and professionals with varied expertise. Program planning and implementation can be difficult when efforts are singular and without support. It is key to the planning process, both in the development of your multiyear curriculum and to programming, that your efforts be focused on assuring collaboration.

   As you begin your process of designing a strategic curriculum, keep in mind that there is value to having multiple perspectives at the table. Making a concerted effort to include others in all aspects of brainstorming, project planning, writing, developing, and implementing projects adds to the chances of success and will yield a collaborative mind-set that continues beyond the life of a project. Build a team of individuals willing to work. Being strategic about prevention efforts requires more than simply making a list of what kinds of programs to consider. It should be a structured process, allowing for open dialogue and multiple perspectives. With that said, be thoughtful about who you should bring to the table. Students are key to your success. Let them be a part of the process.

   Notice in the foregoing case study the establishment of liaisons in key areas on the campus to support prevention efforts. By having established relationships in place, it was possible for the Title IX coordinator to contact those liaisons and have candid conversations about the apparent trends and for those liaisons to help interpret what he was seeing. Instead of approaching each unit with an absolute idea or strategy to employ, the Title IX coordinator shared information and together with the unit identified a strategy for moving forward. This collaborative framework also increases the likelihood of long-term and sustainable prevention efforts in these targeted areas because each unit has buy-in to what the Title IX coordinator is trying to achieve and is willing to implement the various strategies as a part of their ongoing efforts.

4. **Consistent:** When defining consistency, we think of being cohesive, having a standard of form, and the ability to replicate our efforts. Consistency in programming represents a dedication to the work, its messages, and our students. Consistency also requires a commitment to the production, evaluation, and reevaluation of your programmatic efforts.

   Consistency allows for measurement. Until you have tried something new for a period of time and in a consistent manner, you can't decide if it works or not. How do you measure effectiveness if what you are measuring isn't performed consistently? Consistency will make your efforts relevant and provide meaning to the curriculum plans. Your campus needs to see a consistent flow of programming and a commitment to your initiatives. Your programs need to be continuous and visible throughout the year. Consistency maintains your message.

   In the case study, there are several elements of consistency that are important: consistency of messaging, consistency of implementation, and consistency of evaluation. The Title IX coordinator worked to ensure consistency in messaging across the campus related to intimate partner violence by refining the existing policy and increasing dissemination mechanisms and by reviewing reporting protocols to make sure victims received consistent options and resources. By working with other stakeholders on the campus, he could better ensure consistency of implementation because they were involved in visioning the preferred outcomes and because they were invested in the continuation of those prevention efforts. The Title IX coordinator would need to note the changes being made to the timing and content in the online educational module because it would impact evaluation efforts related to that initiative.

5. **Compliant**: Compliance is a fluid, continuous work in progress. In today's hyper-regulatory environment, our prevention efforts must be compliant with applicable laws, regulations, and guidance; our efforts must fulfill the requisite duty of care. Compliance, however, is more than simply checking a box or going through the motions. Indeed, as we noted earlier, our duty of care is a duty to care and prevention efforts should view compliance in this light to truly achieve success. In an effort to reduce the risk of sexual misconduct as well as the crimes of rape, sexual assault, sexual harassment, stalking, dating violence, and domestic violence occurring among its students, your campus should utilize a range of campaigns, strategies, and initiatives to provide awareness, education, risk reduction, and prevention programming.

   The various strategies employed in the foregoing case study help to achieve compliance with Title IX and VAWA. From a Title IX perspective, the Title IX coordinator is monitoring trends and working to remedy the concerns within the campus community even after the individual incidents have been addressed. He is also using those reports to identify pockets of potential climate concerns for the community and exploring those further. To meet VAWA-related strategies for the prevention of dating violence, the Title IX coordinator should document his various efforts in the annual campus security report. By improving victim reporting and resources as well as the policy dissemination, the Title IX coordinator is working toward compliance with both Title IX guidance and VAWA requirements.

6. **Comprehensive**: A comprehensive and strategic prevention curriculum will employ both the entire spectrum of prevention as well as three levels of prevention—primary, secondary, and tertiary, as presented in Gordon's Operational Classification. Certainly primary prevention is the most efficacious in creating change, but that does not mean we can ignore or downplay the impact of secondary and tertiary prevention efforts. If a baseball team relied solely on home runs to score, they would miss a litany of effective, if often more incremental strategies teams use to score runs. Further, Gordon notes that a comprehensive prevention plan will view populations from both a macro and a micro scale—from "universal" (population-wide) to "selective" subsets of the population, to "indicated" individuals. The social-ecological model that

targets individuals, relationships, communities, and societies reinforces this comprehensive approach.

The Title IX coordinator was thinking comprehensively in his approach to prevention. While he considered primary prevention strategies related to encouraging healthy relationships and improving the social norms around sharing of sexual pictures, he did not ignore ways to improve the response to incidents when they occur. He also thought of ways to support the overall campus community as well as special populations and individuals who needed specially focused efforts.

7. **Centrally planned:** We understand, and our campus leaders need to understand, that centralized planning of prevention is an idea whose time has come. Consider now all the different places on your campus from which prevention originates, just on one topic. Let's take sexual assault as an example. The women's center does its work, the survivor support group does its programming, the peer educators are on their message, residential life provides programming, orientation starts things off, the fraternities and sororities fulfill educational mandates from their nationals, athletics fulfills the prevention requirements of their conferences, health educators contribute their messages, some faculty members may be researching prevention implementing their ideas, and so forth. Prevention is coming on many campuses from 20 different, uncoordinated sources whose purposes may align or cross.

The Title IX coordinator orchestrated many of the prevention strategies employed in the case study, but he did not implement all of those strategies. His central oversight of things like messaging, timing, and resource allocation made it possible for other stakeholders to proceed confidently in employing the prevention initiatives while staying aligned with his overall vision for the institution.

FROM THE FRONT LINES

Discussion, Education Needed to Curb Sexual Assault

During my time as a student journalist, I have had opportunities to tell some touching stories. I have spoken with so many inspiring people, and some of these stories have been about survivors of sexual assault or people who deal with preventing sexual assault on college campuses.

I once spoke with a survivor who used her skills to make a documentary as a form of healing. She created a film about the resources available for students and those who help survivors deal with sexual assault.

I have covered a Take Back the Night rally, where people gathered in the darkness of night and marched for all those who have experienced violence or stalking in the night. I covered a SlutWalk, where people unapologetically walked through parts of Lubbock in their "sluttiest" attire with signs reading "still not asking for it," to show that clothing is never an invitation for sex. I have seen college activism against sexual assault on Tech's campus in a variety of ways.

This activism is inspiring—it really is—but the fact that it's 2016 and this activism is still needed is saddening. Denying that sexual assault is happening at alarming rates on college campuses is like denying college students are broke from student loan debt—the difference is it's not being talked about as much. The presidential races are happening right now, all of these candidates are talking about ways to decrease student debt to get the college student demographic vote, but they're ignoring sexual assault.

This is the first step to sexual assault prevention—talking about it. Politicians and administrators in colleges have to do something besides saying Title IX solves it. Yes, Title IX was monumental, but if the sexual assault is still happening at alarming rates, why have we not realized this law was not the end of the road? Trust me, I know talking about sexual assault can make people uncomfortable and cause anger, sadness, or frustration. But if we never talk about it, there's no way we can bring the necessary attention to it.

Those talks need to be productive; they have to address real issues with which people are dealing on campuses, which is why the next step to preventing sexual assault is early sex education. Sex education in public schools needs reform in many ways. For the most part, all that is taught in sex education curriculums is the reproductive system and they ignore sexual assault. If people are taught at an earlier age about consent and healthy sexual communication, I am confident sexual assault rates on campuses will decrease. But this education has to be ongoing, starting at an early age and continuing into college. There is always something new to bring to the conversation and something new to learn, so sex education should not be something that happens only for a couple of years in school.

Obviously there is so much more that can be done to prevent sexual assault besides talking about it and sex education, but these are the two key factors. I think they are the most basic and fundamental steps.

As a student journalist, I love being a storyteller. It is so rewarding to give people a voice. But if there is anything I can do to decrease the number of sexual assault stories I can tell, it is my obligation to do so. I think it's all of ours.

Kristen Barton
News Editor, *The Daily Toreador*
Student Journalist, URGE: Unite for Reproductive and Gender Equity

PROGRAMMING 101

Sometimes we forget the importance of program planning basics. The best program ideas and strategies have failed when not combined with the fundamentals of programming. Programming experts exist on every campus in areas related to student activities, residence life, and student organizations. Even if you feel confident in program planning, these are still critical stakeholders for planning initiatives and should be consulted for coordination of calendars and other insight. Table 3.1 provides a list of other program planning basics not to be forgotten.

Table 3.1 Programming 101

1	Needs assessment	Gather information from climate surveys, program assessments, focus groups, or anecdotal information about gaps in campus prevention strategies.
2	Connect to institutional mission and goals	Ensure that the focus of the program aligns with other institutional efforts and goals. Is there a Title IX–related council or task force at the institution? Are there wellness- or safety-related goals in the campus strategic plan?
3	Consider relationship to compliance	Identify Title IX, VAWA, or other related compliance requirements met by the program.
4	Identify stakeholders and partners	Brainstorm individuals, departments, and agencies that are stakeholders in the initiative. Consider how the program will supplement or duplicate other efforts. Approach appropriate on campus and off-campus partners with ideas for their involvement. Create structures for communicating with stakeholders and partners (meetings, SharePoint).

(continued)

Table 3.1 Continued

5	Agree on program budget and source of funding	Think about financial timelines when seeking financial support from partners; consider sources of funds from local grants and program stakeholders.
6	Determine target audience	Identify if the program is meant for a universal, selective, or indicated audience and describe audience characteristics.
7	Decide on related models or theories	Utilize student development theories, learning theories, and the models listed in this chapter to guide work.
8	Develop program goals, objectives, and learning outcomes	Program goals should be a broad statement about the results of your program. Program objectives should be SMART (specific, measurable, achievable, relevant, and time-bound). Learning outcomes identify what participants should be able to do following participation.
9	Develop program content	Determine any mandatory content related to compliance, consider the 12 risk factors, and think about audience characteristics, method of delivery, consistency in messaging, and sequencing.
10	Coordinate with third-party vendors	If purchasing or using third-party content or presenters, review content for customization and fit for institution. Contact references for feedback on vendor. Follow contracting and procurement guidelines.
11	Select and train presenters or facilitators	If using multiple facilitators or peer facilitators, organize trainings with practice opportunities and role-plays.
12	Confirm logistical information	Identify and reserve locations for program, confirm technology support, order food, coordinate participant parking, secure signage, and so forth.
13	Create marketing and promotional plan	Employ diverse marketing and promotional strategies (print materials, websites, social media, advertisements, and special promotions/incentives, such as academic partnerships for class credit or student org requirements).
14	Present the program	Be ready for the unexpected issues by scheduling time in the day of the program to deal with last-minute needs.
15	Assessment and feedback	Design program assessment and feedback opportunities when you develop learning outcomes. Have a plan for analyzing the data and sharing with program partners. Use this information for continual improvement of the program.

OTHER PREVENTION RESOURCES

National Sexual Violence Resource Center: www.nsvrc.org
Center for Disease Control and Prevention: www.cdc.gov
White House: www.notalone.gov

DISCUSSION QUESTIONS

1. What student, faculty, and staff characteristics are unique to your college or university that will impact your prevention strategies? Consider elements such as background characteristics, developmental and learning characteristics, commuter and residential differences, online and face-to-face learners, type of campus involvement, and employment and family responsibilities.

2. What stakeholders should be involved in prevention efforts on campus and in the community? What obstacles and barriers to collaboration and partnership need to be considered?

3. What resources are available to support prevention efforts? Consider staffing, financial, student, and knowledge resources.

4. Is there support in the campus community for prevention efforts? What attitudes or perceptions may create issues as prevention programs evolve?

5. What elements of the various prevention models and strategies do you think are most important for your college or university?

Part II

Risk Factors

Chapter 4

Objectification and Depersonalization

Now there were some terrible seeds on the planet that was the home of the little prince; and these were the seeds of the bao-bab. The soil of that planet was infested with them. A baobab is something you will never, never be able to get rid of if you attend to it too late. It spreads over the entire planet. It bores clear through it with its roots. And if the planet is too small, and the baobabs are too many, they split it in pieces.

—*Antoine de Saint-Exupéry,* The Little Prince

KEY TAKE-AWAYS

1. Violence, in many of its forms, begins when we see our experiences and our self as different from others. Conversely, when we see our salvation, happiness, and success connected to other people, we are able to empathize with their experiences and treat them with kindness.

2. While focus on self is a basic psychological and physiological survival mechanism, some have taken this focus to an extreme, where their own needs are placed above others not in an assertive way but in an aggressive one. This is not created at college, but rather something our students bring with them from their early childhood and teenage experiences. Some groups on college campuses can reinforce and escalate these tendencies.

3. The path forward involves recognizing the problem and learning ways to maintain a healthy view of self while remaining in connection with the needs and perspectives of others. This should not be seen as something we *have* to do, but rather, something we *get* to do. Something that makes us stronger as a society.

Our main goal for writing this book is bringing educators, staff, and faculty involved in the reduction of gender-based violence on campus better access to the research that helps explain the basis of the underlying situation we find ourselves in. Sexual violence isn't a natural phenomenon in our culture, but rather a result of interrelated risk factors that are very much something we can address and change.

While the factors are not presented in any particular order or hierarchy, we will suggest that this first factor, the objectification and depersonalization of others, is the central concept that draws together the others. The inability to see oneself in others is a thread that weaves its way through the rest of the factors, a keystone that locks and draws all of the other risk factors together.

DEFINING THE FACTOR

The tendency to objectify and depersonalize another group or individual begins with an individual turning away from specific, shared traits and characteristics and instead placing his or her needs and wants in a primary position to the detriment of those around them. When the individual or group attempts to understand others, it is with a negative and critical focus that highlights differences rather than similarities. When there is an attempt to understand others, it is most often a superficial understanding based on their expectations of how the other or others should see the world. There is a pervasive tendency to undervalue the unique aspects of human existence in others and a lack of willingness or ability to see one's thoughts, behaviors, or characteristics represented in others.

This manifests when an individual or group makes remarks or comments designed to undermine self-esteem or diminish or trivialize appearance, personality, or intelligence. Objectification brings the focus on the attributes of individuals at the expense of more fully informed understanding of their psychology, personality, and emotions. Another way to understand this is the distillation of a complex individual into the easiest or most convenient attributes. Others are seen without agency, as actors in a play, present for entertainment and amusement.

The feminist analysis of sexual assault has long indicated that

> a male-dominated society that trains men to use women as objects, and that legitimizes violence as a tool to achieve personal goals with a callous indifference to the feelings of victimized others, could breed a large number of men who openly assault women they know, and in fact may even like.
>
> (Schwartz and DeKeseredy 1997, p. 22)

48

This tendency to see women in particular as "less than" or second-class citizens creates an environment where violence occurs more easily, as the actions aren't really taken against a person or group who feels the same way as the aggressor.

ADDRESSING THE INDIVIDUAL

The objectification and depersonalization of a potential target are well discussed in the threat assessment literature (Grossman 1996; O'Toole 2000; Turner and Gelles 2003; O'Toole and Bowman 2011; Van Brunt 2012, 2014) and translate well to gender-based violence. The parallels are stark and unavoidable when wrestling with this question: "Why do targeted mass shootings seem to always be committed by men?" The first step to carrying out violence is to depersonalize and objectify the target.

The attackers or perpetrators are initially loath to cause harm to someone similar to themselves, and so they engage in a process of separating from the target as a necessary step prior to the perpetration of violence. Elliot Rodger provides an example in his social media postings. Rodger created a 141-page manifesto titled "My Twisted World" and carefully crafted and disseminated his message prior to his murderous spree of knife attacks, vehicular manslaughter, and shooting (Speer 2014).

The language of the manifesto demonstrates a pervasive disconnection from his targets, in this case the women of the sorority he saw as typical of those who rejected him. He writes,

> I cannot kill every single female on earth, but I can deliver a devastating blow that will shake all of them to the core of their wicked hearts. I will attack the very girls who represent everything I hate in the female gender: The hottest sorority of UCSB. After doing a lot of extensive research within the last year, I found out that the sorority with the most beautiful girls is Alpha Phi Sorority. I know exactly where their house is, and I've sat outside it in my car to stalk them many times. Alpha Phi sorority is full of hot, beautiful blonde girls; the kind of girls I've always desired but was never able to have because they all look down on me. They are all spoiled, heartless, wicked bitches. They think they are superior to me, and if I ever tried to ask one on a date, they would reject me cruelly.
>
> (p. 132)

Less extreme examples are rampant in popular media, in productions such as Girls Gone Wild and pornography sites. Women here are seen as one-dimensional objects to be consumed rather than understood. Further examples of this objectification and depersonalization will be shared in chapter 4.

ADDRESSING THE GROUP

While an individual who objectifies and depersonalizes others raises a concern, this concern is drastically increased when it becomes institutionalized and traditionalized by a group. All-male groups, such as athletic teams and fraternities, are most often cited as high-risk populations, but other single-sex organizations and coed clubs/organizations also have the potential to positively or negatively illustrate this risk factor (Berkowitz 1992, 2004; Boeringer 1999; Barnett and DiSabato 2000; Foubert 2000; Carr and VanDeusen 2004; Foubert and Perry 2007; Foubert et al. 2007). While some groups can come together to strengthen the tendency to empathize and see others more completely, others reinforce negative attitudes and serve to reduce understanding and further objectify individuals, creating an ideal environment for this problem to grow.

Schwartz and DeKeseredy (1997) describe K.J. Kanin's reference group theory, which says that perpetrators of sexual violence are

> often men who were highly trained as far back as elementary school to treat women as sexual objects and to use women simply as things to achieve their own desires: "scoring," or engaging in sexual activity. They do not need further training when they arrive in college. They simply need to locate other similarly minded men to make friends, and to tell each other that they are acting properly.
>
> (p. 32)

This observation is an important one as it highlights a problem that has been growing for years, if not decades. There is a mistaken assumption that college and university life creates problems that otherwise would not manifest. Nothing could be further from the truth. While there are certainly exacerbating factors that increase and escalate the risk on college campuses, if we are truly interested in uprooting the underlying causes of our current epidemic, it must start with exploring the values, morals, and worldview of our students long before they arrive on our campuses.

> Men do not grow up in a culture that promises and urges complete equality between men and women. Men who sexually and physically abuse women are not acting in a deviant manner

completely opposite to everything they have ever learned about the way to treat women.

(p. 47)

The authors give the examples of the access to pornographic magazines, the portrayal of women in movies as sex objects, and advertising that portrays women as sexual commodities. They argue that commercials, for example, are not often seen as harmful because they do not show men raping or being violent toward women. However, they do indicate an approval and even an encouragement for the objectification of women (Schwartz and DeKeseredy 1997).

Objectification can occur in a variety of ways, such as sitting outside facilities or residence halls to catcall women walking back to their residences early in the morning, creating a "walk of shame" for presumed sexually active women (Boswell and Spade 1996). Even as we write this example, the pervasive nature of language manifests. What image came forward in your mind when you encountered the phrase "catcalling"? For us, the idea of a playful cartoon wolf from our childhood cartoons manifests. He is wearing silly overalls and his eyes grow wide and appreciative as a female walks by him on the street. He whistles and leers at her, perhaps his heart beats more quickly and tries to pound its way out of his chest. He may drool and howl at her.

And here again is the trouble. This image is engrained for many of us. There is a subtle attempt to take something like street harassment and turn it into a more playful, boys-will-be-boys problem. The true harm of how this behavior creates a hostile and uncomfortable environment for the woman being catcalled isn't really addressed. Or worse, it is seen as a compliment and she should merely shrug it off. Santich (2014) quotes Niki Inclan from her anti-catcalling campaign:

I think it's a general disrespect towards women . . . If she's just trying to cross the street, to get to the parking lot, at a minimum you're interrupting her inner thoughts and internal dialog. On top of that, it's objectifying her. And depending on what is said and done, street harassment can become an act of violence.

(p. 1)

Examples of this phenomenon also include a group of men at a bar or party encouraging the targeting of women based on a certain characteristic as a part of a bet or as a form of entertainment for the group. Specifically, the process of "hogging" has been documented as occurring when "men seek women who are overweight or unattractive to satisfy their competitive or sexual urges" (Gailey and Prohaska 2006, p. 32). The group depersonalizes the overweight woman as lazy, unattractive, or less socially acceptable in order to separate the individual from the potential target of sexual violence. Impersonal sex is documented further in high-risk fraternity members discussing sexual exploits following parties as "faceless victims" (Boswell and Spade 1996).

Recently, another example occurred at an off-campus party. This involved women being asked to wear red, yellow, or green bracelets to communicate to partygoers their current relationship status. Red meant they were in a relationship, green meant they were not, and yellow indicated it's complicated. The underlying message here is that red women are taken, yellow need to be convinced, and anything goes with the green ladies. Women are reduced to colors of convenience for the male partygoers, further helping them avoid wasting their time talking and getting to know someone new, or even worse, wasting time getting to know someone who is unavailable sexually. More common party themes that objectify women are CEOs and Office Hoes, or Pimps and Hoes.

There is a pervasive tendency for organizational behaviors to further objectify rape victims through the acceptance and promotion of rape myths. Sororities, for example, may deny the humanity of the victim and contribute to revictimization. The organization may further isolate the victim by holding her responsible for alcohol- or drug-related behaviors connected to the incident, or by removing her from membership because of the reputational concerns in the community. This modern application of a scarlet letter is an act of depersonalization that builds upon itself where even groups of women begin to "reject their own gender group and see other women in negatively stereotyped ways," thus seeing themselves as exceptions to their gender and believing the woman's behavior provoked the attack (Cowan 2000, p. 239).

FROM THE FRONT LINES

Sexual Assault and the Objectification of Women

Multiple factors are involved in any kind of victimization, whether it is physical abuse, sexual assault, or murder. A fundamental issue is the failure of empathy. As long as we empathize with people, recognizing them as fully human as ourselves, and are sensitive to their feelings and their dignity, we do not victimize them. It is when empathy fails that victimization occurs.

Empathy can be absent for a variety of reasons. In some people, such as extreme narcissists or psychopathic personalities, the lack of empathy can be a chronic state. In most people, however, empathy exists but can be overcome by intense emotion, such as rage. People often do things in a state of rage that they later regret. Similarly, people commit acts under the influence of drugs or alcohol, or in response to hallucinations or delusions, that later cause severe guilt and anguish. All of these can be factors in sexual assaults.

Words and ideas play an important role in the loss of empathy through the process of dehumanizing or objectifying particular groups of people. This is seen in wartime when the enemy is referred to by derogatory terms. During the Vietnam War, the Vietnamese were called "gooks." Similarly, the Nazis portrayed Jews not as people to be killed but as "vermin" to be "exterminated." In a more recent phenomenon, many school shooters viewed their intended victims through the lens of derogatory labels, such as jocks, preps, zombies, idiots, and robots. It is easier to kill people when they are seen not as people but as subhuman creatures.

This comes into play in sexual assaults, with women being viewed as whores, bitches, or bimbos. By dehumanizing them, stripping them of any semblance of personality, autonomy, or intelligence, and viewing them simply as sexual bodies, the empathic link is broken and it becomes easier for the perpetrators to carry out their assaults.

Another factor supporting this objectification is that of perceived injustice. Many perpetrators believe that their victims deserve what happens to them, that "they had it coming." In this twisted view, the perpetrators are simply meting out justice. There are batterers who believe that the women they assault brought the violence on themselves, and there are sex offenders who believe that their victims "asked for it" by the way that they acted.

Rape is often said to be a crime of power and control. It is an attempt to establish dominance over someone who is a threat to the perpetrator's sense of himself. How is a woman a threat? If a man is attracted to a woman, but doesn't have the ability to engage in a relationship with her, he feels powerless. Sexual assault then becomes his method of asserting his sense of masculinity and feeling dominant. For such a man, to be helpless in the face of women is to be a failure as a man. This is intolerable; it is a threat to his identity. He must shift the balance of power.

This dynamic intermingles with anger and a sense of injustice. Some perpetrators look around and see other men succeeding with women where they are failing. In their mind, this isn't fair. It is an injustice, and it makes them mad. If they sense that women are flirting with them but denying them sex, this not only plays into their sense that women are "asking for it" but also generates fury.

Even if women do not flirt with such perpetrators, women's sexual attractiveness alone can be infuriating to them. Imagine a starving man standing in front of a gourmet banquet and being told that he cannot have a bite of food, with people passing delicious dishes under his nose. The temptation would be maddening. For some perpetrators, simply being around attractive women is like being the starving man at the banquet—they can look but they cannot touch. This causes rage. It is not only unfair and infuriating but humiliating, too. In their eyes, the women must be punished. Sexual assault thus serves multiple purposes: to vent rage, to establish dominance and manliness, and to serve justice.

Sexual assault often results from a combination of factors: insecurities about masculinity, inability to form relationships, rage at being denied sex, dehumanizing language and beliefs about women, and a belief that this is unjust—all of these factors contribute to the failure of empathy necessary for victimization.

These factors can be seen in the school shooter Elliot Rodger. Though Rodger did not commit a sexual offense, his rampage was driven by his rage toward women for "denying" him sex. In fact, his autobiographical document provides a remarkable window into the dynamics of a violent offender (Rodger 2014). He wrote extensively about his envy of sexually active men and his outrage at the injustice of his failure with women. His goal was to kill women at the "hottest sorority" on the campus of the University of California at Santa Barbara. His attack was an act of misogynistic violence (Langman 2014).

This discussion has so far focused on one type of perpetrator, but this is not the only type. Let's return to the concept of the extreme narcissist or psychopathic personality. Such people live for themselves, meeting their own needs with no concern for the impact of their behavior on those they encounter. For these perpetrators, sexual assaults are a pleasurable entertainment rather than an act of rage or response to perceived injustice. As one psychopathic rapist commented, "What's a guy gonna do? She had a nice ass. I helped myself" (Hare 1999, p. 88). He violated a woman simply because he wanted to, and felt no guilt or shame in doing so. Despite the lack of rage, inherent in the act is the absence of empathy, the objectification of women as sexual toys, and a disregard for them as human beings.

Both types of sexual offenders—those who are desperate and full of rage, and those who are narcissistic and callous—have common features. Not only do they lack empathy and dehumanize women, but also they have a sense of entitlement. They both begin with the conviction that women owe them sexual gratification. The thwarting of their desire is the root of their violence.

In addition to the types of perpetrators discussed here, there are also the extreme cases of serial rapists who are also serial killers, but that is beyond the scope of this section. It is important to keep in mind, however, that sexual assault is a complex phenomenon with multiple types of crimes and multiple types of perpetrators.

Peter Langman, PhD
Author, *Why Kids Kill*

We wanted to offer a counterpoint here to speak to the issue of sexual violence and the tendency to move forward with negative male perspective where half the student population is seen as demeaning, leering animals incapable of restraining themselves or seeing women as people. The idea of objectification works both ways here, when we fall into the trap of seeing perpetrators or those accused of sexual assault with that same lens of reductionist thinking. While there is no excuse for sexual assault, there is an imperative, codified in VAWA, that we provide support not only for the complainant in Title IX cases but also for the accused. Dr. M.J. Raleigh tackles this often controversial point of view in our second "From the Front Lines" segment in this chapter.

FROM THE FRONT LINES

The Accused

When the call comes in from the director of student conduct with the simple sentence, "I am sending over a young man who has been charged with sexual assault," I never quite know what will walk into the clinic.

The majority of the accused are in shock, confused, and unsure about what this means for the future. Often the first conversation involves recounting the charges and what is remembered of the events leading to the charges. Quickly, on the heels of that recounting, comes the all too common topic of what constitutes sexual assault and how what happened does or does not fit that definition. I have seen the light go on in the eyes of an accused as he becomes aware of what has happened and what will happen next. Calling home to explain to family why they are not in classes or need money for a lawyer is for most accused what brings a look of sheer terror. The media correctly focuses on the multiple-victim sexual perpetrators who are on campus. This does not, however, constitute the majority of individuals accused of sexual assault on campus. The overwhelming majority are under 25 years old, white male, and under the influence of alcohol at the time of the assault. Calling home to tell his mother or father that he has been accused of sexual assault is not a call the student ever imagined having to make.

Although each individual accused is unique and there is no pattern or personality trait that creates a "rapist" profile, there is a set of common events that occur after charges are filed and the conduct process begins. Research on the mental health impact of criminal victimization on women indicates that assault survivors are 8.5 times more likely to attempt suicide and struggle with suicidal ideation, depression, and anxiety compared to women who have not experienced sexual assault (Kilpatrick et al. 1985). The sequelae of sexual assault last for years and it may take a lifetime for the victim to process all aspects of the events. Research on the emotional impact on the person being accused is scarce.

Friends, acquaintances, and family of the accused may express a range of emotions. It is not uncommon for the person accused to experience feelings of isolation, shame, fear of being labeled a monster, disbelief that they could be a rapist, and anger. It is important to remember that a student with no known mental health concerns, excellent coping skills, resilience, solid support networks, and insight will struggle to integrate an accusation of assault into life moving forward. Since few college students will have all of these protective factors, it is more likely that an accusation of sexual assault is emotionally devastating to the accused. Whether the accusation is true or shown to be false does little to reduce the emotional impact for the person accused.

The situation for the accused gets more complex when two pieces of information are added to the unfolding story. If the accused is struggling with a mental health issue before the assault the strain of new environmental pressure will exacerbate existing conditions. The second scenario is the student with an underlying mental health issue brought to the surface by the process of investigation to outcome and adjudication on and off campus. If individuals are found responsible for the assault they may be facing shame, family rejection, and reinforcement of identity as a "monster" on top of the obvious loss of academic continuance, either for a limited period of time or permanently. If the case is brought through the criminal justice system off campus, the possibility of jail time, along with all the lifelong ramifications of being in the legal system, takes the individual's life down a very different track than the one the accused imagined.

Suicidal ideation and feelings of desperation, loss, and anger are common reactions. Emotional isolation is both the result and cause of depression and a very common result of being accused of rape. The student is removed from his normal routine by either his choice or the choice of the victim if they share classes, residence, and friend groups. If the man accused struggles with depression and or anxiety, the isolation from others will exacerbate this condition.

The social reality on campus can be brutal, ranging from being yelled at in public by friends of the survivor, friends of the accused being hostile and violent with others in defense of the accused, social media being used as a weapon, misogynist statements being made as justification, and even encouragement to blame the victim. None of these social reactions help the accused understand or emotionally process the event. In many ways this may move the accused further away from experiencing genuine remorse, understanding, and ultimately behavior change. Moving forward, the accused may experience mistrust in relationships, fear of being accused again, long periods of not being able to focus on academic work, and a struggle to imagine a future that is not defined by the word "rapist." Creating a monster allows us to feel safe, as if we will be able to identify the monster when we see him again and sleep easy at night now that we have removed the threat.

Remember that the majority of sexual assault on campus is not being executed by serial rapists; the reality is that an assault on campus is likely an isolated incident for the accused. It is important to ask the question, what have we done for the person accused of sexual assault? Have we done a mental health screening, have we offered therapeutic support and access to an advocate, and have we helped him develop a support network that does not shy away from the accusation but finds a way to allow learning so the accused can heal?

Mary-Jeanne Raleigh, PhD, LPC, LMHC, NCC
Director of Counseling
University of North Carolina, Pembroke

REDUCING THE RISK

Given the arguments made thus far, how do we address these problems as they occur in both individuals and groups on our campuses? The simple answer is through communication and listening. When we attack a strongly held and developed set of beliefs, the person or persons being attacked will react with a sense of defensiveness and resistance. Change comes at the cost of commitment, patience, and careful conversations.

Think about the last time someone challenged a deeply held belief or thought. Imagine someone coming up to you and saying, "You are wrong! You are contributing to the downfall of our modern-day society! You are enforcing a rape culture. Think of the children!" How would you react to this? If you are like us, probably not very well.

So the challenge here, at the most basic level, is to teach the underlying concept of nonobjectification and personalization. How do we make someone feel unique? How do we help someone feel as if he or she is heard? How do we elicit someone's willingness to be vulnerable and work on changing something that is rooted in who he or she is? We do this through listening. We do this through demonstrating the very behavior we want the individual or group to adopt. We listen, we perspective-take, we empathize. We treat them the way we want them to see and treat others.

This requires a sense of patience and true caring for the other person. We want them to change not merely because their attitudes and beliefs are contributing to a major social and violence problem on our campus, but also because the path they are on is ultimately a self-destructive one. When we care only about ourselves, when we are blind to the perspective of others, when we treat others merely as objects for our enjoyment, we are hurting ourselves.

It has been said that college, above all else, is about teaching critical thinking skills. The central mission for higher education is not sharing knowledge but rather teaching students how to learn, how to think. If acquisition of knowledge was the end goal, there are more effective ways to accomplish this. But instead, we are creating self-actualized members of society: people who can learn, who can understand, who can exhibit compassion for others. All of these traits are core to liberal arts education.

If it sounds like we are suggesting that the teaching of empathy is the solution to the problem of objectification and depersonalization, you would be correct. We spend more time on how to teach active listening and empathy skills to students both individually and in groups in chapter 11.

DEEPER DIVE INTO MORAL DISENGAGEMENT

Albert Bandura's theory (1999) on moral disengagement has been applied in a number of areas related to the prevention of sexual violence. What are the psychological processes at play in which individuals can disengage morally from their behaviors?

There are several ways we separate ourselves from our conduct. We engage in a process of either shifting responsibility for the conduct itself or minimizing the harm of the behavior. In this chapter, we present the factor of objectification as an example, the euphemisms and language applied to women (slut, easy, whore) to frame actions against them as more acceptable. Individuals may also utilize advantageous comparison to justify conduct. Advantageous comparison is when conduct is described in comparison to much worse conduct. An example could be when a perpetrator indicates that his or her behaviors were not rape or violent or forceful when the conduct is actually just that. Consider the following scenario:

> Alan is seen walking a girl into a room at a party. They are alone. He has his arm around her shoulder and is clearly holding her up. He shuts the door to the room. Alan emerges later by himself with a smile on his face, and the girl can be seen with her clothes disheveled as she is lying on the bed asleep. When another partygoer says to Alan that he just took advantage of the drunk friend, Alan comments, "It's not like I raped her. She was coming on to me all night, and she wasn't complaining in there." He shrugs and walks away.

Unfortunately, the more offensive the comparative conduct, then the better we perceive our own conduct. In a group setting, this can result in individuals seeking out others with even worse conduct to associate with in order to feel that their own behavior is appropriate. Then the cycle continues as the social norms around the individual further reinforce the negative behavior.

Individuals may also use moral justification to account for conduct by indicating that it served a worthy purpose. Red flag phrases include versions of the "I am just giving her what she wants" or "She asked for it," or the male who justifies his interactions with a female by saying, "She has been coming on to me all semester. I finally just gave it up so she would stop bothering me." All are forms of moral justification and shift the nature of the behavior.

This brings us to the other way individuals disengage from conduct by shifting the responsibility of the harm caused to others or by minimizing the role we played in the conduct. In group settings, this often means blaming the conduct on being told by an authority figure to behave in a certain way. For college students, authority figures are often their own peers just a few years older, especially in fraternity systems where control over membership status is held by the group. In sexual violence, blame is often shifted to the victim. Unfortunately, not only does the perpetrator shift this responsibility but also society and nonperpetrator groups support these perspectives and do not recognize them as problematic. In Alan's scenario earlier, this manifests in his statement, "She was coming on to me all night." Other similar statements are used to focus the attention on the victim instead of the perpetrator, such as statements related to the victim's behaviors immediately prior to the incident as well as past behaviors and statements about how the victim was dressed or how much the victim drank.

Diffusion of responsibility in group settings is frequent because when the group decides on a course of action, there is no responsible individual. The group is the responsible party. It is common to minimize the harm that is caused by conduct by disregarding or distorting the consequences. In bystander scenarios within a group, if two men decide to collude to drug the drink of a woman in order to obtain sex, the person who drugs the drink is able to ignore the harm of the sexual assault because he was not the person who physically assaulted the woman and because he was not present to see it. With the growth of social media, we often see video recordings or postings of pictures of what is clearly abhorrent behavior. In those cases, the people taking the video or picture often absolve themselves from the harm taking place because they were not directly involved.

Other common scenarios that are described by Bandura's theory include those you might see in dating and domestic violence situations or in stalking incidents. In dating violence incidents, perpetrators may try to attribute the blame to the other party, indicating that they left no choice but to be treated in that way. The perpetrator tries to appear victimized perhaps by taking a defensive act and portraying it as initiating the violence. Stalking incidents can often result from relationship breakups where the stalker is able to rationalize his or her behavior as being something that is deserved because of previous treatment.

Initiatives that consider how moral disengagement occurs would include some of these examples:

- Clearly define and disseminate definitions and examples of conduct that violates institutional standards so that conduct cannot be minimized. Use the spectrum of sexual violence to explain negative behaviors in order to connect behaviors such as objectification to physically violent behaviors of sexual assault. Address that the consumption of alcohol is not an excuse for behavior. Explain the harm in various types of behaviors along the spectrum of sexual violence.

- Watch out for situations where individuals can feel anonymous and blend into the crowd. Why is it difficult to manage fan behavior at large sporting events? Why are so many hateful things shared on social media? Because it is possible to feel invisible in the crowd. Thus, proactive education around large social events and activities related to party themes and other planning can catch some of these practices before they propagate.

- In accountability systems, schools should utilize both group and individual sanctions when poor conduct occurs. It must be communicated clearly across the group that behaviors have the potential to impact the organization as a whole as well as at the individual student level. Officers in organizations have an even higher level of responsibility. If the social chair and the president of an organization sign off on a social event that results in people wearing costumes that are demeaning to women, not only does the responsibility fall to the organization, but also the individual officers and members responsible for approving the decision and participating in the event in negative ways should be sanctioned.

- Bystander intervention programs (covered in chapter 6) must consider what authority looks like to the group of students being trained and give them the skills to challenge or deal with an authority that encourages poor behaviors, especially one of their own peer group. Problematic behavior can be dismissed as an authority figure told a group it was okay or had to be done to be compliant.

DISCUSSION QUESTIONS

1. Discuss some ways objectification and depersonalization are taught to children and teenagers during their development through social media, religion, television and movies, parents, and peers.

2. Where is the balance between focusing on the needs of self and being willing to see things from another perspective? Is there a healthy balance that can be found between pursuing an individual's own needs and desires while respecting the agency and equality of others? What are some ways to teach these concepts to students?

3. Given the pervasive nature of the problem as it comes to our campus, discuss some of the proactive approaches to engage those hosting parties or groups that reinforce depersonalization and eventually change their behavior. What are some of the obstacles to engaging these groups?

4. How should parents, advisors, and alumni be involved in a college's efforts related to objectification? What are the advantages and disadvantages of their involvement in these efforts?

5. Beyond gender-based objectification, what other areas on campus are engaged in this type of dialogue and willing to partner on related initiatives?

Chapter 5

Obsessive or Addictive Pornography/Sex Focus

The more often we see the things around us—even the beautiful and wonderful things—the more they become invisible to us. That is why we often take for granted the beauty of this world: the flowers, the trees, the birds, the clouds—even those we love. Because we see things so often, we see them less and less.
—*Joseph B. Wirthlin, religious leader*

KEY TAKE-AWAYS

1. Sexual behaviors and attitudes are learned from our access to information and from our experiences. If pornography is our primary source of information, an unhealthy view of sexuality can emerge.

2. Obsessive pornography usage leads to desensitization and the further objectification and depersonalization of others. Similarly, the consumption of degrading or violent pornography has the potential to create a practice or fantasy rehearsal for actual violence.

3. This consumption can occur with individuals as well as within a group setting. Each creates challenges for the conduct office to address with students. Having an understanding of the differences among punitive, developmental/educational, and restorative justice sanctions can assist in addressing these behaviors.

The issue of pornography consumption is a challenging one to discuss. As feminist sex educators, there is a reasonable argument that most, if not all, forms of pornography are degrading to women and men and lead to unrealistic expectations. The industry itself has been described as exploitive and harmful to those it employs.

Yet, as educators who value positive sex communication, we celebrate the diversity of sexual experience. Everyone has their own idea of what is offensive and what is puritanical. So as we grapple with this chapter, we ask for some leeway and suggest that our central points are founded on the extremes of the behavior. Our concerns lie in the consumption of degrading or violent pornography or the frequency of the consumption creating difficulties in friendships, completing schoolwork, and maintaining healthy relationships.

It is our personal view that pornography consumption, in and of itself, is not the problem. It is the overconsumption and the use of degrading pornography that depicts rape fantasies, sex with children, sex with nonconsenting adults, or the violent degradation of partners in painful manner that concern us. This consumption creates the potential for fantasy rehearsal. It is this usage that becomes less about sexual gratification and more about practicing and building to violence.

It is also concerning when pornography is the only information about sex available to someone. When there is a gap in healthy sex education and it is filled only with degrading or violent pornography, a person's understanding of what is normal sexual behavior begins to shift. Our sexual scripts evolve more collaboratively and openly, and not just because of pornography, but rather in the vacuum of other positive sexual education and information, pornography is likely to have a greater impact than that which develops through more open discussion and exploration. Sex, in turn, becomes defined in the negative, in the forbidden and scandalous, rather as a naturally pleasurable activity between consenting parties.

An example of this comes from the TV show *Friends*. There was an episode in Season 4 where Joey and Chandler find themselves with free access to cable pornography. After they consume the free content almost nonstop for days, Chandler comes into the apartment and has this interaction with Joey. While a humorous exchange, it does highlight the concern that drove us to explore this risk factor.

Chandler:	"Hey, I was just at the bank, and there was this really hot teller, and she didn't ask me to go do it with her in the vault!"
Joey:	"Same kind of thing happened to me! A woman pizza delivery guy comes over, gives me the pizza, takes the money . . . and leaves!"
Chandler:	"What? No like 'Nice apartment, I bet the bedrooms are huge?'"

Joey: "No! Nothing!"
              They both pause, looking at each other.
Chandler: "You know what? We have to turn off the porn."
Joey: "I think you are right."

DEFINING THE FACTOR

The overuse of pornography is hard to describe without references back to the earlier risk factor related to objectification and depersonalization. There is some intentional overlap between this risk factor and the problems that occur when we stop seeing people as individuals with a sense of agency and choice and instead see them as objects for our pleasure.

It would be reasonable to assume that an individual or group with a tendency toward objectification would likely have a motivation to consume depersonalizing and violent pornography. Inversely, obsessive use of pornography could establish and reinforce the tendency toward objectification. The circularity of the risk factor discussed in this chapter makes it difficult to pinpoint what is the initial cause and what is the resulting effect.

Research has established that exposure to sexually explicit material is moderately correlated with a variety of negative outcomes, including increased sexual perpetration and endorsement of rape myths (Malamuth et al. 2000; Oddone-Paolucci et al. 2000; Jewkes et al. 2002; Carr and VanDeusen 2004). Exposure to pornography may also exacerbate sexually aggressive proclivities in those who are at high risk for such behavior (Kingston et al. 2009). While these studies are compelling, and the role of pornography on the health of a culture is a significant question, pornography consumption does not cause rape (Jensen 2004).

It is worth noting here that all pornography is not the same. Without expanding the premise of this chapter into an analysis of the harm/benefit of the more common forms of pornography readily available, there is an increase in concern for this risk factor when an individual or group is consuming violent pornography (Allen et al. 2006). While the actors and actresses may very well discuss consent, the fantasy of sexual encounters is focused on the dynamics of power and control. For example, rape fantasy or humiliation pornography would increase a level of concern around objectification and also overlap with additional risk factors we will discuss in future chapters, such as misogynistic ideology, lack of empathy, or obsessive and/or addictive thoughts.

As pornography has become more acceptable, both legally and culturally, the level of brutality toward, and degradation of,

65

women has intensified (Jensen 2004). The degree of habitualization, increased novelty, and sensation seeking becomes a larger concern in terms of increased violence in the medium's content. One pornography director was blunt in describing his task:

> One of the things about today's porn and the extreme market, the gonzo market, so many fans want to see so much more extreme stuff that I'm always trying to figure out ways to do something different. But it seems everybody wants to see a girl doing a d.p. [double penetration] now or a gangbang. For certain girls, that's great, and I like to see that for certain people, but a lot of fans are becoming a lot more demanding about wanting to see the more extreme stuff. It's definitely brought porn somewhere, but I don't know where it's headed from there.
>
> (AVN director's roundtable 2003, p. 46)

It doesn't help matters when most of our country is woefully ill-informed when it comes to basic issues of health and sexuality. Young people are not being taught, or are being taught ineffectively, basic information on sex and sexuality (Aronowitz et al. 2012). A study found a shocking lack of information or misinformation: only 25% of the youth surveyed knew that urination and menstruation occurred through different openings in the vulva, 33% knew that withdrawal was an ineffective birth control method, and 37% knew that people could satisfy their sexual needs in activities other than intercourse. The average score on a sexual knowledge survey was 44% correct among college students (Carrera et al. 2000).

As with any of the factors discussed in this text, it is a challenge to wrestle with the spectrum of behaviors along the continuum of a tendency, common usage, and obsessive or addictive usage. While some may argue against the tendency for any type of pornography to cause concern, consumption of pornography with power and control themes that leads to increasing desensitization for the autonomy of the individual and respect for a partner or partners becomes an area of increased concern. It is worth considering that the consumption of this pornography becomes a method of fantasy rehearsal for future action.

Diana Russell has argued that pornography is a causal factor in the way that it can

(1) predispose some males to desire rape or intensify this desire; (2) undermine some males' internal inhibitions against acting out rape desires; (3) undermine some males' social inhibitions against

acting out rape desires; and (4) undermine some potential victims' abilities to avoid or resist rape.

(Russell 1998, p. 121)

Seto et al. (2001, p. 1) highlight an additional concern around pornography: "From the existing evidence, we argue that individuals who are already predisposed to sexually offend are the most likely to show an effect of pornography exposure and are the most likely to show the strongest effects."

Conversely, infrequent consumption of pornography depicting a consenting relationship should be considered within the rich tapestry afforded to our individual freedoms for psychological healthy lives. While it may not be for everyone, there should be a concern for this risk factor becoming a bludgeon against any form of pornographic images.

That is not the premise of this risk factor. Addiction here can be defined from the fifth edition of *Diagnostic and Statistical Manual of Mental Disorders* (American Psychiatric Association 2013), though pornography addiction is not an included medical condition. However, use of pornography that interferes with social activities, work attendance, class or study, financial hardships, or hygiene or an inability to cut back usage or take a break for a period of time should all be warning signs that pornography use may be approaching an addictive level.

ADDRESSING THE INDIVIDUAL

Individual pornography use in an obsessive or inappropriate manner is most common where students become consumed with watching the material or using pornography in an addictive manner. This may become known to the community as students engage in more secretive behaviors, such as: separating themselves from activities like going to dinner with a group of hall mates, locking the door to their room, missing class, or disregarding daily hygiene, like showering or brushing hair or teeth.

With residential life students, it may be easiest to have the first intervention here be with a residence advisor or hall director. Depending on the severity of the problem, there may be an additional referral to the behavioral intervention team or to the counseling center. It can be helpful at this stage to try to reduce some of the shame or potential stigma that would prevent the student from seeking help. If there were a lack of shame or surprise at the confrontation, then perhaps an approach that seeks to develop discrepancy with the student would be effective—for instance, helping

67

the student understand how the behavior is getting in the way of his or her academics, social life, or daily self-care.

Other examples of individuals becoming addicted or overusing pornography typically arise as minor conduct infractions. These may involve public masturbation in a hallway or lounge, discussion of questionable materials in the classroom or other group space, or sharing pictures or videos on a university computer or in a public space. In more extreme cases, the student may attempt to collect his or her own material by secretly recording other students in bathrooms or showers or rifling through laundry rooms for underwear or other perceived stimulation.

Progressive discipline and educational models to address this behavior are discussed near the end of this chapter.

ADDRESSING THE GROUP

Examples that would increase concern for this risk factor would include groups that utilize pornographic imagery or videos in a public setting or an activity that diminishes the target's humanity, such as hosting social events with porn-inspired themes. This could be apparent in the utilization of images that reduce women to body parts or objects to fulfill desire at the expense of their unique personhood. This factor can escalate to the circulation of videos of sexual activity including group members, recorded with or without the knowledge of the participating parties.

Group indicators might include an athletic team that regularly visits a strip club as part of team activities or a climate within the organization that encourages impersonal or coercive sex. This occurred in 2004 when the Associated Press reported strippers to be commonplace at football recruitment parties at the University of Denver (Strippers said to be commonplace 2004). Steve Lower, president of Hardbodies Entertainment Inc. in Denver, said athletes at Colorado and universities around the country have been paying strippers to entertain recruits for years. "It's a tradition, like throwing a bachelor party," he said. It may also include group interaction on social media accounts where posting and sharing of nude images or pictures is encouraged or required.

When a group culture is infused with this unhealthy sex focus, as will be apparent in other risk factors, it can breed a disrespectful and often harassing environment for all women and for men who do not behave in a similar manner. The group activity indicates an approval and encouragement of sexual exploits that look similar to pornographic activities, many of which are not possible in a healthy, consensual sexual encounter.

FROM THE FRONT LINES

A Case Study in Sexual Sadism

Bill and Tina are engaged to be married. Bill is a senior biology major at a major university who plans to attend dental school following his graduation. Tina is a senior who met Bill her junior year, and immediately became infatuated with him, because of his good looks and air of confidence. Bill insisted they move in together shortly after they began dating and within months they were engaged. However, due to Tina's work and class schedule, and Bill's self-described overloaded work and study schedule, they have little time together, particularly during the week.

Over time, Bill slowly has taken over control of all of their money, and gives Tina an allowance for daily expenses. Bill discourages Tina from spending time with family and friends, and wants her to spend all of her free time with him. Bill will show up at places where Tina goes to meet friends, and becomes very jealous when he sees her talking to anyone else. He has followed her when she doesn't know it, and he once put a tracking device on her car.

Because she relinquished any involvement in managing expenses, Tina was not aware of all of the charges Bill accrued on a shared credit card until she saw an e-mail regarding a late notice. She called the credit card company and was completely shocked to learn there were thousands of dollars of charges from pornographic websites that featured bondage, torture, and bestiality involving children, as well as adult males and females. Tina had confided to no one that Bill had expressed an interest in bondage behavior with her during sex.

Tina confronted Bill, but he denied it and told her that the credit card was stolen, and he was working it out with the credit card company. Tina was not convinced and thought about the several nights a week that Bill went out in the evening without explanation, and came home sometimes wearing different clothes, or looking disheveled. When she questioned him, he became very angry with her and punched her in the stomach multiple times.

A series of four unsolved sexual assaults have occurred on the campus since the beginning of the semester. The attacks are blitz-style attacks by an offender who came out of the tree-lined walkways and overpowered the victims. The injuries to these victims are significant and include blunt force trauma to their stomachs, and both vaginal and anal assaults. An item of jewelry is taken from each of the victims who were left for dead. The assaults appear to be escalating in violence.

Dr. Mary Ellen O'Toole
Former FBI BAU Supervisor
George Mason University

FROM THE FRONT LINES

Let's Talk About Sex

I grew up in a household where we did not talk about sex. When a sex scene came on TV, I usually got embarrassed and left the room, changed the channel, or suddenly felt a wave of sleepiness and closed my eyes. In fact, even now, I'm a little embarrassed writing this and knowing my parents might read it.

I was the youngest of my siblings, both of whom were quite a bit older than me, so I grew up in the house alone with my parents. I do not remember having a conversation about the birds and the bees with my mom and my dad, which begs the question: where did I learn about sex, because it was not in the classroom? My church hosted a retreat one weekend when I was in high school where the youth group had a special session about sex and relationships. I am pretty sure the theme was "don't have sex before you get married." I stayed with my cousins a lot and picked up information from them when my older boy cousins started dating. And I learned from my friends during slumber parties and late-night gatherings.

It wasn't until recently as I started to think more about how we learn about sex and how we impact attitudes and behaviors related to sex that I thought more about my own upbringing. Why was I embarrassed to talk about sex? How did the lack of information related to sex impact me?

Laci Green calls it "sex-shaming"—the idea that it's embarrassing or shameful to talk about sex. Why does a word change in such profound ways just by putting the word "sex" in front of it? Assault as opposed to sexual assault. Disease as compared to sexually transmitted disease. Why are body parts related to sex looked at so differently from body parts less related to sex? If you're not familiar with Laci Green, she is a sex educator with her own YouTube following. She presented on my college campus recently about how to have the best sex ever for a group of fraternity men. Her presentation started with basic information about body parts (basically she put several pictures of penises and vaginas on the screen and explained things) and moved through safe sex practices, sexual health, and consent. As I was watching her presentation, other than thinking about how I was going to explain to my university administrators what we were doing if they showed up, I was thinking about why with a group of 18-year-olds, so many of them were getting information they had never had access to before that evening.

When you think about that gap for so many college students in access to correct and balanced information about sexual health and sexual relationships, it helps you to understand why the use of pornography or involvement with a group with a sex focus can be so detrimental to a student's development and understanding of sex. If that is the only information people have access to related to sex or it is the primary source of information, they will draw from that for their own sexual relationships. For victims of sexual violence, if they are already uncertain about what a healthy sexual relationship is or who they can talk about sex with, it is even more complicated.

To me, this chapter of the book particularly speaks to the need for family and school involvement around issues of sex education for students before they arrive on the college campus. Embarrassment around issues of sex just shuts down critical conversations that we need to have in order to prevent incidents of violence and to promote healthy relationships and sexuality.

Dr. Amy Murphy
Assistant Professor, Curriculum and Instruction
Angelo State University

REDUCING THE RISK

Admittedly, this is one of the harder risk factors to address directly with an individual because of the hidden nature of the obsessive usage and the way the school may be made aware. Certainly, there are opportunities within the student conduct system or behavioral intervention team to address pornography misuse when it comes to materials accessed on the university computer system or public masturbation in the residence halls around roommates or peers. This creates potential opportunities for a more developmental sanction involving an assessment for addiction as well as education around the harm such use may cause the individuals. Likewise, there would be off-campus involvement in a criminal process if the pornography use involved children, rape, or animals, given local laws.

The challenge, when addressing this issue, is to avoid the creation of a moral police on campus or the equivalent of a *Fahrenheit 451* type of censorship of individual freedoms. This is not what we are suggesting. Rather, we hope administrators, counselors, conduct officers, and law enforcement recognize this issue as beyond a simple violation of the computer use policy or as part of a roommate conflict. Within the existing systems of student conduct, residential life mediation, and behavioral intervention teams, there should be an awareness that obsessive or addictive use of pornography or the consumption of pornography with rape fantasy, torture, or degradation themes would be better addressed with the addition of developmental and educational sanctions in addition to the punitive ones.

Group settings are more amenable to addressing these issues, as the use of pornography is, by definition, more public because of the multiple people in the group. The added pressure for group viewings of pornography creates the potential for a hostile environment and coercion for students who may not wish to view such materials. Students often engage in shouting degrading or offensive comments during the movies that can also add to the presence of discriminatory or aggressive attitudes.

Group events may also include open parties where materials are showed to those in attendance. These actions could be seen as a pattern of escalating behaviors as well as an attempt at lowering the defenses of those in attendance and creating an overly sexual atmosphere, where sexual advances would be seen as more in line with the party vibe. Schools should adapt a clear policy around the showing of this material at parties, gatherings, or group events, with punitive, developmental/educational, and restorative justice sanctions for violating the policy.

To clarify, conduct offices on college campuses generally have three approaches to discipline when infractions occur. *Punitive approaches* are similar to traffic tickets or library fines. Students who violate a policy are required to pay a fine and then are able to go about their business. Multiple offensives and fines may result in suspension or expulsion, depending on the flagrancy and frequency of the code violations.

Developmental or educational sanctions are additional sanctions that can be placed on a student who violated the code. These may involve reflective exercises or written assignments to aid students in better understanding why their behavior was a problem and create an opportunity for students to learn from their mistakes and behave differently in the future. These sanctions are slightly more time-consuming for the school and are typically reserved for behaviors that are egregious enough to necessitate follow-up to prevent a recurrence. Serious alcohol intoxication to the point where an ambulance needs to be called is a good example for a conduct action that should reach beyond a simple punitive fine and instead include some reflection or counseling to increase awareness for the student to prevent this behavior from reoccurring.

Restorative justice sanctions are yet another tool that can be applied to students who are found in violation of policy. Here, the goal of the sanction becomes finding ways the student can pay back the community for the harm that is done. A student who engages in vandalism behavior in the residence halls may be asked to make reparations to the janitorial staff who had to clean up the damage. These sanctions would often be in addition to the existing punitive (fine) and developmental (essay) requirements. Restorative justice sanctions are more rarely applied on a college campus due to the time and effort it takes to create and enforce them. However, we would like to argue that these are particularly useful in bringing about lasting change following a group event.

Examples of various approaches to student discipline are explored over three different cases involving pornography use on campus with individuals and within a group setting. These are offered in Table 5.1.

Table 5.1 Review of Sanction Options

Incident	Punitive	Developmental/ Educational	Restorative Justice
An athletic team hosts a porn and glazed donuts party where they show sperm facial videos while providing glazed donuts as snacks.	The team is fined and each player suspended one game throughout the season.	The team has to attend awareness and sensitivity training offered by the counseling and women's study centers on campus. The team then writes reflective essays on the experience.	The team has to offer community service to the local women's domestic violence center through hosting a car wash and six months of yard work.

(continued)

Table 5.1 Continued

Incident	Punitive	Developmental/ Educational	Restorative Justice
A student steals his roommate's credit card and runs up charges on a rape fantasy porn site.	The student is required to make repayment to his roommate and placed on probation. The student also must move off campus.	The student is made to attend a counseling assessment around his theft and usage of the pornography on the college's community network.	The student must offer community service to the IT department as well as campus police for the infractions.
A student is missing classes and socially isolating because of 8–10 hours of porn use each night.	The student is placed on academic probation for missing an unacceptable number of classes.	The student is required to complete a counseling assessment to determine the extent of the addictive behaviors and look for ways to address the behavior.	The student is required to engage in one student club or activity each week to become more connected to campus life.

DISCUSSION QUESTIONS

1. What access do the students on your campus have to sex education? What initiatives could focus on sexual health and sex education at the collegiate level? What stakeholders would support these efforts? What obstacles exist?

2. Former Behavioral Analysis Unit (BAU) supervisor Dr. O'Toole shares a hypothetical scenario related to sexual sadism. Assuming you have not had a case of this magnitude on your campus, what are some other ways this behavior may have a negative impact on the individual or the community? Do you think the behavior would have escalated if not fueled by the pornography consumption? How might we address the individual freedom to consume such materials when seen against the risk that some who consume the content may be doing so in preparation and fantasy for an actual event?

3. How much is too much? The authors avoided giving specific details around length or duration of pornography consumption to be considered a concern. Where would you draw the line with a student or student group?

4. Imagine an athletic team is discovered to be hosting a "porn night" each week as a way to blow off steam and relax after Tuesday night practices. Team members pick out a movie and watch together. How might the administration address this from a punitive, developmental/educational, and restorative justice model? What are some of the Title IX implications of this activity?

5. Discuss a policy violation on your campus related to pornography use. Discuss how this behavior could be sanctioned punitively, developmentally/educationally, and through restorative justice. What are the pros and cons of each approach? How do you balance individuals' right to view legal pornographic materials in their own residence?

Chapter 6

Threats and Ultimatums

The tree which moves some to tears of joy is in the eyes of others only a green thing that stands in the way.
—*William Blake,* Night

KEY TAKE-AWAYS

1. Threats and ultimatums are often used to intimidate and deter the likelihood of reporting a concern or leave a relationship. Educational programs should focus on ways to help identify these behaviors, whether subtle or overt, from an individual or group.

2. One approach to addressing these behaviors is teaching your community about the bystander intervention approach. Simply put, bystander intervention makes community members aware of a concerning behavior and then teaches a host of options for the bystander to intervene and stop the risky behavior from continuing. Teaching this approach to students is a current requirement under the VAWA regulations.

3. To reduce the risks related to threats and ultimatums, it is critical to identify vulnerable populations on the campus and the contributing factors in the environment that increase their vulnerability as well as using risk assessments and safety planning when threats and violence are reported.

Threats and ultimatums are a form of sexual violence, not just a risk factor for sexual violence. The importance of this chapter lies in outlining how threats and ultimatums present in relation to gender-based violence. Threats and ultimatums are used to try to influence behavior and to provoke fear in a victim. Threats may be direct and easily observable or may be more hidden and covert. Ultimatums are a form of threat often made conditionally with an "if-then" statement. We use both terms as a risk factor here in order to emphasize the need to recognize the types of threats and ultimatums that occur in dating and domestic violence situations, stalking, and as a type of force related to sexual assault.

While often verbal, threats and ultimatums may also occur in written form or in online environments. There are a number of high-profile examples of online threats being made toward individuals based on the type of work they do, opinions they share, their appearance, and lifestyle. When threats and ultimatums occur in the context of an organization or group and are connected to membership requirements, they may also merge into hazing-related behaviors.

DEFINING THE FACTOR

Individuals groups who make threats and demands to meet their needs are the central concern surrounding this factor. The goal of making a threat or ultimatum for an individual or group is often one of the following: sexual activity, a continued relationship, control over a relationship, power over the individual, or to limit someone from reporting. An ultimatum often concludes with a potential loss of face, financial hardship, impact to social status, violence, harm to self, or outing of sexual identity. In domestic violence situations, threats might involve children and the threat of no longer being able to see them. In dating violence, threats may start with coercive emotional statements to acquire sexual activity—"If you love me, you'll have sex with me"—the unspoken threat being if you do not have sex with me, I'll find someone else and leave you. Stalking behaviors are also closely aligned with threats toward the stalking victim, intimate partner of the victim, or the property of the victim.

There is a critical importance in identifying concerning behaviors at their lowest level because the escalation of threats and ultimatums is well discussed in the violence risk assessment literature (Fein and Vossekuil 1998; O'Toole 2000, 2011; Deisinger et al. 2008; Calhoun and Weston 2009; Van Brunt 2012, 2014; Warren et al. 2014). Threats and the creation of ultimatums become common problem-solving approaches for the individual or the group. They acquire what they desire through coercive action. This may be a learned behavior that has worked for individuals in past relationships in order to obtain what they want in terms of sexual activities or security and guarantees the relationship will last.

The Association for Title IX Administrators (ATIXA) outlines a framework for analyzing sexual misconduct (2011). It indicates that sexual activity should be prohibited by colleges and universities when it is forced, when it is nonconsensual, or when the victim is incapacitated and that is known or should be known to the accused. The construct of force is important to the discussion of threats because a threat is an element of force. Sexual activity that occurs because of a threat should be considered sexual misconduct by college and university policy.

Threats, ultimatums, and implied threats/intimidation are exemplified in these statements:

If you do not have sex with me, I will hurt you.
If you do not stay with me, I will hurt myself.
If you have sex with me, I'll make sure you pass the class.

In domestic and dating violence, threats may come in the form of aggressive behavior or physical violence:

Slamming fist into a wall when angry
Kicking the furniture
Hurting the dog
Grabbing arms and shaking
Grasping chin and face to force head in a certain direction

Another form of force identified by the ATIXA model (Sokolow, Lewis, et al. 2015) that relates to threats and ultimatums and is common on the college campus is the idea of coercion. Coercion is unreasonable pressure for sexual activity, compelling someone to act in a certain way. Threats are often used as a form of coercion. Coercion might also be combined with grooming behaviors, such as isolating someone from his or her friends, using objectifying language (you're such a tease), and using substances to weaken defenses. Perpetrators can minimize coercive behavior by calling it seduction, but coercion is unwelcome and unreasonable in its nature.

Oh, so you're one of those Christian girls who don't have sex before they get married. I see how it is. You show up dressed all skimpy to turn me on but you don't put out. You're just a tease, and everyone knows it.

This coercive statement also offers an implied threat that if you do not sleep with me then I am going to damage your social reputation.

ADDRESSING THE INDIVIDUAL

IPV often involves the abuser or attacker setting ultimatums or threats to a victim through coercion or verbal aggression. This can be done to isolate the target from help or support or to create such a sense of fear and danger that compliance becomes a more likely outcome (Teranishi-Martinez 2014). Individual threats could involve sharing of personal information or a naked photo or video of sexual activities if the target does not comply with additional ultimatums. On a college campus, a threat might involve the use of a position of power to threaten students that they would be discredited if they reported sexual violence or harassment.

Consider the following case example:

Blair is a first-year student who begins dating Jack after they meet at a party early in the fall semester. Blair hadn't dated much before meeting Jack and enjoys the attention he offers. Jack is a junior on campus and a popular, well-liked member of the campus swim team.

The relationship develops quickly over the first few weeks of school and the two are inseparable on campus. Blair often sleeps in Jack's room off campus and rarely sees her roommate. They began having sex on the first night they met. During the first few weeks, they have sex several times a day.

Jack is somewhat possessive of Blair's time. He becomes frustrated when she has to study for classes or spends time hanging out with her other friends. He finds her friends annoying and resents the time they take away from his time with Blair. They have their first big argument when Blair goes home, about two hours away, to visit her parents for the fourth weekend of the semester. While Blair knows Jack isn't happy with her decision to go home, she still goes since it's her younger brother's birthday and her parents want to spend some time with her. Blair is excited to have a break from the academic stress of her classes, which she is falling behind in due to all the time she is spending with Jack.

When Blair returns Sunday night, she meets Jack for dinner on campus in the dining hall. Jack is furious at her. She hasn't seen this side of him before. He demands to know why she didn't text him back immediately at one point during the weekend. Blair tells him she had left her phone upstairs during the party. Jack demands to see her phone and Blair hands it to him. Jack pages through the texts and becomes more upset when he sees she texted with a male friend from home and spent some time with him at the mall on Saturday. Jack accuses her of being unfaithful and Blair says he is overreacting. She says, "I did hang out with a Mark—a friend from high school—but we were with a bunch of my friends."

Over the next week, Blair attempts to make Jack feel better by spending more time with him, going to his swim practices, and further neglecting her academics.

> Her friends on campus express concern that they never see her anymore, and Jack develops an annoying habit of demanding to look through her phone each time they meet, looking for texts she is sending to other men.

In this case example, we can see many of the subtle governing and threatening actions Jack engages in to control Blair's behavior. He isolates her from her friends and family and makes attempts to monitor her technology. As the case example unfolds, it is easy to see how Jack's behavior escalates to physical threats of violence. One of the important lessons here is the emphasis on training and educating community members to identify and engage in bystander intervention techniques to address these behaviors when they are encountered.

> The semester continues and Blair finds herself spending more and more time trying to reassure Jack of her feelings toward him. The more Blair gives, the more Jack demands from her. Jack not only monitors her phone but also now demands that Blair give Jack her Facebook password. Jack says, "I know you are probably talking to that Mark guy again. What do you take me for, an idiot? I'm no idiot."
>
> Blair's friends see her less and less. One evening while Blair is at the library, a friend confronts her and talks about how she misses her and worries that she isn't enjoying college since she is spending all her time with Jack. Blair becomes defensive and lists all the good things about the relationship. She doesn't divulge Jack's phone and Facebook monitoring because she doesn't want to get a lecture from her friend.
>
> Jack doesn't like that Blair has a night class and has to walk across campus alone on Monday and Wednesday nights. He tells her that he will pick her up in front of the classroom building at 9:00 p.m. sharp. He tells her just where to wait for him. One Monday night, the class runs a little long and Blair is five minutes late meeting Jack at the arranged place. She finds him pacing in front of his car. He grabs her by the arms and shakes her. "I just got out of swim practice and I'm supposed to wander around looking for you? Are you fucking kidding me? I'm sitting here in my car worried that you are being raped or something!"
>
> Blair tries to explain the class let out late and he shakes her again. "Then text me! You seem to be doing that all the time anyway! You can't take five fucking seconds and let me know what is going on?" Blair tries to explain that the professor doesn't allow phones in class. Jack becomes more enraged and shoves her into the car.
>
> Several of Blair's classmates watch this unfold. No one intervenes as Jack speeds off with Blair in his car. They can see she is crying. Two classmates decide

that they should say something and they stop by the dean of students' office in the morning to share what happened. The dean listens, then calls a BIT meeting, and invites the Title IX coordinator to consult.

Controlling behaviors may be seen around smart phone monitoring of text messages or through social media sites, such as Facebook. These actions are important to attend to as they often escalate prior to gender-based violence occurring.

ADDRESSING THE GROUP

Threats and ultimatums can also come in the form of intimidation and coercion from an organization. There are few associations that exert the amount of control that fraternities and sororities do on membership in the organization and social status in a community. The pressure for conformity to the group norms and behaviors is extensive (Godenzi et al. 2001). Even in situations where active members believe they are giving a new member the opportunity to choose participation in a certain activity or event, the coercive power and intimidation make it unlikely that a student maintains any choice or control in the situation.

When you transfer this context to issues of sexual violence, the desire to conform to group norms in order to achieve membership creates a dangerous environment for the cultivation of unhealthy attitudes about gender, sex, and relationships. The implied threat of losing social status and membership in the group is very real for a student who is considering reporting an incident related to an organization or one of its members. A fraternity or sorority could threaten that if students make a report then they will no longer be invited to social events, creating a "social suicide" of sorts, and research has even documented pressure exerted by fraternity members on a fellow member to limit his commitment to a girlfriend (Boswell and Spade 1996).

In the book *Fraternity Gang Rape*, several examples are given of how a fraternity might use ultimatums for sex. The author describes a freshman participating in sorority recruitment processes who is isolated by two fraternity members and told that in order to become a member of the sorority, she would have to have sex with a fraternity member, which then resulted in a gang rape. She was told following the incident not to feel bad because another woman has also been there that evening for the same reason (Sanday 2007). The threat of social ostracization is an overt threat that organizations with social capital on college campuses wield with great power.

Military organizations have also been found to have pervasive cultures of threats in order to discourage reporting. Annual Department of Defense reports explore sexual assault in the military and identified threats from senior officers as an obstacle to reporting sexual assaults (2015). On the college campus, we must consider high-risk populations being targeted with threats from those in positions of power. Graduate international students, for example, may be vulnerable to these situations. Consider this scenario:

Jackie is a graduate student in biology at a research university. A biology faculty member, Dr. Lee, recruited her when he was presenting at her undergraduate school in Taiwan. He met her family during his visit and talked about the many opportunities available to her in the United States, including a position in his research lab and a scholarship. Jackie received her F-1 visa to study in the United States and started graduate school. She met a few other graduate students in her program, but it was competitive in the lab so she found it difficult to make close friends. Dr. Lee acted as her mentor and friend, helping her find a place to live and advising her on academic projects as well as research. He agreed to chair her thesis committee and gave her an opportunity to work on a grant with the National Science Foundation.

One evening, Jackie stayed late in the research lab, working on a project. Dr. Lee came up behind Jackie, brushed her hair off her shoulder, and said quietly how proud he was of how hard she worked. He kissed her lightly on the temple and hugged her close to him. He left the lab and Jackie kept working. She felt it was uncomfortable but thought Dr. Lee was just excited that she was doing so well.

A week later, Jackie went to meet with Dr. Lee about her thesis. She was struggling with the research method she was proposing and hoped he could help. He pulled a chair next to his desk and motioned for Jackie to sit by him. He positioned the paper on the desk where they had to lean toward each other to review different portions of her work. When Jackie mentioned how difficult the research was, Dr. Lee put his hand on her knee and moved it back and forth on her upper thigh as he said, "Don't worry, Jackie. As long as we work together, I'll make sure you get through the program." He leaned toward her and kissed her forehead. When she seemed uncomfortable, he looked at her and said, "You like working with me in the program, don't you? You know that I will make sure you do well here, right?" Jackie said, "Of course. I am so grateful for your kindness." She quickly left his office.

You can see how the scenario can escalate quickly as a faculty member or an upper-class graduate student could take advantage of an international student with limited resources and options. Jackie is discouraged to reach out for help or report concerns because of implied threats related to her research lab position, scholarship, grades, thesis project, and visa status. This type of tightly coupled relationship within an academic department for graduate students happens quite often because of recruiting mechanisms for international students into specific academic disciplines. While not a student organization, the climate within an academic unit or department can increase the vulnerability of students and faculty to being victimized by threats related to sex and must be considered in prevention efforts.

FROM THE FRONT LINES

Bourbon Street and Mardi Gras

I was walking along Bourbon Street in my favorite city of New Orleans the night before Mardi Gras. If you haven't had the pleasure of wandering down Bourbon Street anytime near Mardi Gras, it is quite an experience. I was walking down and watched a larger, athletic man grab a young blonde woman by her wrist. Her friend had her by the other arm and they were engaging in game of a tug of war over her. As I got closer I heard the guy say, "Hey, baby, what's your name? You are beautiful. I just want to know your name."

The woman smiled it off uncomfortably and tried to free her hand. I stepped up and took his hand and said, "Hey, man, let her go." He looked at me in his happy state of drunk and said, "I just need to know her name!" By this time, she had already worked her way free and was well on her way down the street. I kept walking and that was the end of the bystander intervention for me.

As I think about what happened, I'm struck by two thoughts. The first is a recurring one about what it must be like to be a woman in society — how my perspective would change and what being a perpetual state of "on guard" would feel like. And if it isn't being grabbed outright by a drunk man twice her size on Bourbon Street, it would be the constant looks. The objectification and sexualization of the individual without her permission. That feeling of taking.

The second thought relates to threat. That all threat isn't what we see in the movies. The ominous rapist jumping from the cover of the bushes and dragging his prey into the woods. The aggressive male telling his girlfriend to shut her mouth or he will shut it for her. These are easier to spot. It was the playfulness in the man's eyes as he grabbed something pretty that walked by him on the street. It was that complete lack of awareness that his behavior could have even been seen as threatening. He believed, without a doubt, that he was justified grabbing her arm as she walked by and asking her name. That he was owed her name because of how she looked. That's the part that worries me more as we look to expose the root causes of violence in this book. Those unconscious behaviors males engage in without even thinking.

And lest you think I am any better for my intervention actions, I assure you, I am not. While I wouldn't grab a woman's arm to ask her name, I noticed she was attractive and little and blonde as well. It's that part of it, perhaps a third thought as I write this piece, that also haunts me. Knowing that I have my own lack of awareness, my own unconscious thoughts and desires.

The way out, I think, is talking about it. I think sharing thoughts like these and becoming more aware of our unconscious and less noble desires offer some attempt at introspection and improvement. I know for myself, and most male students, that applying a *1984* thought police, zero-tolerance policy to these negative thoughts leads to more problems and a lack of change.

Brian Van Brunt, EdD
Author
A Guide to Leadership and Management: Managing Across the Generations
Harm to Others: The Assessment and Treatment of Dangerousness
A Faculty Guide to Addressing Disruptive and Dangerous Behavior

REDUCING THE RISK

It's rare to have a clear path forward in addressing risk factors. However, this is one case where a clear two-step approach is universally agreed. The first step involves teaching the members of our community the importance of noticing and attending to these aggressions, whether malicious or unconscious in their etiology. We cannot start to change these behaviors without first teaching others to identify threats, subtle and overt, and ultimatums designed to coerce and pressure individuals into a certain course of action. A summary of some examples to teach students about is outlined in Table 6.1.

Table 6.1 Subtle and Overt Threats and Ultimatums

	Threats	Ultimatums
Subtle	"Keep making me wait. See what happens." "Maybe I'll go talk to him about what he posted on your Facebook page. Maybe I'll show him what funny really is." "You think you are just going to leave me and that there won't be any consequences for that?"	"If you talk to her again, I can't be with you anymore." "If you break up with me, you should think for a minute of all those photos you texted me. You know I have them all saved, right?" "You've already done just about everything with me in bed, if your friends found out do you think they would judge you anymore for doing this?"
Overt	"Get off the phone or I will smash it." "Be ready after class for me to pick you up or you won't be making it to class the rest of the week." "I will slap your goddamn mouth if you ever disrespect me like that in front of my friends again."	"You think you'll still have any friends after I talk to all of them about our sex life and what you like? Keep your mouth shut or you'll find out." "If you leave me, I'll post that picture of you giving me oral on the class discussion board. It's just that simple."

SAFETY PLANNING

When managing incidents that include threats, there is tremendous value in conducting risk assessments and utilizing safety planning strategies with the reporting party in order to analyze the nature of the threat and to clearly outline the resources and safety options for the victim. These steps can also help to ensure that steps are being taken to try to eliminate opportunity for future threats and violence.

ATIXA outlined a white paper on intimate partner violence that identified steps for a risk assessment and for safety planning (Grimmett et al. 2015). These strategies are part of reducing the overall risk of threats and ultimatums because of the structures they put in place to reinforce a victim's options for support and safety. One of the steps in the risk assessment includes considering risk factors for violence and scenarios in which future violence might occur. The risk factors discussed throughout this book can pair well with risk assessment and safety planning as they are helpful in formulating if, how, and why other threats and sexual violence will occur.

For a student or employee reporting a dating or domestic violence situation where the partner is using threats to create emotional and psychological stress, a safety plan outlines transportation options from a residence to school or work, locations where running into the abusive partner is likely, friends and family who can be with the victim when it is necessary to be in the same location as the abusive partner, emergency planning related to finances, plans for how to alert friends and family that help is needed, and other safety considerations. While the plan in and of itself does not eliminate all violence, it helps to build confidence in the victim that it is safe to use reporting options and that there are viable ways out of the violent relationship.

BYSTANDER INTERVENTION

The second step to the approach, once students have a good understanding of subtle and overt threats and ultimatums, is teaching the bystander intervention approach. Bystander intervention or empowerment helps to engage community members in the reduction of a specific behavior that causes harm to a member of the community. The approach addresses the problematic behavior, from a system and group perspective, by enlisting the community to address the threats and ultimatums.

Once the behavior is noticed, the individual must then take personal responsibility for enacting a change. The problem is no longer the responsibility of the victim, but rather something the entire community takes on as a duty. A spectrum of options can be taught to the students in terms of how to intervene, from distracting the person making the threat to a direct confrontation. In teaching bystander intervention to students, it is essential to give them options based on real-life scenarios and give them opportunities to think critically about how to intervene.

There are a number of bystander intervention programs and curriculums targeting college and universities. Some programs are train-the-trainer–based, where a group learns the curriculum and then brings it back to the campus community. Others focus on passive advertising and education. A few example programs include the following:

- The Green Dot (www.livethegreendot.com)
- Step Up! (www.stepupprogram.org)
- MVP (www.mvpnational.org)
- Prevention Innovations (www.unh.edu/preventioninnovations/)
- Escalation (http://www.joinonelove.org)

DISCUSSION QUESTIONS

1. When considering the case example of Blair and Jack, discuss what ways your campus educates its community about IPV and how to report these behaviors to the Title IX office. What are some of the warning signs that IPV behavior is becoming more frequent? Discuss some ways in which you have seen examples of social isolation, control, or monitoring.

2. Knowing that threats are used to discourage reporting of incidents of concern and as forms of retaliation, what reporting strategies could you consider to assist someone experiencing threats or retaliation? What role can safety planning play in these situations?

3. Consider Jackie's story as an international graduate student. What populations on your campus are vulnerable to threats and ultimatums? What role do academic processes play in supporting the safety of students?

4. What is your definition of bystander intervention? What programs or efforts have you seen successfully implemented on your campus? What are some of the obstacles you have encountered when attempting to apply these techniques? How do the social pressures in a group impact the effectiveness of bystander intervention strategies?

5. What are some of the challenges to intervention when an entire group is exerting pressure on an individual to not report an incident of assault or to "let something slide" instead of making a bigger deal out of it? What are some options we can give students to address this problem?

Chapter 7

Misogynistic Ideology

> The trees that have it in their pent-up buds
> To darken nature and be summer woods
> —*Robert Frost, "Spring Pools"*

KEY TAKE-AWAYS

1. A negative and "less than" view of women contributes to objecti-fication and reduction in value, choice, and agency they have in the world. Society, family, peers, and religious beliefs most commonly perpetuate these views.

2. Patriarchy and unhealthy masculine attitudes contribute to the con-cern around this risk factor. Reducing misogynistic attitudes begins with addressing healthy masculine attitudes as well as addressing an unequal, patriarchal system.

3. Addressing misogynistic attitudes and behaviors in groups can be done by incentivizing self-governance and self-accountability from the multiple stakeholders involved in organizations.

Misogyny is defined as the dislike of, contempt for, or ingrained prejudice against women. This way of thinking is one of the con-tributing factors to sexual violence on our campuses. Misogynistic ideologies are engrained in early childhood messages received from family, media, society, and religion. While there have been steps forward in recent years to make corrections to how women are val-ued and treated, this change has been slow in coming and is not without detractors. Issues of equal pay, fair treatment in the work-place and classrooms, and freedom from unintentional stereotypes and prejudices remain significant challenges and obstacles to be overcome.

Progress in this area has been more forthcoming in higher education settings, though this progress still runs against preexisting expectations and thoughts students have when coming into the classroom. The feminist positive message is accepted in some parts of the country and in others is met with anger from the existing patriarchy. There is an overlap here for many who argue that the United States creates and maintains a rape culture.

Rape myth attitudes have been defined as "attitudes and beliefs that are generally false but are widely and persistently held, and that serve to deny and justify male sexual aggression against women" (Brownmiller 1975, p. 12). Aronowitz et al. (2012) write,

> In a rape-supporting culture there are messages throughout society that allow the majority of sexually aggressive men to claim that they are not rapists. An event that does not qualify as violent stranger rape may not be perceived as a crime at all. College campuses have, in the past, prescribed to the rape-supporting culture by having very little consequences for the men when a rape is reported. This then leads to women's feelings of powerlessness and a perceived lack of confidentiality in reporting.
>
> (Paul and Gray 2011, p. 881, cited by Aronowitz et al. 2012, p. 181)

This chapter outlines the basis of these theories and offers some clear examples of how these attitudes and beliefs manifest on our campuses. Suggestions for addressing these mind-sets are offered for educators and staff looking to continue changing these harmful beliefs.

DEFINING THE FACTOR

This factor embodies a pervasive belief that the female gender is less worthy or deserving of respect or consideration when compared to males. This may include strongly held beliefs that "women are good for sex and not a lot more" or a tendency to disregard their opinions or desires or see these opinions or desires as secondary to the male perspective. This factor is reinforced through support of peers and primary family supports. This tendency is more likely a "nurture versus nature" worldview shaped by friends, parents, extended family, and religious or political ideologies. Numerous rational and structural factors reinforce gender hierarchies. Whether they are certain media depictions, religious and social conventions, or historical experiences, they contribute to the subjugation of women.

For example, research has shown membership in religious groups as a high-risk population for less healthy attitudes around sex and relationships (Zapp 2014). Likewise, others argue that females have certain biological and genetic predispositions that should result in them holding more nurturing roles in the family system and avoiding working outside of the home. While arguing points of religious doctrine or biological predispositions is beyond the scope of this article, these beliefs contribute to the risk factor. More commonly, religious doctrine becomes warped and misappropriated by individuals or groups and used to restrict and denigrate women. An example of this misplaced religious inspiration comes from Henry Ford Community College student Anthony Powell, who shot and killed another student he had tried to date but who had rejected him (Runk 2009). Prior to the attack, Anthony posted numerous YouTube video clips about his frustrations with women, atheists, and others with whom he disagreed. This is an extreme example, but nonetheless one that proves the point.

In some cases, these misogynistic ideologies may be unintentional and demonstrated through microaggressions. These blind spots are well explored by Sue's (2010, p. xvi) work in microaggressions, which are defined as "brief, everyday exchanges that send denigrating messages to certain individuals because of their group membership." Microaggressions are often unintended slights that have serious implications and impact those of a different country, ethnicity, culture, sexual identity, disability, or mental illness (Sue 2010). Microaggressions are discussed in more detail at the end of this chapter.

Even in our Disney happy place, the movies we watch and stories we read provide examples of how women are subjugated to the role of prize or object to be quested after. Sleeping Beauty is eventually freed from her trap by the kiss of her one true love. Belle, from *Beauty and the Beast*, has long been described as an example of this tendency. Mendelson (2012) writes, "On the surface, the young and beautiful Belle is imprisoned by the monstrous beast and rather quickly comes to love him as he gradually begins to go from captor to protector, friend, and then finally theoretical lover" (p. 1). The beast eventually wins Belle over after locking her father in his dungeon and begins to treat her with some modicum of human decency. As Mendelson (2012) writes, "He doesn't so much become 'good' as stop being 'bad'" (p. 1).

In a groundbreaking meta-analysis, Murnen et al. (2002) found that most measures of masculine ideology were significantly associated with sexual aggression. The strongest support emerged for hostile beliefs about women, the desire to be in control, and an acceptance of violence against women. In addition, the fear and shame of not living up to existing standards of the hegemonic masculine ideology can be connected to deeply personal secrets that even the one concerned hasn't discovered, but has felt in his life. Gaston, indeed.

In a funny and insightful blog posted on www.feministing.com, author Reina Gattuso (2016) writes on the concept of patriarchy:

> Ever heard of a thing called patriarchy? It's a handy, fancy name feminists (we beautiful, beautiful people) have invented for systems of power (= societies) that favor men. Bear with me now. Patriarchy is a system that works at every level. It structures not only overt instances of gender discrimination, but also the way we understand the world. It affects the way we are taught to act and exist in the world. It affects our behavior. It affects our behavior at levels we can't see or understand because we take them for granted. It sets a pattern of beliefs for how we understand and interact with the world. Thus we can say it comprises or structures our behavior. Patriarchy, or a system that privileges men, is like food for our brains and hearts and social experiences: We ingest it in our homes, in public space, in school, in pop culture, in relationships, through the media. We digest it, and it becomes the building blocks of our thoughts, our behaviors, our beliefs about what is right and wrong . . . But it also structures consensual sex: It helps determine what we believe sex is, and how we experience it. It helps determine who feels entitled to sexual pleasure and who doesn't, whose desires are met sexually and whose aren't, whose desires are even assumed to exist.
>
> (p. 2)

The author's point is well made. Understanding patriarchy is important for a number of reasons—in particular, the way we are conditioned to view sex and sexual behavior.

Many writing on gender and to a certain extent the prevention of sexual assault have also indicated that one of the contributing factors is the systemic conceptions of masculinity and what it means to be a man (Jhally 1999; Murnen et al. 2002; Kimmel 2008; Harper and Harris 2010; Kalish 2013). The work in this area confirms the influence of the peer group effect on male sexual scripts and relationships. We chose not to utilize the concepts of hypermasculinity as a stand-alone factor in this book, but in many ways, the concept can be seen interwoven with a variety of factors. Most specifically here related to misogynistic attitudes, research indicates that men are concerned with how they are perceived related to masculinity, and media and other societal messages indicate that masculinity is achieved only by devaluing females or feminine objects. The authors continue that men articulate feeling under attack by feminist systems, but the fear they actually have is not being able to meet the social standards set around masculinity (Schwartz and DeKeseredy 1997). Prevention strategies that embrace diversity in gender representation, diversity in membership within closed communities, involvement with positive role models, and healthy conceptualizations of ourselves become an important aspect of this work.

ADDRESSING THE INDIVIDUAL

Negative individual examples of this behavior most often occur when preexisting thoughts or negative attitudes around women and feminism occur in the residence hall or within classroom discussions. Interpersonal violence incidents often include behaviors that devalue the partner by not listening when the other person is talking, shouting at them, or controlling their actions. Students come to college with experiences and worldviews that are often hardened and entrenched in their cultural experiences. This is often exacerbated with first-generation college students, who may have a more starkly drawn difference between their home experiences and the liberal arts environment of most college and university campuses.

College exists in large part to challenge existing worldviews, stretch perspectives, expose students to diversity, and hopefully, in the end, inspire a higher level of critical thinking and appreciation for various perspectives. Students should demand a refund from campuses that fail to challenge them and simply reinforce existing ideologies. To that end, the campus community is uniquely suited to have conversations with students who engage in offensive or hurtful speech. While it is the right of the student to have these thoughts, it is the responsibility of the college to push back against ideologies that harm individuals, fracture the community, and further marginalize groups.

Much has been written about the current state of mental health and how college counseling centers are particularly overwhelmed, addressing a host of issues that are coming to our campus communities, such as students struggling with homesickness, balancing academic responsibilities, experiencing depression and anxiety, or struggling with bipolar or schizophrenia; it is apparent college counseling centers have a lot on their plates. It is with this appreciation that we suggest another area where our counselors, therapists, and psychologists can be helpful working with students who exhibit hardened and fixated ideologies. Who better to address irrational thoughts or angry comments than those trained in establishing rapport, addressing defensiveness, and exploring new ways of thinking? Given the workload most college counseling centers are struggling with, an alternative could be to engage in train-the-trainer–type programs where the counseling staff teaches nonclinical staff some of these techniques and approaches to meet with students who exhibit hateful or negative attitudes toward women.

ADDRESSING THE GROUP

In groups or organizations, the reinforcement of misogynistic attitudes can become present in how they indoctrinate new members, in the support of rape myths and rape-supportive attitudes, in social events and group terminology, and in their treatment of one another. While the idea of a "hookup" culture is not in and of itself indicative of sexual violence, there is a disproportionate impact on women when it comes to social environments created to promote the casual "hookup." When communication within the group focuses on the idea of finding women who are "asking for it," "wanting to get laid," or "ready to get fucked," the underlying message is that women are good only for sex and not worthy of additional respect.

Groups that are highly sexualized may socialize men to consider sex and women as commodities or possessions. Similar to the examples given in chapter 4 around objectification, this can result in pressure for a member to sleep with a certain number of women, to brag about sexual exploits, or to engage in certain sexual activities as a game. Think about the member asking another member if he "scored" with a girl the previous evening. With the use of social media, group interaction can take place online, providing forums for the exchange of pictures and other information as proof of a member's sexual exploits.

When some members begin to question the attitudes and behaviors of the group, the organization devises other means for distancing themselves from negative behavior. Groups also create objectifying terminology to lessen feelings of guilt that some members may have about certain attitudes or behaviors (Schwartz and DeKeseredy 1997). Examples might include "booty calls," "fair game," or "getting some action." Look back to chapter 4 for a more extensive discussion of moral disengagement in organizations.

Unfortunately, research indicates that these types of group activities may serve only to recruit more members with similar attitudes and behaviors, growing the size of the group and the social acceptance for the activities. In domestic violence situations, research has

93

also indicated that males who abuse their wives are often members of groups that reinforce standards of gratification through dominance (Schwartz and DeKeseredy 1997, p. 38). The group may say things like "she deserved what she got," or praise the abuser for "taking care of business," or discourage thoughtful behavior by saying that someone is "pussy-whipped."

Group examples of these hateful, misogynistic messages frequently make front-page news in the higher education community. Phi Kappa Tau Fraternity at Georgia Tech was suspended for a pattern of sexual violence that included a requirement for new members to sing a song titled "The S&M Man" with lyrics that included, "Who can take a bicycle, tear off the seat, impale a virgin on it, and push her down a bumpy street," and "who can take two jumper cables, hook 'em to her tits, turn on the juice, and electrocute the bitch" (Somani 2014). Numerous fraternity parties have been shut down or brought through the campus conduct process for including messages such as the one at Texas Tech University reading, "no means yes, yes means anal," or the inclusion of a vaginal sprinkler that was supposed to simulate a female ejaculation (Kingkade 2014).

Another aspect of this factor, particularly in groups, is the negative attitudes, threats, and assaults that occur toward men who are deemed to be effeminate in appearance or mannerisms. To the individual or group who engages in these beliefs and attacks, the core frustration seems to come back to the anger and irritation that come from a male behaving in a "female" manner. This acting "less than his maleness deserves" drives feelings of anger and rage that, while directed at a male, are ultimately directed back to a stereotypical female mannerism daring to be appropriated by an effeminate man. Franklin (2000, p. 1) writes, "during the course of my research I came to conceptualize the violence not in terms of individual hatred but as an extreme expression of American cultural stereotypes and expectations regarding male and female behavior."

FROM THE FRONT LINES

Red Herrings and Straw Men: Nice Guys, Bad Boys, and Blurry Distinctions

Many people are familiar with the "stranger in the bushes" trope conjured up in discussions about the problems of gendered violence and sexual assault. The concept suggests that evil strangers lurking in dark corners are the primary perpetrators of such acts. These faceless characters—and the terror they represent—hold tremendous power in society, undermining the agency of women and those with subaltern gender and sexual identities and their ability to move about freely and without fear of harm.

Even when such an attacker is caught, prosecuted, and convicted, the influence of the trope is reinforced in two ways. First, those who minimize and dismiss the prevalence and impact of gendered violence are gifted with fodder for "one bad apple" and "isolated incident" clichés that deny the systemic nature of the problem. Second, since the proverbial bow is tied on the single case, those most vulnerable to such violence are made to be even more "careful" in their movement, and their relationships with peace and trust are further compromised.

Of course, research and statistics demonstrate that intimate partners and acquaintances are most often the perpetrators of gendered violence, and these situations overwhelmingly involve males harming females. Pointing out these facts often elicits defensive qualifications that most men do not commit such violence and that some women do— both of which are true. Yet, given the facts and the gendered nature of this intractable and systemic problem, we must engage the question of how masculinity and misogyny figure into what is happening.

Lately I have been thinking about the ideas of "nice guys" and "bad boys" in regard to gender-based violence. With regard to the former, I have often seen men—and women—come to the defense of a man accused of sexual coercion or assault, arguing that he is a "nice" guy. Sometimes that is the entire argument, leaving the "and so he probably didn't do it" or "it's not as bad as she said" implied, but unsaid, and therefore more potent. Alternatively, I have noticed that when men are thought of as "bad boys," oftentimes this is said with ironic affection or admiration, implying a cute rascal who isn't really so bad as to do something as sordid as hitting or raping a woman. In either case, it seems inevitable that the woman in the story will be suspect, having her clothing, demeanor, honesty, or competence questioned, and assumed to be at least partly culpable for what happened. When the alleged perpetrator or victim have subaltern gender or sexual identities, are people of color, or live in poverty, a number of other complications arise in the discourse, almost always diminishing the veracity or worthiness of those involved.

Another way in which the "nice guy" and "bad boy" expressions serve the interests of misogyny is found in their flexibility as symbols.

The meanings of "nice" and "bad" are relative, both in reference to each other and to any number of other ideas. For instance, a man who sneers at his partner may be deemed to be "nicer" than the one who yells at her, is "nicer" than the man who slaps her, is "nicer" than the one who assaults her. Even if progressive-minded people object to such a continuum, enough people hold such beliefs that it is entrenched and has consequences in the social milieu where violence occurs. It may arguably enable such violence by inspiring rationalizations on the part of perpetrators, victims, or witnesses. Similarly and strangely, it is not uncommon to hear something to the effect "well, he's a bad guy, but not *really* a bad guy," comparing bad against itself and splitting the mythical difference, or comparing one bad deed to a worse one, minimizing the former and pointing to the latter as the "real" problem.

The implication of all of this is that we need to name gendered violence—both individual acts and patterns of behavior—as real, harmful, and unacceptable without qualification. In the face of rhetorical devices intended (consciously or not) to distract, minimize, or deny, we must call bad ... well, bad—and demand that it is replaced with good as defined by the person on the receiving end of the equation.

Jason A. Laker, PhD

Professor, Department of Counselor Education &

EdD Program in Educational Leadership

San José State University

REDUCING THE RISK

So, given the broad and expansive nature of this problem, how do we address it on our college campuses? The temptation to charge headfirst at these engrained attitudes and beliefs, while momentarily cathartic, will likely not lead to lasting change. Education and communication remain the most effective tools in changing deeply held beliefs. Direct assaults have not proven as effective. Instead, there should be an effort to make the idea of seeing women as equal and this movement be seen as what it means to be a man. We can accomplish this by not only tolerating but indeed celebrating feminism. Here we create a society that is more focused on diversity, tolerance, and acceptance.

What we are currently doing isn't working. Look to the work of Jackson Katz (1995) and we can better understand how masculinity defined by aggression and dominance isn't a positive vision of masculinity philosophy. It has led to a male generation lost in defining itself apart from aggression, competition, and being seen as strong men, or to borrow from Katz, Tough Guise (Jhally 1999). Jean Kilbourne has long been vocal about the dangerous and insidious methods by which the media portrays women in advertising, as in her groundbreaking film *Killing Us Softly* (Lazarus et al. 1979).

There needs to be a shift that holds women as equals in every respect, and perhaps this effort starts to flourish more at our colleges and universities. Here we have an opportunity, a coming together of men and women who will be in positions of influence and power in the next decades. Who better to spend our educational capital on to bring forth a more egalitarian and just society? One where concepts such as empathy and compassion are seen as having equal value as assertiveness and competition. One where a combined sense of humanity is discussed, rather than relying on out-of-date gender-based stereotypes. One where there are children's toys and not gender-based representations of what boys and girls are supposed to like.

So what does this look like practically? An example of this shift could be explored through the idea of masculinity, sexual conquest, and performance in the bedroom. Assume a group perpetuates the idea that success in the bedroom equates to dominance and exerting power and control. The other perspective here is that being truly sensual involves the ability to reach beyond one way of being (dominating) to having an entire range of abilities and options. The accepted myth is the idea that the best you could have is someone who truly "fucks like a man." Is this the pinnacle that we desire? Is there a biological imperative that demands a dominant and subservient liaison? We'd like to suggest no, this is not a fait accompli. There is another way of doing things.

Reina Gattuso (2016) writes,

> I'm saying this because we need to know—you, human male lying next to me; you need to know—that the way you conceptualize pleasure and its choreography is not the way sex inevitably is. You can fuck differently. You can fuck like a girl. Because I don't feel like the primary distinction between my lesbian sexual experiences and my hetero ones is a matter of anatomy. Rather, it's overwhelmingly a matter of gender and the way we're trained to get off. Women tend to be trained to think about other people more,

to care for other people and to provide things to them, and to demand their own gratification less (this is why you think I currently sound like a selfish bitch for simply asking you to consider me your equal). The best partners I've had, of whatever gender (but step up your games, guys, because I mostly mean women), asked questions. They were creative. They were kind. They played with me. We collaborated. If one of us came and was so goddamn tired we needed to fall immediately asleep and could not bear to flick our wrists another moment, we said so, and that was okay, because it was not merely assumed as par for the course.

(p. 3)

We don't offer these comments merely as sexual advice, though it is good sexual advice, but rather as a creative example of how to approach this issue in a fun and innovative way with students. Too often, we approach a negative belief in a way that challenges and draws up immediate defensiveness from those who hold the belief. The issue of addressing the patriarchy isn't designed to bash or take away from masculinity, but rather strengthen masculinity by including a more diverse definition that respects individual differences and celebrates the diversity found in gender identity. Not an easy message, particularly in geographic areas where this is seen as primarily a religious issue; however, it is a noble issue to tackle and worth the extended conversations.

Working with individuals, in some ways, is an easier task then addressing an entire group of men.

ORGANIZATION ACCOUNTABILITY

Groups hold power. Any lasting change must address the social impact of the misogynistic beliefs being supported and undergirded by groups on campus. This is not always an easy task, addressing a group's poor behavior and aligning them with the more prosocial, women-positive viewpoint. Here are items to consider related to organizational accountability, particularly when addressing a concern that surfaces in an inter/national fraternity on a campus.

1. **Understand the organizational and governance structures of the fraternities on your campus.** Not all fraternities are the same. Some will have inter/national headquarters with professional staff and volunteers and others will have regional

headquarters with part-time volunteers. Some fraternities were founded to serve multicultural communities. Some fraternities are coed. For the purposes of this section, I refer ahead primarily to those all-male fraternities associated with the North American Interfraternity Conference (NIC). NIC is the trade association representing 70 fraternities located on more than eight hundred college campuses. Problems exist in other fraternities and organizations, but this portion of the chapter is to help you understand the complicated aspect of facilitating change in the NIC fraternity community on your campus.

2. **Recognize that fraternities have multiple stakeholders and this makes communication structures complicated.** Fraternities have multiple decision-making levels—the undergraduate chapter, which could range from 20 to 200 members, the undergraduate officers and leadership team, faculty or staff chapter advisor, local alumni chapter advisor or alumni advisor team, alumni advisory boards (housing corporations and scholarship boards), chapter alumni, headquarter volunteers, headquarter traveling consultant staff, and headquarter professional staff. Bottom line: each step in prevention planning and organizational accountability needs to consider who is influencing the organization decisions and the information flow, and additional communication steps will be necessary for positive resolutions to occur.

3. **Believe it or not, the NIC and inter/national fraternity headquarters staff have some common interests with the college or university.** They are interested in maintaining organizations on the college campus, and they are interested in avoiding litigation and bad press related to incidents involving alcohol, sexual assault, and hazing. Since the reemergence of Title IX efforts nationally, some fraternities and the NIC are identifying opportunities to implement prevention initiatives related to sexual violence for their members. By no means are we in perfect alignment and in some areas we are in opposite corners, but as a fundamental concept, it should be possible to find common ground in most situations.

4. **Create incentives to support the fraternity ideals of self-governance and reward organizational accountability efforts.** The idea is that you want the fraternity leadership actively identifying problematic behavior, reporting it to you, and addressing it before it escalates. This means helping them to recognize what behaviors are concerning, giving them options to report, and outlining the type of response that you expect from the organization.

5. **Work collaboratively to respond to incidents of concern.** Communication to fraternity headquarters should be frequent and not just when problems occur, but when problems surface, there are usually opportunities to resolve situations collaboratively from investigation to resolution. Create communication and accountability structures that support collaboration, which means having flexible structures to consider ideas from headquarters about how to address concerns.

6. **Individual member conduct is treated as individual conduct until it becomes organizational.** Fraternities espouse the ideals of brotherhood and members will go to great lengths to support a brother. This can be a positive idea, but it turns negative when that support becomes collusion to protect a brother from criminal or university conduct charges. Fraternity leadership must be told that individual member behavior is addressed as individual behavior until it becomes organizational behavior. An individual member makes a choice to sexually assault another student. This is individual member behavior that is generally not related to the organization. When the organization members begin to act to hide evidence or fabricate stories, this becomes an organizational situation that requires organizational accountability and should result in university conduct proceedings against the organization.

7. **Sanctioning of organizational conduct should consider self-accountability efforts and collaboration.** Conduct proceedings should reward chapters that hold individual members accountable for behavior that is not in alignment with chapter values and university policy as well as organizations that respond quickly to negative behaviors and take reasonable steps to remedy organizational climate concerns.

8. **Use sanctions that make sense and relate to the root factors.** Hearing boards and hearing officers have a tendency to try to do too much with organizational sanctions, which can result in a list of required activities that are virtually impossible to enforce and track in terms of completion. In addition, the sanctions can end up running a small group of officers in circles, trying to comply, and have little impact on the overall chapter climate or membership.

9. **Closing a chapter is not always the answer.** It is common to be asked why we even allow fraternities to exist on the college campus and why we don't just close the chapter. It may seem like the easy answer to just shut down a chapter, but that decision does not necessarily remedy the areas of concern. Often, suspending a chapter just shifts how and

where the behavior is occurring, and you lose the opportunity to work with organizational leadership that do want to do the right thing. Closing a chapter is valuable when there is no way to remedy the membership's attitudes and behaviors with reasonable sanctions, and there is a need to halt chapter activities until the existing membership has left the campus community. Closing a chapter is most effective when done in coordination with headquarter staff.

In the case study ahead, the concept of "tagging" is described. Unfortunately, there are several social media sites that encourage sexually explicit or nude pictures to be submitted and promote the idea of writing Greek letters or other brands on women's body parts and posting pictures of them online. For college and university staff, when coming across these types of pictures related to a report of sexual assault involving an incapacitated student, there follow multiple levels of investigation and accountability measures that must be considered, including organizational remedies.

> While investigating a sexual assault, the police department takes photos from cell phones of students involved that show pictures of the complainant in her bra and thong-style underwear only. She is bent over and men are drawing what appears to be Greek Fraternity letters on her butt with a magic marker. Two different fraternity names are identifiable. There are also pictures of her upper breast/cleavage with her hands covering her breasts with a third fraternity written on it. A closeup photo of her exposed vaginal area shows the words, "James was here." The location where this occurred is unknown and appears to be a house party. The respondent in the sexual assault allegation is not in any of the photos. The information indicates that other members of the fraternity may have been involved the night of the assault and may have information about what occurred.

In this case, gathering information from organizational leadership about social events that occurred around the night in question could be helpful. There is a risk in disclosing what is being investigated because this could prompt communications to membership to erase and delete digital images and videos on phones, so the timing and nature of these communications need to be strategic and need to consider criminal processes. More than likely, this is a situation where after the majority of the individual sexual assault investigation is complete, contact would be made to discuss the involvement of the organization in the incident with the headquarters staff and local advisors.

Discussions should include: if completing a collaborative investigation is feasible, what information is available to indicate that the organization leadership had knowledge related to what occurred, and did organizational activities contribute to the incident? There are a number of considerations related to the privacy of the victim and what information would be released to the headquarters in a collaborative process. In some cases, the headquarters staff could be given an opportunity to present a plan for remedying concerns within the organization and see how it aligns with institutional sanctioning. If this was found to be a pervasive attitude in the organization related to the "tagging" and mistreatment of women, this would minimally require a series of educational initiatives, bystander intervention, social event restrictions, and empathy-based service requirements, and may require more severe sanctions and penalties depending on the severity of the involvement. The question is always whether the climate within the organization can be remedied with the sanctions outlined.

RESPONDING TO MICROAGGRESSIONS

A central challenge for educators working with students who express unintentional misogynistic comments is the importance of understanding and responding to microaggressions. Microaggressions are defined by Sue (2010) as "brief, everyday exchanges that send denigrating messages to certain individuals because of their group membership" (xvi). Sue et al. (2007a) further divide microaggressions into three categories: microassualts, microinsults, and microinvalidiations. By definition, these are often unintended slights that have serious implications for students in the classroom and residence halls.

Imagine an instructor asks the class to break up into groups and a group of male students proceeds to ignore a female student who requests to join their group as they have a number of things in common related to the assignment. This would be an example of a microassualt. The slight might not have been intended, but the failure to include a classmate in a group based on gender sends an unacceptable message in the classroom.

Microinsults are actions that disrespect or demean a person based on his or her group status (Sue et al. 2007a, 2007b, 2009; Boysen 2012). An example of this could be a student who makes generalizations about women and their level of intelligence or that all women are at college only to try to find a husband. Again, these comments may come out of ignorance, poor access to teaching or information about gender and culture, or simple stupidity. In any case, the instructor has a responsibility to address these microinsults as they have a strong impact on women and those who witness these comments.

A student in a public speaking class who congratulates a well-dressed female student on a presentation by saying, "I'm really surprised at how well that went. You were very well spoken today. I just thought you were another pretty face," is an example of a microinvalidation. This kind of comment sends the message to the female student that "I thought you were capable of looking good, but that was about it" (Sue et al. 2007a, 2007b). Another example of a microinvalidation may be a student who says, "I don't really pay attention to gender at all; we are all the same." While probably unintentional, this conveys the message that the experiences unique to a woman are not valid and worthy of a discussion.

So, how do we address these behaviors in the classroom and around campus? The challenge here is addressing a potentially insulting, invalidating, or assaultive comment or action by a student or group of students who may not have an awareness that the behavior or what they said has been taken poorly. One approach to addressing this conflict in the classroom is addressing students early on in the class with examples of microaggressions and then creating an opportunity for a discussion and remediation. This is the idea of getting out in front of the issue.

Sue et al. (2009, 2010) offer research that demonstrates that students want professors to engage in these kinds of discussions and for instructors to facilitate an open dialogue that validates their experiences of bias and racism. Professors should be involved in this process and not let the students dominate the discussion and take it away from the lessons of microaggressions. Instructors who are not trained or prepared to discuss these issues with their students might lean on the women's center or university office of diversity programming or counseling or ask a psychology professor versed in microaggressions to discuss the topic. Boysen (2012) suggests brief, minute-long response essays after the presentation in an attempt to gauge how students receive the information.

The issue of microaggressions, related to race or gender bias, is not easy to address for faculty or staff. Increased training to identify, intervene, and manage these behaviors and comments is needed. Sue (2010) suggests that knowledge and awareness are key to recognizing and effectively handling microaggressions. It is unlikely that all faculty and staff will become experts in gender studies, feminism, diversity issues, or multiculturalism, but with increased exposure to the importance of this topic it may be an area about which staff and faculty can learn more in order to successfully engage students in these kinds of discussions.

When addressing microaggressions, Sue offers a five-step approach that can be useful in training students to practice when they find themselves having said something that was offensive. First, it is essential to apologize. You can resolve differences of intent and impact by apologizing as quickly as possible. It doesn't matter what you meant; it matters what you said and how the other person perceived it. Reflect on what just occurred and try to understand why what you intended was different than what occurred. Look at ways you can take responsibility and explore ways you can do better in the future. Be honest about your intention and discuss with the other person his or her perspective.

When attempting to avoid microaggressions in the first place, Sue (2010) offers five steps to address the problem. The steps are explained in Table 7.1.

Table 7.1 Addressing Microaggressions

Constant vigilance of your own bias	Pay attention to the way that you perceive the world. We all have biases based on our experiences. Be open to seeing things from a different perspective.
Experiential reality: interact with those different from you in terms of race, culture, and ethnicity	One way to address bias and become more informed of other cultures, genders, and those who are different from your own way of seeing things is to interact with those who are different from you.
Don't be defensive	Microaggressions are particularly difficult to address as the person committing the microaggression is often unaware that what was said was perceived as offensive. Adopting a defensive posture or an unwillingness to explore how a statement was received is a difficult barrier to overcome when addressing the problem.
Be open to discussing your own attitudes and biases	Given that the microaggression was unintended and that we all have biases when it comes to groups different from our own, being open to understanding the etiology of our comments is a helpful step in being able to move forward.
Be an ally and stand personally against all forms of bias and discrimination	It is the responsibility of people in positions of privilege and authority to spread the message of microaggressions. This doesn't mean ''white knighting'' the problem and making it yours to solve, but rather using power and influence to ensure there is stage time for this important issue to be addressed.

Source: Sue (2010)

DISCUSSION QUESTIONS

1. In what ways have you seen negative behaviors against women on your campus? What are some of the underlying negative attitudes and beliefs that fuel these behaviors? What factors influence these attitudes and beliefs? Where do they come from?

2. The authors make the point several times that a direct frontal assault on the patriarchal or misogynistic beliefs may not be the most effective way to bring about lasting change. However, when a group or individual behaves in a public way that directly impacts women, is there an obligation we have to respond in step with the severity of behavior to not appear soft or accepting of their behaviors?

3. What time periods, events, and activities on your campus are ripe for misogynistic attitudes and behaviors to surface? Are there proactive ways to alert stakeholders to problematic behaviors and ask for their help in preventing the occurrence?

4. Several tips are provided in the chapter for working with fraternities to address issues of concern. What are benefits and disadvantages to implementing the suggested strategies? How could you incentivize self-accountability structures? What organizational sanctions make sense on your campus and which sanctions need to be changed, revised, or eliminated?

5. The authors introduce the concept of microaggressions. Talk about a time you have been the recipient of a microaggression because of your gender, skin color, physical or mental health disability, socioeconomic status, or sexuality identity. What are some of the challenges in addressing microaggressions with people who aren't consciously aware that what they are saying is offensive?

Chapter 8

Grooming Behaviors

Trees there were, old as trees can be, huge and grasping with hearts black as sin. Strange trees that some said walked in the night.

—Neil Gaiman, Sandman

KEY TAKE-AWAYS

1. Grooming behaviors are well understood in stalking and sex crime cases as the individual lowers the target's defenses and lures the target into a location for an abduction or attack. Grooming behaviors in domestic violence can be more subtle, designed to lower defenses over time.

2. Abusers who engage in grooming behaviors may be consciously aware of them or display less insight into and awareness of what they are doing and how these behaviors affect others. Part of the solution for those unaware of their behaviors and the corresponding impact is educating the community to identify these behaviors and intervene when they occur.

3. It is not sufficient to educate students about bad behavior, but also important to educate them about healthy relationship habits.

Ominous, right? Grooming behaviors sound like a pedophile trying to lure a child to his van with candy and promises of puppies and kittens. And the term is best understood in that context, lowering the natural defenses by playing on themes of attention, fun, pleasure, and flattery. While some grooming behaviors are rather unsophisticated, such as coercive pressuring or aggressive flirtation, others are subtler, like slowly isolating a person from his or her support group and friends or making negative comments about the way the person dresses or behaves to lower his or her self-esteem.

We would argue these behaviors can be applied either consciously with malice or simply learned over time as practices that naturally allow the abuser to obtain what he wants from the other person. In a more malicious and conscious application of these behaviors, we are dealing with a potential serial attacker with narcissistic and sociopathic tendencies. Here the focus would be a referral to behavioral intervention team (BIT), law enforcement, or student conduct personnel.

As with threats and ultimatums, the path forward to reduce these behaviors is teaching and educating the community to identify these behaviors and develop bystander intervention approaches to intervene. Grooming behaviors can be seen as setting the stage for further stalking, sexual assault, or domestic or dating violence through disempowering and terrorizing the target. In addition to teaching intervention techniques, the behaviors should also be seen as a "tip of the iceberg" and reported up to the campus BIT, law enforcement, or student conduct personnel.

DEFINING THE FACTOR

This risk factor for sexual violence, stalking, and domestic/dating violence addresses the behaviors that are used by an aggressor to lessen a victim's ability to advocate for his or her safety. An individual attempting to disempower a partner or reestablish a relationship that has ended may use the grooming behaviors. Individuals or groups may also use these behaviors to increase the vulnerability of an individual as a target of sexual violence.

Examples of grooming behaviors include the following:

- **Stalking or tracking a person's movements or location** (Meloy and Fisher 2005): Here the individual monitors the target's behavior through his or her smartphone, GPS, or social media profile. He or she memorizes the target's schedule and follows him or her around on campus. The impact of this behavior creates a feeling of omniscience where victims feels as if they cannot escape the reach of the person or group that is monitoring them. This process also further isolates targets from existing social supports as they worry they will be observed in this as well. It creates a sense of worry and paranoia, commonly described as "having to walk on eggshells" in all aspects of their life to avoid confrontation with the abuser.

- **Blocking an exit through physical presence or threat of violence** (LaViolette and Barnett 2000; Armstrong et al. 2006): Here the individual prevents exit from a location, often feeling justified as the individual has not yet finished saying what he or she needs to say or feels as if the target isn't listening or understanding in a way he or she would like. This behavior can cross the threshold to kidnapping or criminal threatening, depending on laws in the state where it occurs. It also would be a violation of the student code of conduct at most schools.

- **Isolation of individual or group away from friends or acquaintances** (Humphrey and Kahn 2000; LaViolette and Barnett 2000; Armstrong et al. 2006): This more subtle behavior often occurs over a period of time and has a cumulative effect as victims become further and further isolated from their support network. This is not often a planned act but rather comes from the individual's desire to limit other opinions or outside threats to the relationship. They monitor phone calls, forbid visits, begrudge outings with friends, and may emotionally manipulate the victim by saying things like "You don't spend time with me anymore" and "Why would you need to talk to them—you have me. Aren't I enough?"

- **Insulting or embarrassing an individual (or group) or attacking his or her self-esteem through disparaging remarks** (Armstrong et al. 2006): Embarrassment in front of a group of friends is a grooming behavior designed to reduce the self-esteem and self-worth of the target in efforts to drive him or her back to the abuser. This creates a cycle where the victim's worth is limited to comments by the abuser and the only value the victim has is found in the abuser's gaze. This grooming behavior also has the side effect of further embarrassing, and thus isolating, the victim from his or her social group or any activities nor expressly approved of by the abuser.

- **Objectifying an individual or group** (LaViolette and Barnett 2000; Armstrong et al. 2006): This can be seen as a subset of the prior grooming behavior. Here, the value of the individual being targeted is limited to the extent the abuser desires. The victim could be valued as a "pretty girl" but not seen as very smart or worthy of deeper discussions reserved for those with more to offer. The victim could be seen as useful in the sense of providing a service to the group, such as making food, hosting an event, or bringing drinks, but unworthy of being an equal at the event. As mentioned earlier in the book, the act of objectifying takes away the agency, choice, and personhood of individuals and reduces them to a one-dimensional shadow of their true self.

- **Emphasis of power and control themes, reduction of individual or group choices, and infantilizing behavior** (LaViolette and Barnett 2000; Teranishi-Martinez 2014): In this collection of behaviors, we see power and control exerted over an individual. This may be achieved with threats of direct harm or more emotionally manipulative tactics that intimidate and control the victim. This could involve a threat to expose nude photos or racy sexting messages if the victim doesn't comply with the abuser's demands. The central concept here is the abuser takes control of the victim and guides his or her behavior through threats or dismissive behavior.

ADDRESSING THE INDIVIDUAL

Individual examples of grooming behavior occur most frequently within domestic and dating violence scenarios where one party attempts to control and manipulate the other party by isolating them from their friends, lowering self-esteem, and reducing the ability of victims to defend or protect themselves. These relationship dynamics are typically observable to those who know what to look for and are often first seen by students who have experience with intimate partner violence (IPV).

While overt pushing, shoving, taking of a phone, yelling, or threatening behaviors are easier to spot and quickly become known to campus police and student conduct personnel, subtler controlling behaviors are of particular concern when discussing this risk factor. Take the following scenario as an example:

> David is sick and tired of dealing with McKenzie's flightiness. He has told her too many times to count why it is important for him to see her every day, and she just seems oblivious to this rather simple and reasonable request. Hell, other women on campus would kill to have this kind of attention. What makes her think she is so goddamned special?

He waits for her outside of her last class and will get an answer to why she thinks she can just ignore him. He has sent her over a dozen text messages and she responds with nothing. Like he doesn't have anything better to do but wait around for her. It's her selfishness that bothers him most right now. He wrings his hands and anticipates the fight that she, once again, is making him have with her. Students begin to trickle out of the classroom and he sees her near the back talking to another student.

David rubs his eyes as if to clear the thoughts bubbling up in his head. Is she seriously talking to that guy across the room instead of responding to the text messages he just sent? Who the hell does she think she is? Part of him relishes the fight they will have. How she will pathetically try to defend her actions, yet again. And how he will rip her excuses down to the bone. He wonders if it is really worth it. Then he looks at her standing there in that short skirt and he reminds himself that she is worth his time. She just needs to learn some better manners.

McKenzie touches her friend's arm in the back of the classroom and laughs at the joke he made. The professor mixed up a pretty basic idea in class tonight and he joked about what else he might be getting confused on when they have the exam next week. She glances at her phone and sees the text messages from David. Shit, she thinks, and looks around the classroom. She sees him waiting by the door, looking at her.

She excuses herself from her friend and meets David at the door. "I'm so sorry. I didn't see your messages in class. The professor makes us turn off . . ."

Davie interrupts her. "Let's just talk about it in the car. I don't want to do it here."

That cold and distant voice. McKenzie shivers, knowing the conversation won't be a positive one. She's learned not to argue with him in public, though. She did that once before and the six-hour argument that ensued when they got back to his room still gives her headaches to think about. Sometimes it is just easier to go along with it.

McKenzie's friend stares at her as she walks away with David. He worries about her. Something seems off with that guy.

While there is no direct threat, no pushing or shouting, the controlling nature of students like David fundamentally have the same impact on students like McKenzie. Her choices are limited, her free will to leave the relationship curtailed, and you can feel the way her self-esteem decreases and her paranoia increases. These kinds of situations don't develop overnight, but rather grow over time, like that old story about the frog in the pot of hot water. If you put a frog into a pot of boiling water, it will jump right out. If you put the frog into a pot of cool water and then slowly turn up the heat, it cooks to death, unaware of the danger. Grooming behaviors are hardest to intervene with when they occur like this, slowly wearing down targets' common sense and willingness to resist until they find themselves agreeing and doing things they would have never imagined they would have consented to under normal circumstances.

ADDRESSING THE GROUP

Grooming behaviors desensitize potential victims from awareness of the behaviors occurring around them and decrease the alternatives to access safety. While grooming behaviors are most often thought of as individual behaviors, groups can create environments that are prone to sexual violence by isolating participants and removing protective factors. In a study by Boswell and Spade (1996), they documented social settings created by fraternities and describe conduct and social event planning that lessen the safety options for participants. Environments are created with an unequal mix of genders participating in the party, gender segregation throughout the event, and men treating women less respectfully, with degrading jokes and conversations. The settings also included loud music, which limited conversations, and providing access to "filthy bathroom" options only. All are examples of creating a climate that lessens a person's access to support and safety.

When combined with open sources of alcohol, the social environment has been molded to create a setting where sexual violence can easily occur. There are several famous examples of organizations sharing educational information and advice with its members concerning the creation of environments and activities that have the potential to lure unsuspecting students into dangerous situations. A Georgia Tech fraternity member sent a "how to" e-mail to his organization members that included the "7 E's of Hooking Up." He gave them grooming advice that consisted of encountering a group of girls, engaging them by talking to them, escalating by asking them to dance or go to a room or a couch, getting an erection, ejaculating, and expunging them out of the room when finished. He provided additional details about conversation and talking points, how to encourage them to drink alcohol, how to dance with them, and how to begin making out with them. His final line includes, "If anything ever fails, go get more alcohol. I want to see everyone succeed at the next couple parties. In luring rapebait" (Willingham 2013).

Grooming behavior within organizations can include this blatant type of attitude and behavior as well as strategic social environments, but grooming behavior also occurs related to the treatment of members within the organization. Younger members are particularly vulnerable to what they perceive that the group requires in order to be socially accepted. Unfortunately, other unhealthy new member activities related to hazing can make some organizations even more vulnerable to the power of social norms.

The ritual process in these cases humiliates the pledges in order to break social and psychological bonds to parental authority and to establish new bonds to the brotherhood. The traumatic means employed to achieve these goals induces a state of consciousness that makes abuse of women a means to reinforce fraternal bonds and assert power as a brotherhood.

(Sanday 2007, p. 43)

New members are groomed to adopt the predominant attitudes and behaviors of the organization. New members often become isolated from previous friends, family members, or intimate relationships because of the demands of membership requirements and time constraints, the natural transition to college and drifting away from parental expectations, or discouragement from other members about having a long-term, committed relationship. This strengthens their bonds to the new organization. Thus, when even just a few members exemplify attitudes that are harassing or violent, the entire organization can be at risk.

FROM THE FRONT LINES

A Case Study in Stalking and Rape

Tom is a 21-year-old sophomore at a major Midwestern university. He is majoring in sports management, and is planning to go on for an MBA. His grades are average, around a C+, which will make it difficult for him to get into a top-tier MBA program.

Friends describe Tom as a little arrogant and self-absorbed, particularly when he is drinking, at which time he becomes loud, and can even become abusive, particularly with women.

Tom is not involved in an exclusive relationship; however, his good looks attract lots of girls. He doesn't date much, claiming it's hard to find girls who meet his standards. Tom volunteers at a local youth center, giving swimming lessons to male and female teens and tweens between ages 10 and 15.

Last month, one of the mothers of one of his swimming students unexpectedly took her daughter out of class and told the pool manager that her daughter felt uncomfortable with Tom because he touched her too much. Tom completely denied any wrongdoing when confronted by the manager, and in fact was indignant when he was questioned.

Another student confided to some of her friends that Tom had sexted her some provocative photos of himself swimming nude. The student thought it was funny and didn't go to authorities.

Tom had an internship the summer between his freshman and sophomore year. However, he was "let go" before the internship ended for misuse of a computer. Tom told the university it was all a misunderstanding, and that he had accessed some photos a friend sent him attached to a personal e-mail that involved some nudity. He explained that his supervisor was a prude with no sense of humor and was out to get him, so he decided to end his internship early.

During his freshman year, Tom was stopped late at night and questioned by police for loitering behind a girls' dormitory. Because he was 17 at the time and considered a juvenile, he was released by police and no investigation ensued, and no charges were filed. This dorm was located in an area where there was a recent rash of apartment burglaries. Some of the victims reported missing items of underwear. No suspect was identified.

Dr. Mary Ellen O'Toole
Former FBI BAU Supervisor
George Mason University

FROM THE FRONT LINES

Alcohol 101

One of my favorite jobs at New England College was teaching the "oh shit, I just got in trouble with alcohol class" (not the actual name for the class) for students who had a first infraction of the school's alcohol policy. This included students who were caught with a beer in the residence halls, were found drinking underage, or drank to the point of needing police or hospital care. Basically, anyone who had run afoul of the college's student conduct code for alcohol violations.

I enjoyed teaching the class because I'm a bit of a sadist. It thrilled me to see their sad faces first thing Saturday morning, angry and remorseless, ready to receive their just punishments. Just kidding. I really enjoyed teaching the class because it was offered at a reasonable hour after classes during the week and it was my 90-minute chance to make a positive difference in a student's life.

The way I taught the class was different from the typical punishment model. Instead, I focused on the biphasic curve and the harm reduction approach and taught the students how to drink smarter, if they choose to drink. The first slides we reviewed encouraged the students to think about the qualities of successful drinkers—people who drank as adults and did so without negative consequences. What made someone able to drink and not get in trouble? What qualities do lifelong drinkers possess that keep them away from health problems, social missteps, and criminal or legal problems?

This approach worked because it focused on what they should be doing (if they choose to drink), rather than what they should avoid doing. We focused on positive behaviors, like drinking slowly, enjoying and savoring the beverage, drinking with food, keeping track of the number of drinks you have, knowing your tolerance level, and having social events and fun with friends who didn't always rely on alcohol. The students appreciated being talked to like adults and I believe they learned some important things during our time together.

The lesson here, I think, for addressing grooming behaviors is a similar one. You certainly could take the list offered at the beginning of this chapter and make posters and awareness campaigns and videos to demonstrate these bad behaviors. And I think we should do exactly that. But as we have said before in this text, that approach is necessary, but not sufficient. What we also need to do is teach the qualities of a healthy and successful relationship, a relationship that is not based on manipulation, coercion, and exploitation or is repetitively harmful to either party. What does that look like?

The following section in this chapter offers what Amy and I would suggest are some of the key qualities of healthy relationships. We've included some discussion questions and starting points to engage students on these issues. These observations and qualities are based on our combined work as a counseling center director and a dean of students. Together, we have worked with a wide array of students in relationships, some in couples counseling in my center, others in front of conduct boards or in mentor relationships. It is our hope that these examples create some positive dialogue with students to foster opportunities to reduce negative behaviors (like high-risk drinking or grooming behaviors) through teaching healthy alternatives and exemplars.

Brian Van Brunt, EdD
Author
A Guide to Leadership and Management: Managing Across the Generations
Harm to Others: The Assessment and Treatment of Dangerousness
A Faculty Guide to Addressing Disruptive and Dangerous Behavior

REDUCING THE RISK

When working with students who have severe alcohol abuse or dependence, it is important to teach them not only the trigger and warning signs of falling back into a pattern of alcoholism, but also ways that people exist and live happy lives without alcohol. In the same way, we would argue that teaching students the dangers of grooming behaviors and negative and controlling warning signs found in unhealthy relationships involves teaching how people maintain healthy relationships. Unhealthy relationships based on threats, pressure, isolation, and manipulation would then stand in stark contrast.

Healthy relationships, in all of their wonderful diversity, are based on concepts of open communication and respect for each other's autonomy and connectedness. In those healthy relationships, there is a cultivation of each individual's value and self as well as a willingness to sacrifice and give to the relationship itself. There is a sacrifice that each makes to the relationship and to the betterment of the other. Great relationships live in this balance, one person giving and loving the other, wanting the best for him or her, and this, in turn, being given back.

For our students, those unique, special little snowflakes that they are, sharing with them the ways healthy relationships work is, arguably, part of that critical thinking and citizenship education liberal arts educations are known for. Teaching empathy, positive communication skills, reasonable expectations, how to communicate when angry, and how to realize that the relationship may not be worth saving are all topics we not only should but also must be having with our students.

So while creating workshops and lectures on the dangers of unhealthy relationships and teaching students what to avoid lest they end up in an abusive relationship are part of the solution, this should not come at the expense of engaging students in a more relationship-positive conversation. This is the same with consent-based conversations; the education cannot end with "get consent before you have sex or it is rape" but rather should address the ways students should engage in open, sex-positive conversations with their prospective partners, discussing both desires and boundaries.

So, what makes a healthy relationship? The following examples are drawn from the author's experiences in teaching workshops, offering couple's counseling, mentoring, and holding disciplinary conversations with students. Readers are encouraged to adapt the following into programs and use the corresponding discussion questions to inspire conversation with students. While we refer to couples in the following section, these principles also apply to polyamorous relationships. These relationships, in many ways, require an even more advanced and nuanced ability for all involved to communicate, listen, focus on others, strive for balance, and have a mutual respect.

Communication: It all starts here. Talking openly with your partner about the good, the bad, and the ugly of the relationship not only is the first quality of having a healthy relationship but also outshines all other qualities we are about to discuss. It also happens to be, unfortunately, something that requires vulnerability, experience, humility, self-acceptance, dedication, and commitment to do well. Nurture communication in a relationship and it becomes easier and easier to accomplish. Neglect communication and you find yourself traveling quickly down the longest chute this side of the gumdrop forest (yes, we are mixing board game metaphors here, but we do so with reckless abandon).

1. What are some of the easier things to talk about in a relationship?
2. Discuss some ways communication might get harder the longer the relationship lasts. Discuss some ways communication might get easier over time.
3. What are some obstacles to good communication in a new relationship? Think about a time where you wanted to say something but you didn't. What kept you from sharing?
4. It can be helpful to think about sharing in a relationship being like pouring milk from a container into a glass. It is more difficult to pour all the milk from a gallon jug into a small glass. Think about times when sharing was prevented because the container (the attitude or ability of the other person) wasn't able to handle the liquid (information) you had to share.
5. Are there times where emotions or the location of the talking makes it more difficult to share with another person? Think about talking about feelings of jealousy at a busy restaurant. Share an example in which this went poorly.

Active listening/empathy: A healthy relationship requires those in the relationship to know the wants and desires of the other person. This is accomplished through active listening and a sense of empathy and understanding. These qualities come easier for some people, more naturally, but the skills of active listening can certainly be taught. This begins with clearing away distractions, such as a phone, computer, television, or other people, and truly listening to what your partner has to say. Open-ended questions, those that avoid a simple one-word or short-phrase answer, also can help bring about a more empathetic understanding of a partner's needs or wants.

1. Think about a time when you were fully understood by another person. What did that feel like? Can you share the example?
2. What are some obstacles that keep you from listening actively to another person? Think of some that are physical (phones, computers, friends) as well as emotional (tired, angry, resentful).
3. Pair off with another person in the group and practice listening to them without giving advice or direction. Simply repeat back what they just said word for word. After doing this for several minutes, try summarizing what the person said rather than simply repeating his or her words back to them. After several minutes of that, ask a question designed to get the person to share more details with you. Switch back and forth as you work on this exercise.
4. How might you address the problem of one partner being overly empathic to the other partner's needs and desires, but the other partner is not willing to act in the same way? In other words, what if you empathize and listen actively and your partner does not reciprocate?
5. Think about a time where you asked someone you were in a relationship with a question that helped clarify, in an empathic way, what he or she wanted or needed. How did that feel?

Focus on the other's happiness: There really should be a word for this in the English language. It seems close to the idea of empathy, understanding another's experience from his or her perspective, but that's not quite what we are talking about here. Healthy relationships exist when there is a desire on the part of one person to make the other person's life shine more brightly. When there is a willingness to focus on the other's needs rather than your own needs. Perhaps this concept is more akin to altruism. There is an investment in the other person having a complete life, one full of what he or she desires and without the partner begrudging or guilting the other person into submission or given in a tit-for-tat manner, where it is less a gift and more a barter for future payback.

1. Think of a time when someone had your best interest at heart and did something for you without an expectation of getting something in return. How does that reflect in your past relationships?

2. A problem certainly can occur when one person gives all of him- or herself in a relationship for the other person and there is little offered in return. Think of a time or an experience where someone took without giving in return. Is it possible to have a relationship that lacks this balance? What does that look like?

3. A requirement in giving to another for his or her happiness is the ability to empathize and understand what might make the other person happy. What experiences have you had where someone tried to make you happy, but really didn't know what you liked or wanted? How did you communicate with that person around this disappointment?

4. What has been your experience in thinking about other people when things are stressful and upsetting in your own life? Are there times when caring for another person had a positive effect on your mood?

5. It can be difficult when the person you care about has needs or desires that do not line up with your own. What are some ways to talk about these potential "hot spots"?

Equanimity: One of our favorite words. It means to have a sense of balance in the chaos of everyday existence. Relationships work well when there is a natural sense of give-and-take, back and forth, a sharing between partners that is informed by a desire for the other's happiness and a desire for your own. Within the context of open communication, partners can discuss their desires and find a sense of compromise and balance on issues that goes beyond a ledger sheet or sense of keeping score. It's a sense of balance and fairness found in the mother's simple wisdom of helping two hungry children share a sandwich. She simply says to one, "You cut the sandwich," and to the other, "You pick which side you want." It's a balance that leans on the parable of the commons. What is good for you is also good for me. What is bad for you is also bad for me. We rise or fall together.

1. What has been your experience with finding a balance in past relationships? When was this more difficult? When was this more straightforward?

2. What are some topics that are difficult to find balance in? Some examples might be finances, flirting with other people, and how to spend free time.

3. Think about a time when the balance was off in a relationship. What are some ways that you regained a sense of balance? How did you communicate with your partner? What do you wish you had done differently?

4. Over time, habits can develop where one person has a larger sense of control over certain issues in the relationship. Talk about your experiences with this.

5. Are there ways to know when a relationship isn't getting better, but getting more out of balance, falling further away from something that is positive? How have you addressed trying to fix a relationship that is out of balance versus walking away from it?

Social connection: This one is particularly difficult for college students. We all have different needs and desires for social interactions and connections. Some of us enjoy parties and spending time with multiple friends. Others enjoy "hamster-balling" in the quiet of an evening with a good book and some favorite snacks. Healthy couples find a balance between their needs and build upon the previous qualities of communication, active listening, empathy, the other's happiness, and equanimity. While some couples have similar desires in how they share their time socially with others, some are paired differently and have the opportunity to communicate about ways they can work together to find a mutually agreeable middle ground.

1. Do couples who share an outgoing or at-home approach to social connections have an easier time of it? What arguments have you seen (or had) with couples who have a similar desire to be extroverted versus introverted?

2. What are some tensions you have experienced in talking with a partner about going out and spending time with friends versus staying home? How did you resolve these? What would you have done differently if you could go back in time?

3. How do you interact with a partner when you don't see a situation the same way? For example, if you are tired at a party and feel like it is time to go home? Or if you have been cooped up for a while, how do you ask your partner to go out and spend time with friends?

4. Have there been times when the desire to spend time with friends apart from your partner has created tension in the relationship?

What are some ways you've tried to address this with your partner? What worked or didn't work? What would you do differently?

5. What are some examples of compromises you have found with your partner to develop middle ground?

Mutual respect: This is the quality of caring for and respecting your partner and his or her choices, outlook, and experiences. This is the idea of looking at the other person and feeling proud and content that you are with him or her in a relationship. You care for your partner and want the very best for your partner's future. This quality is one that is in balance, where each partner has a respect for the other's interests.

1. Can you think of a relationship (dating or otherwise) where you had a feeling of mutual respect? What contributed to that feeling?
2. Is mutual respect an immediate quality of a relationship or something that develops over time? In your experience, is it a quality that either exists or does not, or is there more of a spectrum of mutual respect that develops over time?
3. What factors strengthen a sense of mutual respect in a relationship? What are some things that can erode a sense of mutual respect?
4. How does the concept of trust support the idea of mutual respect between partners in a relationship?
5. Think of a time when you lost respect for someone you cared about. What was the process involved in reestablishing that mutual respect again? Is it always possible to reestablish mutual respect? What are some things that would be more difficult to negotiate back to a place of mutual trust?

We hope the previous examples offer some starting places for conversations with students or groups of students to discuss the aspects of healthy relationships. We would encourage you to end the exercise by asking the audience to think of other qualities they think are important in a relationship and develop some of their own discussion questions related to those qualities. The concept here, again, is talking about healthy relationships in the hopes that students will learn what to look for in addition to spotting those warning signs and grooming behaviors that make up unhealthy relationships.

DISCUSSION QUESTIONS

1. What are some examples of grooming behaviors you have seen on your campus? What are the obstacles to intervene with these behaviors?

2. Grooming behaviors are particularly challenging to address in group scenarios. What are some experiences you have had where grooming behaviors occur at parties and other on-campus events? What are some approaches to addressing these problems?

3. In the author's example with David and McKenzie, what keeps students in the classroom, particularly McKenzie's friend, from confronting the situation? How do we overcome this hesitation?

4. In the case described by Dr. O'Toole, we see an escalation of Tom's behavior. He seems adept at talking his way out of situations that might otherwise begin to establish a clear record of sexually based behavior problems. How might your campus handle a case like Tom?

5. What opportunities exist on campus to promote healthy relationships? How can efforts incorporate perceptions of the "hookup" culture on college campuses?

Chapter 9

Using Substances to Obtain Sex

> It's the point at which, as we say in the language of the desert, one dies of thirst just when the palm trees have appeared on the horizon.
>
> —*Paulo Coelho*, The Alchemist

KEY TAKE-AWAYS

1. Alcohol has a long history of being used to calm and ease people's nerves in group settings and as an aphrodisiac of sorts for sexual activity. Some use alcohol to reduce a person's natural defenses and take advantage of them sexually in a way they would protest more vehemently when less intoxicated.

2. Sexual violence prevention is closely linked to alcohol prevention efforts. Education related to consent and incapacitation is important for students as well as conduct officers and hearing boards reviewing Title IX incidents.

3. Victims who were under the influence of substances during an incident of sexual violence often blame themselves for what occurred. Training for the campus community needs to include how to support reporting parties and include cautionary information on questions and statements that can add to self-blame and victimization.

As we developed the risk factors for this book, we knew that alcohol intoxication was an aspect that occurred again and again in cases of sexual assault on campus. Studies have typically pointed to upwards of 50%–75% of sexual assault incidents involving alcohol or drugs. It has been our experience at two separate large institutions that close to 90%–95% of cases of sexual assault on campus involved alcohol intoxication. It is difficult to overstate the enormity of the problem of substances used to impact the sexual violence on campus.

A separate issue, we contend, is related to women's choices and rights to become intoxicated and not to be taken advantage of during this time. There tends to be two major camps in this argument. One group says firmly and unequivocally that women can drink whatever they want, wear whatever they want, and are not responsible for men who attempt to have sex with them without consent or sexually assault them. The other camp talks more about risk mitigation and teaching women to be aware of their high-risk choices of drinking to a point where they are less able to protect themselves or have a heightened awareness of the risky situations they are putting themselves into.

We would suggest there is a middle ground here. No matter what a person is wearing or how much he or she has had to drink, no other person has the right to take advantage of another sexually. However, it also should be part of our prevention message that intoxicated individuals don't make the best risk managers. In this chapter, we emphasize the danger when alcohol is used actively and with a malicious intent to reduce people's decision-making capacity and ability to defend themselves.

This process of using substances, both alcohol and other drugs, to overcome a person's hesitancy to engage in sexual activity is both an obvious and pervasive one in our society. At best, alcohol is used as a social lubricant to relax and make a potential partner feel more comfortable in a situation. At worst, alcohol is used to drug and numb a target's natural defenses and reduce his or her ability to escape sexual advances. Our concern is more the latter, both with individuals and systemically as part of a group's strategy to create an environment more primed for sexual assault.

DEFINING THE FACTOR

Some individuals or groups make use of alcohol or other drugs in an attempt to lower the resistance and defenses of those they target for sexual behavior. It recalls the classic Christmas song "Baby It's Cold Outside," in which alcohol is used to lower the defenses of the woman to give sexual consent. It would be reasonable to see this as connected to the previous chapter, as the use of alcohol and other drugs to reduce someone's ability to make conscious choices could also serve as a grooming behavior. Given the frequency and devastation to which this particular grooming behavior is used on college campuses, the authors chose to create this as a unique factor. The use of alcohol is well established in the literature on college sexual assault with indications that 50%–75% of incidents are associated with alcohol or other drugs (Abbey et al. 2001; Krebs et al. 2007; American College Health Association 2008; Zapp 2014).

Alcohol use by college students is well documented, including high-risk alcohol use, such as drinking games, pregaming, and binge drinking, as well as the negative consequences associated with alcohol, such as taking advantage of someone sexually or being taken advantage of sexually. Alcohol and other substances are frequently ingested by college students to relax, reduce social anxiety, and increase their enjoyment. College parties have a long history of involving alcohol to reduce inhibitions and help those in attendance have a good time.

As mentioned in the introduction, the challenge here is sorting out the difference between one or two drinks to feel more relaxed and comfortable and the practice of drinking to the point of intoxication. The level of alcohol intoxication is affected by a number of factors, including the frequency and potency of the drink, the consumption of food, an individual's body type, gender, and alcohol tolerance, given past drinking behavior. Through the case studies, we hope to better illustrate the difference between drinking to become more socially relaxed as part of a typical courtship or dating experience at a party versus those individuals who use alcohol more directly as a tool to allow them to take advantage of another person.

ADDRESSING THE INDIVIDUAL

The research indicates two different relationships between alcohol and sexual assault. Perpetrators of sexual assault are more likely to be problematic users of alcohol, but victims of sexual assault are also more likely to indicate high-risk or problematic drinking (EverFi 2013). While the use of alcohol should never excuse sexually violent behavior, it is clear that the tightly coupled relationship between alcohol and sexual assault must be addressed in prevention efforts. Victims drinking alcohol when assaulted may be more hesitant to report than other victims, and they may blame themselves or experience trauma in different ways than victims not consuming alcohol when assaulted.

Only a few [people] would suggest that a woman who passes out from alcohol abuse in a bar shares responsibility for having her purse stolen and would therefore argue against prosecuting the thief, even after he was caught using her credit cards. When the topic is sexual relations, people often find the "facts" confusing. (Schwartz and DeKeseredy 1997, p. 49)

With that, victim support efforts have to acknowledge the strong possibility that a victim was drinking when assaulted and provide reassurance and encouragement that he or she is not to blame and help is available.

The use of alcohol also provides an excuse to perpetrators of sexual violence.

> They admitted they had committed an act that on the surface seemed to be rape, but said that they were drunk or high, and therefore not completely in control of their actions. It is not unusual to argue that many men drink heavily on campus before a date rape not to loosen their inhibitions, but to give themselves the excuse that they were not in control of their actions.
>
> (Schwartz and DeKeseredy 1997, p. 74)

"Although few would claim a direct causal relationship, alcohol is related to woman abuse in many ways" (Schwartz and DeKeseredy 1997, p. 48). Schwartz and DeKeseredy (1997) indicate that alcohol is often connected to stories that support misogynistic ideologies and the objectification of women. These experiences are easily relatable to male locker room discussions where women are discussed in crass and objectified ways. The idea of men gathering, drinking at a bar, and talking respectfully about women they like is, unfortunately, a bit of a laughable image. The reality is alcohol reduces men to their baser instincts and often removes filters, leading to an increase in objectifying and sexualized depictions of women.

Alcohol is also linked to reports of misperceptions of sexual interest between parties, leading to ignoring cues of refusal and contributing to victim blaming around regretted sex (American College Health Association 2008). Consider the following scenario:

Margie is a senior in college. She is enjoying her last year of football games, parties, and road trips with friends. She has traveled with her best friend, Jamie, and Jamie's boyfriend, Chris, to an away football game. Chris introduces her to one of his friends, Taylor, who happens to live in the town. Margie and Taylor spend the weekend together, having a good time, and flirting openly with one another. The first evening at a bar, they kiss in a dark corner and talk about how turned on they are, but they go to separate houses that evening. On the last night, following the football game, the foursome attends the game together and bar hop and party throughout the evening. Margie is having fun with Taylor. She likes him, and she wants to make out with him more. Taylor thinks Margie is cute, and

> he wants to have sex with her that evening. Neither is necessarily interested in a serious relationship, but they like each other.
>
> Both have had a variety of alcoholic beverages throughout the evening, including at least one shot at each of the bars they visited. When they get back to the house where she is staying, Margie realizes she is probably about to pass out and heads toward the bedroom she was using. Jamie and Chris head toward their bedroom and tell Taylor that he can sleep on the couch or whatever, and they "wink" at him. Taylor eventually follows Margie into her room. Margie has undressed and is in a t-shirt and shorts under the covers of the bed. Taylor says to her, "I know you're not asleep. Come here, I want to mess around." Margie sighs and says, "I'm so sleepy. I really want to, but it's so late." She sits up in the bed and Taylor leans down, and they kiss. Margie is responsive to Taylor's kisses and initiates oral sex. When Taylor begins to pull Margie's underwear off, she mentions again that she is not sure and that she is tired. Taylor uses his hands on Margie and then begins to have intercourse with Margie. Margie participates and seems to enjoy it.

Alcohol is related to interpersonal violence. In dating violence and domestic violence, the initial aggression may be nonsexual. It may include grabbing, shoving, hitting, or threats. In a similar manner to sexual assault, perpetrators of sexual violence are often high-risk or problematic drinkers (Zapp 2014). These are the cases that exist on today's campuses and are drawing the attention of the media and appearing on the front pages of magazines. Student conduct officers, law enforcement, and Title IX investigators struggle to work together to resolve these cases through an on-campus process, off-campus criminal process, or a combination of both.

ADDRESSING THE GROUP

EverFi's research indicates that the majority of our students have generally healthy attitudes and behaviors related to alcohol and sexual assault, but they are able to identify a much unhealthier minority who continues to decline in negative consequences related to alcohol after arriving on the college campus. They are also the group that is more likely to sexually assault another person, according to their findings (EverFi 2013). In other words, students who report more negative consequences of alcohol use have less healthy attitudes and behaviors related to sexual assault. This unhealthy minority is most often male members of fraternities or athletes (Zapp 2014).

The nature of alcohol use in an organization is, in and of itself, a possible predictor of problematic behaviors related to sexual violence. In group settings, alcohol use increases conformity to group norms by reducing inhibitions and individual judgment, and increasing group bonding (Jewkes et al. 2002). In fact, the more popular or the more social capital held by an organization, then the greater the pressure to conform to peer norms related to alcohol (EverFi 2013). This same pressure to align with the group norms translates beyond alcohol, such as negative attitudes around the treatment of women.

In more extreme cases, an individual or group uses substances to facilitate sexual assault. This could be a systemic issue for a group or a more focused tactic by an individual or smaller group within a larger social setting. Subtler methods of substance abuse include hosting social events that provide high volumes of free alcohol and serving alcohol to underage students, who are more vulnerable during their transition to college. At group events and parties, communal alcohol sources, such as "trashcan punch" or mixes, could be made significantly stronger or adulterated with illegal or prescription drugs. In a story reminiscent of carnies marking rubes with chalk to be targeted for robbery later in the evening, some organizations make use of X's and special marks on partygoers to indicate that person for future exploitation.

These systemic actions by a group or organization on campus contribute to the risk of sexual assault and gender-based violence by creating and nurturing an environment conducive to exploitation. The premeditated nature of abusing alcohol at these parties and gatherings can no longer be seen as a "boys-will-be-boys," unfortunate behavior. Rather, these should be seen as planned actions to aid in the commission of an assault.

FROM THE FRONT LINES

The Alcohol Quandary

I don't know about you, but I have felt nervous talking about alcohol and sexual violence because it is a topic that can easily shift toward victim blaming or giving perpetrators an out for their behavior. As I write this, I find myself critically considering each sentence for its subtle meanings and implications. Thinking critically about our prevention efforts is one thing, but it cannot be to the detriment of dialogue around sometimes confusing social situations. It also cannot keep us from talking to students about this relationship and how to navigate realistic social settings.

127

Since 2011, I have found it intriguing to watch the development of various programs and online modules related to prevention of sexual assault and how they handle the issue of alcohol. Some online programs have created integrated modules, whereas others have split alcohol and sexual violence into two separate components. Some educational presenters take on the complicated issue of consent and alcohol use, while others instead indicate that sex and alcohol use cannot occur together in any safe way. If we have learned nothing else from prevention efforts related to high-risk alcohol use, we should know that we have to be realistic about the alcohol-related behaviors in our college communities and give students concrete tools for having sexual relationships in this environment. Pretending that students are not going to drink will not work, and pretending that students are not going to drink and have sex will not work either.

How often at Title IX investigator and coordinator trainings do we hear the question of how you handle cases in which both parties are drunk. Some trainers argue that a man who is incapacitated can generally not sustain sexual intercourse, but that often feels like an oversimplification. Instead, we train on breaking down the elements of the interaction, creating a timeline about what occurred and when, and unwinding elements of who if anyone was incapacitated and if the other party knew. From a prevention perspective, it can start to feel like the only way to educate students is to have them treat their partners who have been consuming alcohol or other substances with only caution and hesitation, which by themselves are not elements that generally lead to healthy interactions.

Some sororities have also tried to identify ways to support the safety of their members in alcohol-related environments by changing the way they interact with fraternities at social events. Most sorority houses are alcohol-free or the sorority has more restrictive alcohol policies than other groups, which means for the organizations to participate as a group in social events with alcohol, they often have to participate at fraternity houses or third-party establishments. Interestingly, one of the reasons sororities let fraternities plan the events is because they take on more of the liability and risk, but they also take on more of the expense of purchasing alcohol. Since this put the power in the hands of the fraternities to control the environment of the social event, some sororities decided a possible solution was to host their own events and take back the power to control the environment. At one school, the sorority community also decided to limit sorority new member socials during the first four weeks of the semester, resulting in some arguing that it was just a form of telling women not to drink as much or not to go out. I share these examples to illustrate the complexities of what we are dealing with on college campuses when it comes to sex and alcohol.

In Cassie's scenario, before we know that she did not remember anything from the night before, is it possible she was just more assertive and flirtatious because of the alcohol use and was finally telling her friend Doug that she wanted to be with him? Absolutely, it's possible. Should Doug be educated to push her off of him and leave? What are realistic tools and techniques to help students in these situations?

I think there are several options for further examination as we proceed as a prevention community. First, we have to utilize realistic contexts and cases when we are educating students. It frustrates me that so many case studies and educational videos show scenarios where the incapacitation level of one of the parties is obvious (meaning he or she is passed out). Generally, students understand that level of incapacitation. It is much more difficult when one party is still actively participating and in some cases initiating sexual activity. What would students say about the Cassie and Doug scenario ahead when considering the different options available to each of them in navigating what occurred? That case scenario is a realistic example of what students may experience.

Second, consent education has to include the element of the hookup. Some students are going to participate in sexual activity with no relationship history with a person or with no intention of an ongoing relationship. Including this aspect of student relationships in educational efforts in a nonjudgmental manner allows you to include in education around consent and incapacitation the idea of how well you know someone and how that relates. Last, we have to include skill building related to patience and examining our needs for instant gratification. We can help students explore ideas around the positive aspects of delaying sexual activity and how they can enjoy the moment without risking hurting someone or themselves.

Students are surrounded by imagery that indicates the only way to make a connection with someone is an evening out with lots of alcohol use to break down barriers. I am from Texas, where country music dominates most radio stations. Just by quickly searching the top country songs on the radio right now, I can find example after example of how alcohol and sex are portrayed in ways that confuse casual freedom to engage and get to know another person while enjoying an alcoholic beverage with alcohol-laden misogyny, mistreatment, and objectification of women. Sexually violent behavior feeds off alcohol just like tree roots feed off water. We have to help students, and our campus communities for that matter, develop the critical thinking skills to consider for themselves the complicated nature of sexual activity in college and the harm that having sex with someone who is incapacitated has on that person.

Dr. Amy Murphy
Assistant Professor, Curriculum and Instruction
Angelo State University

REDUCING THE RISK

In order to prevent the occurrence of sexual violence, we have to be willing to have difficult and often uncomfortable conversations about the role of alcohol in our social lives, relationships, and sex lives. Consider this scenario:

Cassie and Doug have been friends for years. They have always flirted with each other, but they have never pursued a relationship, sexual or otherwise. They usually see each other at the same bar on Fridays and will hang out together, usually with other friends around as well. One Friday night, they stayed at the bar throughout the evening. It was common for them to order multiple rounds of shots throughout the night while also drinking other drinks. On this evening, Cassie was drinking whiskey sours, and Doug was drinking beer.

Cassie and Doug were sitting at the bar together. Cassie was leaning into Doug, laughing with him, and touching his arm and leg flirtatiously. Doug was telling Cassie what a great friend she was and how any man would be lucky to be with her. Doug said that if he was not so messed up then he would want Cassie to be his. Cassie told Doug that she thinks he is amazing and sexy. Several of Cassie and Doug's friends suggest they go back to Doug's place to play cards. During the card games, everyone continues to drink beer late into the evening.

When people start to leave, Cassie stays behind, sitting on the couch. She launches herself at Doug when he walks over to the couch after everyone has left. They proceed to have sex. The next morning Cassie wakes up in Doug's bed naked and does not remember everything that happened. Doug's memories of the evening are clearer.

The two scenarios presented in this chapter illustrate why alcohol is such a complicating factor when it comes to sex. In fact, some prevention programs indicate that anytime alcohol is a factor, then sex should not occur. That philosophy, while easier perhaps, is too similar to other abstinence-based prevention efforts, and it is not realistic or an effective way to educate about alcohol and sex.

There are other options to consider, and the following sections are offered to give some insight into the details of how best to navigate the murky waters when alcohol and sexual consent collide with individuals and groups on campus.

DEFINE CONSENT, INTOXICATION, AND INCAPACITATION

From a policy perspective, recommended practice currently educates students on the construct of incapacitation: "a state beyond drunkenness or intoxication, where decision-making faculties are dysfunctional" (Sokolow, Swinton, et al. 2015). From a training perspective, this is often described as not being able to understand (1) *who* you are having sex with, (2) *what* type of sexual activity you are engaging in, (3) *when* the sexual activity is occurring, (4) *where* the sexual activity is occurring, (5) *why* the sexual activity is occurring, and (6) *how* the sexual activity is occurring. Incapacitation occurs at different points for everyone depending on how much alcohol was consumed, tolerance levels for alcohol, food intake, voluntary or involuntary use of drugs, if vomiting occurred, and other personal factors related to health and body type. The time frame and amounts of alcohol, food, and drugs consumed can also shift when someone becomes incapacitated.

When you consider Cassie's example in the previous section, it presents the potential concept of a blackout. The scenario indicates that Cassie woke up with little memory of the occurrence. Cassie initiated the sexual activity, but according to recommended policy, even if she removed her own clothes and demanded sex, if she was incapacitated, she could not consent to sex. What about Doug? If Doug was incapacitated, then he could not consent to Cassie's initiation of sex.

During conduct hearings, institutions are told to evaluate two factors: (1) Is there a preponderance of evidence that the alleged victim was incapacitated by alcohol, other drugs, or unconsciousness? and (2) Did the accused student know as a fact, or should the accused student have known from the circumstances, that the alleged victim was incapacitated? (Sokolow, Swinton, et al. 2015). Understanding these elements does not necessarily help in the prevention of sexual assault. In fact, you can find yourself feeling as though you have given perpetrators a guidebook for "getting away" with an assault instead of educating them on the prevention of violence. Chapter 16 focuses on ideas related to consent education to combat some of these concerns.

ENGAGE IN ALCOHOL-RELATED PREVENTION EFFORTS (MINDING YOUR P'S AND Q'S)

Prevention efforts related to sexual violence should be closely linked at least in part to prevention efforts related to alcohol at both the individual and group level. Just as with sexual violence, alcohol prevention should also focus on risk factors for high-risk alcohol use and adopting evidence-based practices in a comprehensive manner. For individuals, utilizing programs that help students to develop skills related to alcohol use, such as how to find the perfect buzz or Alcohol Skills Training Program (ASTP), can be a helpful way for newer students to create better habits early in their college transition. These types of programs recognize that college students are likely to consume alcohol and focus instead on safer choices and decreasing the negative consequences of alcohol use. This provides an opportunity to address the risks associated with alcohol and sexual activity.

For students found in violation of alcohol policies, institutions should have a clear sanctioning plan to assess and intervene with high-risk users. This could include BASICS (Brief Alcohol Screening & Intervention for College Students), a research-based motivational interviewing and alcohol/drug assessment. EverFi research suggests that sexual assault prevention efforts should target high-risk men identified by predictors, such as alcohol use, aggressive behaviors, and unhealthy attitudes toward sexual assault (2013). They caution that this group appears resistant to current prevention efforts and is quickly developing unhealthier attitudes and behaviors during the first semester of college. BASICS sessions with individual students can provide that opportunity to screen for those types of high-risk attitudes and utilize motivational interviewing and educational information to address those concerns.

MONITOR SOCIAL EVENT PLANNING

For organizations, the development of social event planning skills for organization leaders can be an effective way of beginning to shape safer social environments for group activities. When an organization uses appropriate planning processes for events that include alcohol, the opportunities for perpetrators to take advantage of women decrease. The Risk Management Policy of Fraternal Information and Programing Group, Inc. (FIPG), provides minimum standards for planning safer social events, and virtually all national fraternities should be complying with these or higher standards as part of their national rules.

FIPG requires that organizations do not purchase alcohol with chapter funds and bulk quantities or common sources of alcohol (e.g., kegs or trashcan punch) are not allowed. By supporting this type of rule, it can decrease the amount of alcohol available at events and the access to open sources of alcohol that can easily be drugged or altered. Social event policies require organizations to utilize third-party vendors or strict BYOB policies that again place parameters on how alcohol is being served at the event, who it is being served to, and how much is being served. Organization leaders also learn that drinking games automatically increase risks and are not an appropriate activity at an organizational event.

While social event planning does not solve all problems (e.g., pregaming, the trend of drinking large quantities of alcohol before an official event or activity where alcohol is more restricted), it is at least a feasible way to train organizational leaders on how to have safer events. Put yourself in the shoes of a 20-year-old college student who is also the president of his fraternity. Think how frustrated you sometimes become working with a group of college students. Now imagine being 20 years old with an organization that may include more than 100 members. These officers often want to do the right thing but need the skills training and also the support from adult advisors and university staff to assist them in implementing these types of policies. They need help articulating to the chapter members why it is important to follow the policies in a way that is appealing to college students.

TRAIN FACULTY AND STAFF TO SUPPORT VICTIMS

Since sexual assaults often occur that involve the consumption of alcohol, and victims may struggle with how their alcohol-related behaviors will be received when they report, it is important to have victim's services and reporting options that acknowledge these types of struggles. Institutions should adopt and publicize clear *amnesty policies* for victims and bystanders. Amnesty policies are policies placed in student handbooks and codes that indicate the options to report incidents of sexual violence without concern for the reporter's policy violations, such as underage alcohol use or drug use.

In addition, faculty and staff have to be trained to expect disclosures from students with information about alcohol-related activities. It is not enough just to tell faculty and staff that they are mandatory reporters and should alert a Title IX coordinator upon receiving a disclosure from a student. That initial interaction between a reporting student and a faculty or staff member sets the stage for how the student perceives the resources and options available to him or her at the institution. Training for faculty and staff must include how to respond sensitively to student disclosures and should provide specific words and phrases to transition that student to a Title IX administrator. When the handoff goes poorly, it is less likely that the reporting party will utilize the resources available.

Using scenarios like the one ahead with faculty, advisors, and staff can be a good training tool for helping them to know their obligations related to reporting but also for responding to a complicated disclosure from a student.

> After missing several classes, Brook visits your office and indicates that she missed class because she was hospitalized for a suicide attempt. When you express concern, she further explains that she tried to kill herself because she was raped after attending an off-campus party. Additionally, she shares that her mother and others have blamed her for "causing it" by drinking too much the night the rape occurred.

Once faculty consider the scenario, give them specific words and phrases to help when receiving reports from students about sexual violence:

> Thank you for trusting me and telling me.
> I am glad you talked with me.
> I want to help get you connected with someone here who knows all of the resources and options available to you.
> I know you are hesitant for anyone to know about what you are going through, but at our college we have a specialized staff member to help you navigate the options available to you. I am going to contact them to help you.

DISCUSSION QUESTIONS

1. What are your thoughts on the role of alcohol and its place in courtship and easing anxiety in dating or romantic situations?

2. Think about the Margie and Taylor scenario. Would this be considered rape or sexual assault under your college conduct code? What additional information would you need to obtain in order to answer this question? If you had a conversation with Margie or Taylor before this happened, what kind of information would you share with them? How might Chris and Jamie have intervened in this situation?

3. Discuss your reaction to the idea that any alcohol creates confusion or the inability to consent fully. If some alcohol is considered socially appropriate and not overtly problematic, how do you decide how much is too much?

4. Discuss the differences between being intoxicated and incapacitated. What are some of the physical signs and symptoms that would indicate the difference? What are some of the factors that make it more difficult to differentiate between the two (e.g., if one person had been drinking earlier in the evening apart from the other person)?

5. What are some of the key elements, in your mind, related to training for faculty and staff in terms of working with victims of sexual assault or gender-based violence?

Chapter 10

Hardened or Inflexible Point of View

Of all the trees we could've hit, we had to get one that hits back.
—*J.K. Rowling*, Harry Potter and the Chamber of Secrets

KEY TAKE-AWAYS

1. A hardened point of view is a way of thinking that reduces a healthy community on a college campus. It primarily separates people rather than bringing them together. Inflexible beliefs create barriers to understanding and diversity.

2. Hardened perspectives about gender increase the risk of sexual violence, stalking, and IPV. Inflexible assumptions about the roles of males and females in society, on campus and in relationships, lead to conflict, objectification, depersonalization, and misogyny.

3. The most successful way to engage inflexible thoughts and hardened points of view is through circular questioning that doesn't raise the defenses of the other person and instead encourages the person to explore his or her beliefs with a more critical eye.

The risk factor describes a process, rather than a specific content. In the violence risk and threat assessment literature, the idea of a hardened point of view is an early cause for concern as it sets the foundation for perseveration, angry and hateful debate, and a movement to acting out rather than talking about differences. Simply having a strongly held belief isn't necessarily a problem; in fact, having strongly held beliefs is part of what makes us human. The risk factor is the tendency to have an inflexible point of view paired with other factors, such as a misogynistic ideology, expectations around what is owed to a person in regards to sexual activity, and, at the very center of the concern, a lack of willingness to take into account the perspective of another person or group.

The old joke applies:

A schizophrenic patient comes to a doctor and says. "I'm dead." The doctor thinks for a minute and says, "Well, if you are dead, then you won't bleed." The patient agrees and allows the doctor to prick his finger. Blood flows and the doctor says, "See, you are bleeding; you are alive." The schizophrenic patient responds, "Well, what do you know, dead men do bleed."

The schizophrenic in the joke is unwilling, and arguably unable, to empathize or see things from another point of view. A hardened outlook starts with an unwillingness to have a sense of humility and curiosity for another person's or group's perspective. The only thing that matters is the self-assurance of the individual's way of seeing the world. This inflexibility is the antithesis of learning, growth, and development. The risk factor here applies to those who are predisposed to close off other perspectives, double-down on their ideas without consideration of viewpoints, and, in the extreme, develop a martyr-like outlook that is resistant to any questioning, critique, or opinion.

We'd like to stress here, once again, that it isn't holding a belief that is the problem. Diversity of opinion and differing beliefs and ideas are positive things in a society. The problem is the unwillingness to have a belief questioned when the belief creates expectations concerning another group or person who has been marginalized or discriminated against. Some might argue that an appreciation of diversity and the encouragement of perspective taking are, in themselves, inflexible or hardened perspectives. The issues we return to in defense are that our viewpoint does not take away rights and perspective of others, but rather encourages a diversity of perspectives. A group on campus makes signs stating that women shouldn't be surprised that they are raped when they dress a certain way or drink to excess is harming a marginalized group (women). As we ask the group consider their perspective, the harm they are causing by holding these beliefs becomes the concern.

DEFINING THE FACTOR

We are focusing on situations where an individual or group has a steadfast and intractable point of view or belief system that is highly defended against change or further rational debate. These beliefs may include the misogynistic ideology mentioned earlier in the book. Any argument or attempt to dissuade the individual or the group from their beliefs results in a "double-down" of the belief and a perceived sense of attack.

Dr. Glasl, a professor at Salzburg University in Austria, developed the "model of conflict escalation" that offers nine stages of conflict escalation useful in understanding how an individual begins to escalate toward violent action (Glasl 1999). The first of these stages is defined as hardening. In a 2014 white paper, "Threat Assessment in a Campus Setting" (Sokolow, Lewis, Schuster, et al. 2014, p. 9), the concept is broadened and applied to targeted and predatory violence that occurs in a university setting. The authors write, "The individual begins to selectively attend to his or her environment, filtering out material or information that doesn't line up with his or her beliefs. Stances begin to harden and crystalize. There is some oscillation between cooperative and competitive."

The concept of hardening as it applies to threat assessment is supported by a wide number of research articles and published works (O'Toole 2000; Turner and Gelles 2003; Association of Threat Assessment Professionals 2006; Randazzo and Plummer 2009; Sokolow and Lewis 2009; ASIS International and the Society for Human Resource Management 2011; Meloy et al. 2012; Van Brunt 2012; Sokolow, Lewis, Van Brunt, et al. 2014). This hardened viewpoint expands to sexual assault as perpetrators engage in victim blaming as a rationale for the assault (Krahe et al. 2007; Bieneck and Krahe 2011).

Another attribute of the hardened or inflexible point of view is the minimization and denial of the validity of other points of view. Not only must the individual's worldview be valid and accepted by others, but also this worldview is often offered as the only reasonable perspective. Individuals often seek out others who share their perspective for reinforcement and further validation. This has the potential to create groups that become self-reinforcing and immune to alternative perspectives or viewpoints. This in turn creates opportunities for pressure to maintain conformity and groupthink.

IPV incidents may include these hardened points of view around themes of control and jealousy. This is the idea of the partner as the property of the perpetrator and the need to control the partner's behaviors, social environment, and access to information. Researchers have shared examples of statements demonstrating the entitlement of the perpetrators and the desire to link themselves permanently to their partner: "I'll never let you go" and "If I can't have you, no one will" (Teranishi-Martinez 2014, p. 2).

ADDRESSING THE INDIVIDUAL

A particularly negative example of this factor is exemplified in the murder of Grace Rebecca Mann at Mary Washington University in April 2015. Mann was part of an organization called Feminists United that uncovered a chant by the school's rugby team that referenced necrophilia, rape, and violence against women. Following the suspension of the team, and prior to Mann's death, one supporter of the team warned "feminists would burn" if the team was suspended and that "there will be no survivors" (Jackson 2015, p. 1). In the light of her tragic death, viewpoints remained hardened and fixed. Sympathy and compassion for Grace Mann were lacking and cries of misandry against the rugby team persisted.

These inflexible beliefs are often learned behaviors from parents, peers, and religious education. They may center on the subjugation of women into a particular set of actions or behaviors, such as "women are made to have children and to care for families." When these beliefs are challenged in higher education settings, individuals often come back with well-rehearsed responses or an unwillingness to change their opinion. If someone was to ask, "What about women who are unable to have children? What should they then do?" The all too common response would flow out of the hardened perspective: "Well, then they should be teachers or day care workers. They should find other ways to use their natural gifts of supporting children in our society."

This thinking is concerning for several reasons. There is the obvious limitation this creates by restricting women's potential to childcare. There is the secondary harm that implies men will never be as good as women in caring for children. This secondary harm can be seen as having an effect on many men in terms of how their masculinity is defined and, in some ways, directly related to the conversations raised in this book. Men should be strong, men should not cry, and men should earn the money and protect the family. Women should be nurturing and emotional, and they should take care of the children and make a nice home for the man. These hardened views of gender contribute to problems of gender-based violence and often to domestic and dating violence when equal communication breaks down and stereotypes and outdated expectations take the forefront of the discussion.

ADDRESSING THE GROUP

Sometimes hardened and inflexible perspectives can be identified in the group setting. In the membership selection process, organizations filter out members with perspectives that are different from the predominant attitudes of the organization (Murnen and Kohlman 2007). The group may then have the tendency to create alternative narratives about the attitudes and behaviors of the group with disregard for the impact of their behaviors on others in the community.

Hardened perspectives can suddenly present in the midst of your prevention and education programming for organizations. I was observing an educational session for a large group of organization members recently when the behavior of the audience became unruly and the treatment of the presenters became disrespectful. The presentation was on issues like those presented in the book, and the members of the audience were shouting out inappropriate statements that were misogynistic and horrible. Now, there are a variety of things to consider that impacted this behavior, but it was at minimum an indicator that within that community of students, there were hardened perspectives and opinions that were not going to be shifted in that large-group setting. This is insightful for prevention work on the campus.

For organizations with long-standing histories on campus and extensive rosters of alumni, the hardened perspective of alumni can also impact the undergraduate members even after they graduate. When role models and mentors are exhibiting behaviors, this influences the attitudes of the individual member. An opportunity to reduce the risks associated with inflexible perspectives is to infuse positive adult role models and advisors into organizations. It is common for colleges to require organizations to have a faculty or staff advisor, but so often, that person signs off on paperwork and is not involved within the organization. Many fraternities are beginning to include nonmember and female advisors on their rosters to engage with membership.

The current system asks 19-year-olds to run large, multifaceted organizations, often with access to significant financial resources and the ability to regulate their membership, with little external involvement. Take a moment to look back at chapter 3 and consider the developmental stages of many of your students. Is it surprising that we would see the types of leadership struggles that we do? Are we surprised that an emerging leader would struggle with confronting an inflexible perspective from a senior member? Also, consider being a college student athlete, with the attention given to some players by the campus community, and the demands placed on students. The athlete's relationship with coaches who role-model positive attitudes and behaviors is also important. Positive adult mentors in organizations and activities can watch for hardened individual and organizational perspectives that are detrimental to the groups and the campus community.

FROM THE FRONT LINES

One-Track Mind

David came to university from a local high school and had college-educated parents who had dreams of their son graduating from college. The diagnosis of autism at four years old did not deter David or his parents from that goal.

His first day of orientation quickly became the bellwether of what was to lie ahead. David did not leave the parking lot until his mother walked with him to the check-in; she signed him into his classes and helped him find his orientation leader. Kelly was a junior studying special education who was very excited to be an orientation leader, and she welcomed David into the group of new students with a warm smile and handshake.

Over the next few days David followed Kelly around campus and would go to sleep only after she had walked him back to his room. Incidents that occurred over the week of orientation concerned Kelly and she reported specific incidents to her supervisors.

The second day of orientation Kelly was eating with other orientation students when David insisted on sitting next to her. Kelly asked David to sit somewhere else at the table. David threw down his tray of food and left the cafeteria. Campus police were called when he was found slamming his head against the brick wall of the cafeteria building. Kelly was able to calm David down and walk him to health services. On the last night of orientation, the evening before classes started, Kelly came out of her room to find David sleeping in the hallway. He said that his roommate threw him out because his pacing was keeping him up. David was sleeping outside her door because he didn't know where else to go. Kelly walked him back to his room.

When they approached his room David grabbed her arm and tried to kiss her. When she pulled away, with her hand on his arm to keep him at a distance, he started to cry and punch himself in the face, repeating, "I am so stupid." This behavior frightened Kelly and she tried to avoid any contact with him from that point forward.

Over the next few weeks of the academic year Kelly would be walking to class to find David following her. He started to leave notes on her door and was frequently found sleeping in her hallway. Kelly spoke with her parents, her friends, and the residence hall director. Everyone told her to just let him know that she was not interested in him and that she would report him to the police if he continued. When she executed this plan David became overwhelmed and crumbled on the sidewalk, throwing his head against the sidewalk cement. As blood was running down his face David kept repeating Kelly's name and saying that he knew she loved him because she smiled at him, touched his arm, and was nice to him. Campus police took him to health services.

Three weeks later Kelly reported David to campus police for sexual assault. She recounted for police that David was sleeping in the lounge of her residence hall and when she went into the lounge to ask him to leave, he demanded that she walk outside with him. When Kelly refused and picked up her cell phone to call the RA on duty, David pinned her against a wall, grabbed her breast, kissed her, and ran out of the building. Kelly pleaded with campus police to find David but not to charge him with any policy violation. When police found him he was in the woods near campus, pacing in a clearing. He was not cooperative with police and his parents were called to take him home for the night.

The student conduct officer, after reading the police reports, requested a meeting with David, at which point counseling services was asked to meet with him. The staff counselor described a young man struggling with spectrum disorder, confused by his own emotions, and exhibiting limited understanding of the charges he was now facing. Kelly confirmed the information on the incident reports, and David was charged with policy violations through the office of student conduct. Charges were filed in criminal court, and David was suspended from the university pending the outcome of the campus judicial process. Ultimately the director of counseling determined that a conversation with David's parents was the best course of action. The goal of this meeting was to explore how to help David understand the specific behaviors that are not acceptable on campus and to determine the support he needs for the upcoming judicial process. The following year David was attending a local community college, living at home, and awaiting a court date for his criminal hearing.

Mary-Jeanne Raleigh, PhD, LPC, LMHC, NCC
Director of Counseling
University of North Carolina, Pembroke

REDUCING THE RISK

Critical thinking is the hallmark of liberal education. It can't be just about content knowledge, but rather teaching students how to think. Following this logic, there is little room for inflexible thoughts or hardened points of view in any capacity on campus.

However, as we have stated before, the direct assault may not be the most advantageous. The attack creates a heightened defense. We would encourage, rather, a more logic-based, circular-questioning, Socratic method of engagement. This creates a more disarming interaction that allows the individual to feel less accused and more open to having his or her thinking challenged.

Remember the TV show *Columbo*, starring the late, great Peter Falk? He played the short, cigar-smoking detective with the rumpled trench coat who had a way of catching a criminal with his guard down. The criminal doesn't suspect Columbo is smart enough to catch him, so he relaxes and ends up caught in his own carelessness. Columbo is the quintessential example to teach others that the direct approach is not the only way you can persuade others to change their position. The character demonstrates the power of circularity in a creative manner to accomplish your goals.

Let's put this concept into action. On the following pages, we have offered several strongly held beliefs by students, along with suggested Socratic, Columbo-type questions.

"Women should focus on raising children and running the house."

- I understand where you are coming from. Many religious groups make these arguments about the role of a woman. What are your thoughts about women who cannot have children or are interested in another career?
- In some ways, having predefined expectations about what we are to become in life is somewhat limiting, no? While women might feel constrained by childcare, men might also feel overwhelmed by the prospect of having to provide for a family. Is there room to be more collaborative, working together based on each other's strengths?
- While this might be what some women choose, is it fair to require that of all women? It seems the same kind of idea as requiring

143

all men to play sports. Some men might like sports, but others might not.

"Some women say no at first; it's the man's job to flirt and convince them to say yes."

■ You make some interesting points here. Where might you draw the line between flirting and coercion? While someone might not be sure about what they want to do at first and asking them clarifying questions is part of healthy communication, can we agree that pestering or nagging the person for hours or days until they give in isn't really the same?

■ Isn't it exhausting, at some level, to always be the assertive one around sexual behavior? Have you ever had or seen a relationship where this was more of a balanced discussion between two people?

■ What are some ways you can talk to your partner about the difference between flirting and pressuring? How might that conversation go?

"Men are more naturally aggressive and getting angry is part of their biology."

■ While there is some truth to the idea that men and women are different biologically, doesn't this idea of falling back to our primal selves kind of excuse a wide range of behaviors? Like men don't have a choice but to yell when they get frustrated? Or women can't help but cower and get emotional when upset? I'd like to think we have grown beyond these ways of interacting as our only option.

■ Does your attitude change with more athletic women or more feminine men? Is it merely physical size and presence that govern our behaviors? Can women be aggressive? Can men be emotional?

■ If men are more aggressive because of their biology, does this then translate into them being able to behave more aggressively without consequence? For instance, wouldn't it be reasonable to assume that in today's society a more primarily aggressive male has some responsibility to learn ways to keep his aggression in check? Like how a bigger guy learns quickly that his playful punch to a friend leaves a bruise and he has to tone it down some?

"Women are ruled by emotions, so they don't listen to logic."

■ I hear what you are saying, but I struggle with the idea that because we have a preference or predisposition that this then means we can't grow or adapt. It feels a little bit like a cop-out that this becomes the only way men or women can act.

■ What are your thoughts on which one is better? For me, logic and emotions are best when they go hand in hand to figure out a situation. Like Kirk and Spock from *Star Trek*. There is a place for emotion and a place for logic. Shouldn't our goal be having the ability to change between the two perspectives as needed?

■ I guess it may just be me, but I like the idea of everyone having some adaptability and flexibility in how they see and behave in the world. The way you are explaining things feels like it limits my choices.

"This is college. Lighten up. It was just a party that got out of hand with some silly posters and signs. We didn't mean anything by it."

■ I get that. I don't think your group set out to offend people on campus or end up on the six o'clock news. But it really isn't your intention here but the impact of your action that caused the problem. Does that distinction make sense? Can you think of a time when you didn't mean to cause harm, but the harm was still caused? I'd agree that it would be even worse if you set out to be offensive, but it still isn't okay just because you didn't mean it.

■ Again, I know this wasn't your intent, but another way to think about this is the message you sent to the community as a leading campus group. While you didn't set out to be offensive or degrade women, that was the result. People look up to your group on campus and the messages you send, intentionally or otherwise, carry weight.

■ Let's play this out. What would happen if everyone on campus adopted this attitude of taking it easy and lightening up? What would happen if your professor didn't give out a syllabus with the same kind of rationale: "It's college—you should be able to figure this out. Read the textbook. Be ready for the test." Or if someone put up a sign that called you names or insulted your family and then they said, "It was just a joke. I didn't mean anything by it. Your mom really isn't a whore. Don't be so serious." Do you see the problem with your way of thinking about this?

VALUES CLARIFICATION

It may be that you know this already, but when working with organizations exhibiting negative behaviors, the best way to begin is by talking with the group about why they were founded, what core values are held by the organization, and why the individual members chose to join. Just as with individuals, this is done by illustrating to the organization membership how their actions do not align with the group goals. Unfortunately, this is a delicate area because often not only do the organization members reinforce bad behavior but also the campus reward systems can support maintaining social status or privilege over a willingness to change.

Thus, organizational change often starts with individual member motivations and interests. Break the group into smaller subsets of members for structured, social norms education in which members share their own values and goals. More often than not, individual members are underestimating the positive attitudes of other members. This type of dialogue and values clarification activity can help individuals to feel more assured that their positive views are shared over negative ones that are reinforced in larger, social settings.

Organizational leadership must also buy in to the educational initiative, which means specific, skills-based training for organization officers and senior members. One of the setbacks that can occur is to have an engaging event with an organization, but the members return the following week to hear how worthless it was from the leadership. Senior leaders should be educated on how to recognize problems within the organization and how to address them with individual members and groups. The more buy-in and involvement that can be achieved from the organizational leadership, the greater likelihood of successful organizational change.

It's also critical to engage the support of positive adult mentors in organizations and educate them on how these hardened perspectives of gender and sex are in many ways the "gateway drug" for higher-risk sexual misconduct and sexual violence. It can be a tough conversation because often alumni members are socialized in similar ways. In what other settings do you find 19-year-olds with unfettered membership selection power and control over financial resources in large organizations? This does not exist anywhere else to the extent that you find in a college environment. Adult involvement, oversight, and role modeling from both male and female mentors and advisors are the most powerful ways to begin shifting the climates of organizations at foundational levels, as described here.

As an example, what follows is an interaction I had with the president of an organization.

It was the third time I had met with the student about concerns related to the organization and the expectations we had for the leadership of the organization. We had previously discussed the importance of utilizing the accountability structures within the organization to hold individual members responsible for their behaviors and to set expectations that were more in alignment with university and organizational values.

Upon finding out that the president had disregarded our discussions and had in an additional incident been specifically involved in the misconduct, I was very disappointed. Some of his comments were that other organizations behaved the same way and "got away with it," and that the organization had to act in the way they did because everyone else did it too. I shared my disappointment with his behaviors because I thought he was a student leader who shared and supported the goals of our office to ensure that organizational experiences were positive for students.

Unfortunately, the conversation got worse and turned to the student attempting to "negotiate" his organization's way out of trouble. He offered to turn other organizations in for misconduct if it would lessen the consequences for his group, and when I declined, he offered multiple other options, such as giving up individual members who were involved. It was not one of my better moments as an administrator in that my frustration boiled over. I share the example because hardened perspectives do not have to emerge specifically tied to attitudes around sexual violence, but they can also emerge from group leaders and organizations inflexible in their perceptions and intentions related to the organization. When combined with other risk factors for sexual violence, they create an incredibly dangerous combination.

Dr. Amy Murphy
Assistant Professor, Curriculum and Instruction
Angelo State University

DISCUSSION QUESTIONS

1. What are your thoughts on hardened points of view? Are there times when this concept is more reasonable and not as problematic? What are some of these? What are the times when hardened or inflexible points of view cause problems in our society?

2. College is a time when your worldview is challenged. Think about ways you had to question the way you saw the world when you were at college. How did these challenges help shape your thoughts and feelings now?

3. Discuss some ways you have seen hardened or inflexible points of view contribute to gender-based violence on your campus.

4. The authors suggest a more circular approach to addressing an individual or group presenting with a hardened or inflexible point of view. Do you agree with this approach? How might you handle it differently?

5. Suggestions for addressing inflexible perspectives in groups include utilizing values clarification activities and adult role models. What examples do you have of where those techniques have worked or not worked on your campus?

Chapter 11

Pattern of Escalating Threat

> The woods always look different at night . . . as if the daytime trees and flowers and stones had gone to bed and sent slightly more ominous versions of themselves to take their places.
> —*Suzanne Collins,* The Hunger Games

KEY TAKE-AWAYS

1. Escalating behaviors should be seen more as an action and less as a specific set of behaviors. These include deviations from an existing baseline or a lack of remorse or escalation following a disciplinary intervention.

2. Stalking and interpersonal violence are most often in an upward trajectory, meaning the next action is likely to be more severe without intervention and assistance.

3. Behavioral intervention teams (BITs) can be a resource to help in identifying problematic patterns, assessing behaviors, and providing interventions to assist students and maintain safety in the campus community.

This risk factor captures the idea of movement and intensification of threat. While much of the book has focused on the static factors that increase the risk of gender-based violence, this chapter explores how behaviors, both individually and as part of a group, can escalate and should be a focus of intervention.

Escalating threat implies that there is an understanding of a baseline interaction between individuals or a group. When there is a departure from this baseline with an escalation, we should be concerned about this and intervene accordingly. This may be a couple that never really communicated well with each other around campus now becoming physical in their arguments. This could be a group on campus known for its wild parties with offensive themes now extending to rumors of isolated bedrooms and spiked drinks. What once was a mild concern seems to be increasing in severity.

One place these escalations occur is following an intervention for a lower-level behavior. One would expect a student or group called out on their concerning behavior to behave with some remorse, or at least caution, as they move forward beyond the disciplinary meeting. A group or individual who then escalates following an intervention should be seen as a particular cause for concern. Likely, they have a hardened and inflexible point of view that is resistant to change.

DEFINING THE FACTOR

This factor describes an individual or group that continues to escalate behavior toward a higher level of violence. There are examples of predatory thinking (Turner and Gelles 2003; Association of Threat Assessment Professionals 2006; Meloy et al. 2012; Van Brunt 2012, 2014), grooming behaviors (as mentioned in chapter 8), and practice and testing behavior designed to "test the waters" prior to a move toward more dangerous behaviors.

Elliot Rodger demonstrated this escalation prior to his murderous assault in California (Speer 2014). We learned that the attack was primarily motivated by Rodger's self-described frustration at his failures to obtain sexual relationships with his peers. He became enraged at a couple showing affection. As a result, he threw a soda on the couple and ran away. It would be reasonable to assume that this escalation from an angry thought at a happy couple to throwing a soda helped desensitize Rodger to prepare him for something more ominous in the weeks to follow.

In this risk factor, the concepts of movement, intensification, and acceleration are key. There is an increase in the behavior of concern (misogynistic statements, stalking behavior, threats or ultimatums, using alcohol to lower a victim's defenses). This often occurs despite attempts by the institution to address the concerns through conduct action, education, or prevention efforts.

In the predatory violence literature, the individual can be described in the context of Meloy et al.'s (2012) approach behaviors. An individual or group becomes determined in their focus on a pathway to violence and, despite efforts to dissuade them from negative actions, they continue to move toward a negative outcome.

Stalking behaviors typically fall into an upward trajectory from initial, exploratory behaviors to more intensive and invasive techniques, including hyper-intimacy, proximity/surveillance, invasion, proxy pursuit, intimidation and harassment, coercion, and constraint and aggression (Meloy and Fisher 2005). For a frustrated ex-boyfriend, following his ex around campus may initially be enough to satisfy him. As his obsession deepens, however, he may purchase a magnetic GPS device to attach to her car in order to follow her more closely.

In sexual-addictive predatory or paraphilic behaviors, we may see a student who is initially comfortable flashing private parts anonymously in public places escalating to masturbation or masturbation with contact with unconsenting others. In both of these cases, the idea of behaviors escalating provides an opportunity for more intensive involvement. At the end of the chapter, we will discuss in more detail how the behavioral intervention team (BIT) can be a helpful tool in disrupting the escalating behavior.

ADDRESSING THE INDIVIDUAL

Stalking, intimate partner violence, and dating/domestic violence are the most common forms of escalating threat. Behaviors begin to test the thresholds of response for an individual.

Carter is a flirt and has a reputation on campus as a bit of a player. Carter is attractive and pitches on the campus baseball team. He is fun and gregarious at parties and tends to drink quite a bit. Carter often uses his drinking as an excuse for his flirtatious and aggressive behavior with women.

Carter begins his seduction by focusing his attention on a female student he is interested in. Being charismatic and outgoing, Carter often makes the other person feel special and cared for. He compliments them, makes subtle contact at the bar as they are having conversations by touching her arm, shoulder, and leg. Typically, the woman goes home with Carter after several drinks and he ends up sleeping with her. Carter does this with multiple students around campus during a given week.

Carter meets Ellie at a bar and is flirtatious with her. He compliments her, and they joke about shared interests and friend each other on Facebook. They laugh at each other's pictures when they were younger. Ellie has several drinks, as does Carter, and she reluctantly agrees to go with him back to his apartment for another drink. Ellie decides to have sex with Carter, and as they begin, Carter tells her he likes it when he can choke her. Carter then puts his hands around Ellie's neck while having intercourse with her. Ellie doesn't like the experience and tries to roll away from Carter. He becomes frustrated at her and they stop having sex.

Ellie says, "I'm sorry, I'm just not into that kind of stuff. We can have sex, but not like that."

Carter regains his composure and responds, "That's okay. Let's just go back to what we were doing."

They resume having sex and Carter is more aggressive, holding Ellie down, and bites at her shoulders. Ellie isn't sure about this either, but goes along with it and starts thinking more about leaving. Carter slides his hands back around Ellie's throat and she tells him to stop and get off of her.

"What?!?" Carter says. "I thought you were into it more when I was holding you down and biting."

Ellie says she is not and then gets dressed and leaves. Carter sees her outside of class the next day and acts like nothing has happened. He invites her over again that night to finish what they started. Ellie refuses politely, just wanting to get away from him. She tries to walk away from him.

Carter holds her back by grabbing her arm. "Hey, wait a minute." Ellie doesn't want to make a scene and waits. "I just thought we had a good time last night. I feel like we have some unfinished business." Ellie tells him that she has to get to her next class and they should talk later. They make plans to meet by the library.

Ellie doesn't show up at the library and Carter is furious. Ellie just doesn't want anything else to do with him. She goes back to her room and checks onto Facebook with her laptop. She sees a message on her wall that reads, "Hey, missed you tonight. Let's meet up again and this time I'll bring the handcuffs;)." Several of Carter's friends have posted comments under the message about rough sex, thumbs-up, and 50-shades-of-Ellie. Ellie takes a screen cap of the post with her phone, deletes the post, defriends Carter, and walks down the hall to talk to her RA about the situation.

This kind of snapshot scenario is all too common on today's campus, with the poor communication and expression of sexual desires against the backdrop of alcohol intoxication. Carter makes demands of Ellie and she refuses. Carter then ignores the underlying message of what she told him and what her comfort level is, and proceeds to look at ways to have his own needs met sexually. This escalates to Ellie wanting to avoid Carter the next day, and Carter and his friends escalating on social media. Carter is likely known to the campus conduct or behavioral intervention team on campus, and this behavior should be seen as a concerning escalation in his typical baseline behavior.

ADDRESSING THE GROUP

These patterns of escalation can also originate from groups or organizations. While subtle hints or vaguely intimidating threats may be the initial action, noncompliance from the target may result in an escalation in threats. An athletic team may attempt to intimidate a woman to keep her from reporting an assault by a team member. This intimidation may begin with notes and phone calls and could escalate to social media attacks (creation of a website attempting to discredit her reputation) and team members driving by her apartment and throwing a brick at her window.

The grooming behaviors mentioned earlier create environments conducive to patterns of escalating threats and increase the likelihood students will allow the threatening behaviors to continue. Social organizations may follow a pattern of escalation in regard to their use of intimidation and coercion. Parties may start with more open and inviting environments for guests, progressing to more elite environments, reinforcing the need to conform in order to be socially accepted.

It may be helpful to visualize this risk factor as it requires a sense of movement forward and an intensification of behaviors. While the original thought or behavior could be centered on misogynistic thinking, using substances to obtain sex, or obsessive pornography usage, this factor is about an increase in the amount or intensity of the behaviors. For example, where the misogynistic thinking was once private jokes among group members, it becomes aired in a public blog or article in the school paper.

A group that was disciplined for offering free beer to underage students could escalate to using a Rohypnol in a drink to incapacitate a partygoer. An individual who masturbates to pornography by himself for one to two hours on a normal night may begin hosting "jack off" parties, where groups are encouraged to watch pornography together for longer periods of time. Whether individual or group behaviors, the concern is the escalation of these behaviors as clear warning signs that should be heeded by the campus administration.

FROM THE FRONT LINES

A Case Study in Stalking and Rape

Steven began his academic career at a small, private Midwestern college near his hometown. He was recruited there to play on their football team. He had a full scholarship, but was still undecided about his major. Steven was a good-looking young man, but had problems meeting people and forming close friendships. Some thought he was just shy.

Steven went out with a few coeds, but these dates never went beyond the first date. One of the coeds made an allegation of sexual assault against Steven, but the college investigated it and determined that alcohol was involved and it was a "he said/she said" situation. There was no campus police department, and the local sheriff was never notified of the allegations, so no criminal investigation of the incident was conducted.

Shortly after the allegations, Steven quietly left that college and subsequently enrolled in another similar-size college several hundred miles away, but in the same state. He left that college after one semester, following a similar sexual assault allegation made by another coed. That college investigated the allegation, determined that alcohol was a major factor in the allegations against Steven, and characterized the incident as "he said/she said." This college closed its case, the local police were never notified, and no subsequent criminal investigation was conducted. College #2 had not been made aware of the original allegations made against Steven at his first college.

Steven relocated across the country to live with a family member and work as a nurse's aide in a local hospital. There was a small college in this new city where Steven lived, and his plans were to enroll in the college after a year's residency, in order to qualify for state tuition.

Shortly after his relocation, a coed from the local college was walking alone at night near the campus when she was attacked and sexually assaulted. However, due to the severity of the attack and the extensive injuries she suffered, the victim could not identify her assailant.

Several months later, another coed went missing following a night of partying with her friends. Her body was never found, and no suspects were identified.

Dr. Mary Ellen O'Toole
Former FBI BAU Supervisor
George Mason University

REDUCING THE RISK

The best way to reduce the risk of escalating threat strategies is attending to behavior as it occurs around campus and looking first for concerning baselines of behavior and then escalations of this baseline. No other group on campus is better situated to do this kind of work than the campus behavioral intervention team (BIT).

154

The conceptual purpose of a BIT is caring, preventive, early intervention with students whose behavior is disruptive or concerning. A BIT has three primary functions. A BIT gathers information, analyzes this information through an objective rubric or set of standards, and then develops and engages in an intervention plan with the student. Each phase is spelled out more here:

Phase 1. A BIT must gather information from the community. This means advertising the team well to the community and teaching them what they should report. This means nurturing the referral source and communicating back to ensure future reports.

Phase 2. A BIT must have some way of analyzing the information once it comes in. Simply stated, this involves rating the information into low, moderate, and high categories, with corresponding action items for each of these risk ratings. This should be a consistent and objective process that can be repeated and addresses the full spectrum of information shared with the team.

Phase 3. Finally, a BIT sets in motion interventions to mitigate the risky behaviors. These may include psychological assessments, violence or threat assessments, case management, or conduct meetings. The intervention is chosen based on: (1) who is best trained to intervene, (2) who is most likely to engage the student in a positive manner, and (3) who is best positioned to increase the likelihood the intervention may lead to future positive connections.

Each of these three steps is essential. And this is a circular process. Once the information is gathered, the analysis is complete, and the intervention is conducted, then we return to the information gathering stage to begin again.

Let's talk through how a BIT would handle the following case:

Kristen and Lisa meet their first year at college and live above each other in the same residence hall. Kristen has been out as a lesbian since her first year of high school, and Lisa has always struggled with feelings of liking both men and women, but has dated only boys at her high school.

Kristen and Lisa are in the same sociology class and end up making out at a party the second weekend of school. Kristen isn't really looking for a serious relationship and had several bad experiences in her past with dating women who either weren't fully out yet or had bisexual desires.

They end up making out on several other occasions, and Lisa has fallen fast for Kristen. Never before in her life has she connected so well with someone and she can't help but share her feelings and excitement. Kristen is put off some by Lisa's enthusiasm and starts to distance herself from her.

Following a GLBT support meeting on campus, Kristen and Lisa get into a big argument because Lisa announced to the group that Kristen is her girlfriend. Kristen does not see their relationship as monogamous or committed and tells her she needs some space. The argument was very public and split the group, with half of the members of the support group paired off with Lisa and the other half supporting Kristen.

The argument continues on Facebook, with Lisa sending private messages to Kristen that are ignored. Then Lisa posts publicly on Kristen's wall, saying, "I just need to talk, can't we talk?" Kristen doesn't respond well to this and defriends Lisa on Facebook. Lisa starts texting Kristen and gets no response. She leaves her increasingly disturbing voicemails, demanding that they talk. Kristen ignores her and skips class the next day to avoid running into Lisa.

The next night, Kristen goes out with some friends to have some drinks and get away from the situation. Lisa waits for Kristen to return outside of her dorm room. Kristen flips out that she is outside of her door and yells for her to leave her alone or she will call the campus police. Lisa yells, "I just want to talk to you. I love you and you won't even talk to me! That isn't okay. You have to talk to me."

Kristen goes into her room and slams the door, yelling back, "The only thing I have to do is to go to bed and get the hell away from you, you psycho bitch."

Lisa slumps down in front of the door, crying. The resident advisor comes out and tries to talk to Lisa to calm her down. Lisa eventually calms down and goes back to her own room.

The case of Kristen and Lisa is a good example of where behaviors escalate between two individuals and provide an opportunity for members of the community to share their concerns with the campus BIT. This could have occurred following the initial argument at the GLBT support group, when a student was concerned over the Facebook posts on Kristen's wall, or during the scene that occurred in the residence halls. The hallmark of successful interventions is early gathering of data by the BIT. The sooner the BIT is involved with this case, the sooner interventions can be put into place to prevent an escalation in violence. This could involve a supportive referral for Lisa to counseling to work through her emotions or a discussion with Kristen and her RA about how she could handle the situation differently.

Educate faculty, staff, and students about the risk factors for sexual violence. By having conversations around behaviors and attitudes across the spectrum of sexual violence and addressing the hesitancy that is often present when reporting, people are empowered to respond and report incidents. Many people's concept of violence, including sexual violence, is often that a person just snapped and acted out of character. However, violence is evolutionary, and there are indicators along the way that someone is becoming sexually aggressive.

DISCUSSION QUESTIONS

1. What behaviors have you encountered that started out at baseline and then increased in intensity or duration? How does your campus monitor these changes in baseline?

2. In the scenario of Ellie and Carter, discuss potentials for bystander intervention or reporting the behavior to law enforcement or the campus BIT.

3. While the case of Steven is certainly a more extreme escalation, resulting in multiple assaults and death, consider the initial baseline behaviors that then escalated throughout the case. Where would the campus BIT, residential life, or conduct office have opportunities to intervene?

4. How would you address the scenario with Kristen and Lisa? What support would you put in place for those involved? What would your Title IX or conduct process look like in this case?

5. Beyond IPV and domestic/dating violence, how have you seen escalated threat tied to sexual assault and rapes?

Chapter 12

Lack of Empathy

> Only with a leaf can I talk of the forest.
> —*Visar Zhiti, Albanian writer*

KEY TAKE-AWAYS

1. The lack of empathy leads to a pervasive lack of ability to understand the perspective of others. This is related to gender-based violence as it gives fuel to objectification, threat, and harm to other groups.

2. A lack of empathy can occur on the individual level or in group settings. A lack of empathy may be an active choice to put individual or group needs ahead of those of the person impacted or it may be a lack of ability or willingness to attempt to see actions from a perspective different from the individual or group.

3. A ten-meeting educational training module is included that has been helpful with helping those involved in domestic/dating or IPV learn about the impact of their actions and change their behavior. This training module could be used by counseling staff or those trained in IPV support and advocacy.

Empathy is the process of connecting to the experience of another, seeing things from his or her perspective, and having a sense of concern and compassion for him or her as a person. Empathy differs from sympathy, which is a more cursory awareness of how another person or group is doing. If sympathy is watching someone dig a hole, empathy is climbing in the hole with them and helping.

As Professor Snape described his potions class in *Harry Potter*, empathy is a subtle science and exact art. There is a process to being empathetic that involves both psychology and compassion for others. Empathy is used to build relationships and connect with others to move to a common purpose. Empathy allows a person to take the perspective of another and share that perspective taking together.

A lack of empathy is a disregard for the experience and perception of others. It is not merely a lack of awareness but a lack of desire or effort to see things beyond an individual's own perspective. A lack of empathy could be a learned behavior cultivated over a student's developmental years. It is a harmful narcissism that puts the needs of the individual above the needs of others unless there is some personal benefit. As related to this book, a lack of empathy contributes to objectification, depersonalization, and misogyny. A lack of empathy drives individuals to escalate threats and use substances to obtain sex. A lack of empathy is a threat that binds together many of the concepts we have discussed.

DEFINING THE FACTOR

This risk describes an individual or group that fundamentally lacks empathy for others (Caputo et al. 1999). This lack of empathy could be seen as a hardened and inflexible point of view. The needs of the individual or group become narcissistic in nature and lack awareness of the societal, community, or personal harm they may cause others. Another manifestation of this lack of empathy is a patronizing or paternalistic regard for others in which they presume to "know" what the other one needs, and hence impose actions on them.

A lack of empathy for others can grow through a preexisting worldview or a reinforced perspective through their current group memberships, in which the individuals minimize the impact of how their behaviors affect those around them. They see the world in a way that makes it more difficult for them to see from another's perspective.

This lack of empathy often results in feelings of frustration and surprise in the individual students being questioned about beliefs or behaviors. They struggle to see the relevance of viewpoints different from those informed by their personal experiences.

This factor also plays out on the larger stage, with groups failing to appreciate how their behavior or attitudes are a problem for others around them. They may feel a sense of entitlement to have the freedom to think what they want to think and bristle at the idea of taking responsibility for seeing how their actions may impact others. If their belief system includes intolerance, sexism, and acceptance of oppression, this may contribute to rape attitudes (Bendixena et al. 2014).

Sexual assault perpetrators were identified as having higher levels of hostility toward women and lower levels of empathy, and were more likely to hold traditional gender-role stereotypes (Seto and Barbaree 1997). Meloy and Fisher (2005, p. 7) note this pattern of behavior in stalking cases where "pathological narcissism suggests a sense of grandiosity and entitlement that diminishes any empathy for the victim; and the stalker's focused attention."

Addressing a lack of empathy, whether in the individual or the group, is key to behavioral change. Change occurs when an individual or group sees the benefit for their own good. By assisting an individual or group in developing the ability to understand the perspectives of others, it helps them feel more in connection with those around them. When that connection occurs, the potential to take responsibility for poor behavior increases.

ADDRESSING THE INDIVIDUAL

Efforts that focus on the healthy development of empathy in college students have the potential to influence various aspects of the campus community to reduce sexual assault (Hamilton and Yee 1990; Schewe and O'Donohue 1993). Foubert and Perry (2007, p. 2) write, "Low rape proclivity and high empathy toward rape survivors are strongly linked (Osland et al. 1996), which suggests that finding ways to increase men's empathy toward survivors may lower their likelihood of raping." Students with more sophisticated development of empathy skills are more likely to respond positively to peer disclosures of victimization and to respond negatively to attitudes supportive of rape myths.

Foubert and Perry (2007, p. 13) share a particularly interesting aspect of their study describing participants' reaction to a male-on-male rape scenario and its impact on participants. They write,

> The most overwhelming result of the present study is the consistent, passionate, and detailed comments participants made regarding the changes in their attitudes and behavior that they attribute directly to seeing a videotape describing a male-on-male rape situation. Participants said this video helped them believe they could better understand what rape feels like, were able to apply this newfound understanding to what female survivors might feel, and reported connecting this newfound understanding to helping survivors and confronting rape jokes.

A lack of empathy for another student's perspective is a thread that runs through many of the examples and scenarios we have presented. Table 12.1 provides some further examples in which a student's lack of willingness or ability to think about the needs of others plays a role in gender-based violence. The theme of many of these examples involves a focus on self over others in addition to

Table 12.1 Examples of Individuals With Lack of Empathy

Behavior	Example	Underlying Problem
Stalking	A male student struggles with why a female isn't interested in him. He has asked her out several times and she has turned him down. He tried to be Facebook friends and she refused. He decides to learn more about her by creating a fake Facebook account and friending some of her friends and then trying to friend her to see what her interests are.	▪ Focus on needs of self over the needs of others ▪ Lack of respect for the female student's desire to not pursue a relationship ▪ Crossing of boundaries by trying to access her Facebook account
Harassment	A graduate student teaching a class tells an undergrad that she isn't smart enough to be in his class because girls are bad at math and that she should spend her time picking out some better outfits and marry someone with money.	▪ Objectifying and stereotypic thoughts and actions ▪ Abuse of power ▪ Lack of willingness to see how comments would affect a female student
Domestic Dating Violence, IPV	A female student pushes and shoves her girlfriend when she gets angry and feels she isn't listening to her. She yells over her during arguments and slaps her in the face when she continues to disagree with her perspective. She blames her for getting her so angry that she can't help but hit her.	▪ Not listening to the other person in the relationship ▪ Using threats and physical violence to silence different opinions ▪ Disrespect for the idea that there might be other perspectives than hers
Sexual Assault	A male student has several drinks and meets a female student from his sociology class at a party. She has had too much to drink and has been vomiting and slipping in and out of consciousness. He has sex with her while she is passed out. She makes Title IX and assault charges the next day. He says she consented and she is crying rape because she felt bad about her choice the next day.	▪ Male student puts his own sexual needs over the safety and agency of the female student ▪ He lacks appreciation for how she sees what happened and how he took advantage of her

an inability to understand the perspective of others. When addressing a lack of empathy, the challenge becomes understanding which issue is central and should be addressed first: a narcissistic focus or inability to see the perspective of others.

ADDRESSING THE GROUP

In group settings, this lack of empathy is often demonstrated by a lack of ability to understand the perspective of the victim. A sorority may struggle to see themselves in an assault of one of their members if they distance themselves from her with the rationale that she had a drinking problem, a lengthy sexual history, or promiscuous personality. Armstrong et al. (2006, p. 493) describe it this way:

> The most common way that students—both women and men—account for the harm that befalls women in the party scene is by blaming victims. By attributing bad experiences to women's "mistakes," students avoid criticizing the party scene or men's behavior within it.

In addition, the process of justifying or denying sexual violence or denying personal vulnerability often involves limiting which behaviors are considered to be rape and blaming rape victims for their own victimization (Peterson and Muehlenhard 2004). Iconis (2006, p. 47) describes it this way:

> Men may use rape myths to justify or deny men's sexual violence and women may use them to deny personal vulnerability to rape. For example, a man may endorse the myth that if a woman does not have bruises, she cannot claim she was raped. He might, then, regard coercing a woman to have sex as acceptable as long as he does not leave bruises on her. If a woman endorses the myth that only promiscuous women get raped, she might feel that she can avoid rape by not "sleeping around."

Groups may also underplay their involvement or the applicability of climate surveys to their particular group. With no specific complaint, the organization may downplay the concern and its impact. Some argue that fraternities are unfairly singled out as a source of the problem rather than a tool useful for reducing sexual assault (Shastry 2014; North 2015).

Examples in which groups put their needs ahead of the needs or experiences of the individual are provided in Table 12.2.

Table 12.2 Example of Groups With Lack of Empathy

Behavior	Example	Underlying Problem
Creating a Hostile Environment	The tennis team at a university makes homophobic slurs and comments after the matches. One student who is gay feels threatened and insulted by these comments and goes to the coach.	■ The team's lack of awareness regarding microaggressions and the impact of their insults on others ■ Inability to appreciate the power of language to hurt or marginalize others
Sexual Assault	Four members of the football team have been drinking heavily with a female cheerleader at a party. She initially agrees to having group sex with four men, but when they take her to the back room of the party she changes her mind and wants to leave. The men continue to undress and have sex with her, saying, "You already said yes, you can't back out now. Besides, you just said you always wanted to do this. It's college, do something crazy."	■ The football players putting sexual needs and sensation seeking above the desires of the woman ■ Disregarding her withdrawal of consent and raping her ■ Objectifying her and trying to convince her this is what she wanted
Destroying Property and Making Threats	A group of men on campus are frustrated about all the attention sexual assault and other feminist issues are getting. They purchase a bunch of dildos and condoms and break into the Women's Center and leave them lying all around, with notes like "Lesbians just need a deep dicking." When they are caught they claim this wouldn't have happened if the group hadn't gotten special treatment from the school.	■ Inability or unwillingness to see how this attack on the center creates fear and a lack of safety for women on campus ■ Lack of respect for the lesbian population on campus in terms of their sexual orientation ■ Putting their own thoughts and politics ahead of another group because they don't feel heard
Intimidation	A sorority member on campus comes to her chapter president to report that she was raped by a fraternity member the night before. The president tells her that she was "too drunk to know what happened" and that "your moment of regrettable sex isn't going to get our parties shut down." The chapter president has other sisters in the group pressure her to not make a report about what happened and just get over it.	■ The chapter president shows a lack of empathy and awareness about what happened to her sister ■ Keeping the Greek system out of the papers takes priority over reporting what happened ■ The sorority puts itself ahead of offering support, counseling, and caring to the member who was assaulted

FROM THE FRONT LINES

An Exercise in Empathy

Empathy is recognizing, understanding, and appreciating how other people feel. Empathy involves being able to articulate your understanding of another's perspective and behaving in a way that respects others' feelings. At the core of empathic behavior is being able to perceive and appreciate what, how and why people feel the way they do—being able to emotionally "read" other people—while demonstrating an interest in and concern for others.

(Multi-Health Systems 2011, p. 5)

Empathy challenges us to manage our initial thoughts in order to be present for others. Listening and considering the other person's perspective instead of judging or fixing can be very challenging. "Unfortunately, empathy often falls by the wayside because when we need it most, we're least open to using it—that is, when we're under stress, misunderstood, irritated, or defensive" (Stein, Book, and Kanoy 2013, p. 130). By analyzing incidents of sexual assault through an empathetic lens, we direct the learner to take on the perspective of another. The process of perspective taking while developing skills related to empathy can aid in creating focused and intentional discussions regarding sexual assault myths and facts.

Until we learn to hear victims, to witness their testimony and learn from them, along with them, from their ordeal, to stand in solidarity and offer them our sincere and abundant empathy, we simply cannot hope to end the travesty of sexual violence. Empathy with victims is the first step on the path to a better, and safer, world for all of us.

(Ravenscroft 2011)

Can empathy serve as an antidote to victim blaming? Can empathy create enough space for each of us to enter a difficult conversation?

They met during transfer orientation; both students were trying to navigate a new university. He commented on the schedule, she laughed; their friendship began as many do. Each of them came to the university from different places and for different reasons. She met his girlfriend, he met her boyfriend; both lived in other towns. Their circle of friends grew, and they trusted each other. Fast-forward two years, and they are planning for graduation. Nothing romantic ever occurred between the two of them—they were friends.

One evening, they were hanging out and decided to have a few shots. Another friend (male) joined them. They were waiting for her roommate and her roommate's boyfriend to come over. They planned to go out as a group; waiting for the others, they took shots and talked about the week. Her roommate was late, so they hung out and waited. He turned to her. "I left my charger in the car, walk outside with me." They went to the parking lot. When her roommate arrives, she finds her on the bathroom floor, and her pants are down. She immediately goes to her aid and is with her when EMS and the police arrive. Her roommate is holding her hair as she vomits.

"Why are her pants down?" the officer asks him. "She threw up on them and was trying to take them off," he responded. The officer asked if they had sex. "Yes, she gave consent," he responds. The officer listens. After a brief pause, he asks the officer, "Am I in trouble?" The officer responds, "I don't know that she is able to give consent—she is really drunk." "I'm drunk, too," he retorts.

The next morning, while in the hospital her roommate recounts the events of the evening before. She tells her roommate that she doesn't remember anything after she left the apartment to walk out to his car. Her roommate tells her she was looking for her in the parking lot, and she saw him on top of her in the back of the car. After hearing the details, she says, "I would have never done that had I been sober."

How do you expect the roommate to respond?

Option 1:   I know, it's not your fault.
Option 2:   I know, but you got drunk and walked out to his car.
Option 3:   I know, you hardly ever drink; especially not liquor.
Option 4:   I know, but he said you gave consent.

What form should empathy take for her, for the roommate, and for him in this scenario?

Candice Johnston
Associate Dean of Students
University of North Carolina—Wilmington

REDUCING THE RISK

So, how do we fix this problem when students or a campus group lack empathy for another's perspective? First, it is helpful to realize there are two groups that would benefit from assistance. The first would be students who have not broken the student code of conduct; however, they have trouble seeing beyond their own experience. In many ways, the generation of millennials is often accused of lacking empathy for others around them. They are seen as burying their collective noses in technology and are either unwilling or unable to see beyond their viewpoint.

The second group is those who have violated the student code of conduct and are now in the Title IX or conduct sanctioning process. Here we have a real opportunity to address behavior through facilitated conversations, educational sessions, and programming designed to increase awareness and change behavior. This process, certainly, needs to be balanced against the severity of the case in question with regard to punishment versus rehabilitation.

TEACHING OTHERNESS AND EMPATHY

For students coming to campus who have not run afoul of the student conduct code, the teaching of empathy is best tied to the overall mission of the college. For many liberal arts institutions, this mission involves the ability to think critical and diversely about the world around us. To this end, faculty and staff could reasonably teach basic empathy and perspective-taking skills to students in their classes, workshops, and orientation events.

Carl Rogers (1961) offers the following: "when someone understands how it feels and seems to be me, without wanting to analyze me or judge me, then I can blossom and grow in that climate" (p. 62). Rogers teaches therapists the importance of empathy and congruence to encourage change in their clients. Empathy means seeing the world from their eyes, understanding from their perspective. Congruence is about conveying a sense of genuineness and authenticity. We tend to trust those whom we can understand and who seem honest and direct about their goals.

Empathy starts with a willingness to put your needs as a person aside and focus instead on how others view the world around them. When we do this for our students, they learn how it feels to have another person take a moment to appreciate their perspective. This becomes a powerful teaching tool when helping others see the

166

value of becoming more empathetic. As Rogers (1961) put it, "An empathetic way of being can be learned from empathetic persons" (p. 150).

Rogers argues that the heart of active listening is the ability to understand the underlying message communicated from one person to another. When we demonstrate the ability to listen in a nonjudgmental manner, this allows students to tell their story free of defensiveness and hesitation. Imagine a normal household glass. Have your students think about coming into today with a gallon's worth of liquid. Then they see you have only a normal household glass. It is more difficult to share with another person when they can see you are unable to handle the volume of information they need to share.

To be empathetic we must first adopt an open, nonjudgmental, active listening–based stance. People are more comfortable sharing parts of their lives when they are passionate and feel sure of themselves. We can reassure them through active listening and demonstrating that we truly care about what they are saying.

Carl Rogers summed up these ideals best in his book *A Way of Being* (1980):

> [Empathetic listening] means the therapist senses accurately the feelings and personal meanings that the client is experiencing and communicates this understanding to the client. When functioning best, the therapist is so much inside the private world of the other that he or she can clarify not only the meaning of which the client is aware but even those just below the level of awareness. This kind of sensitive, active listing is exceedingly rare in our lives. We think we listen, but rarely do we listen with real understanding, true empathy. Yet listening, of this very special kind, is one of the most potent forces for change that I know.

(p. 116)

If our goal is to help students as an entire population learn to be more empathetic, this process should start with teaching them some basic skills of mindfulness and active listening. In a group setting, students could be paired off and asked to spend some time with another student, answering some questions about their background—for example:

Pair off students and have both them answer these three questions:

1. What is your favorite TV show, movie and music artist?
2. Think about a fond memory with an animal. It could be a pet or an encounter. What is the story?
3. What is one famous thing your hometown is known for?

Questions like these icebreakers give students the opportunity to talk with each other in the safety of a structured interview. At the end of the exercise, have the students introduce the person they just learned about. For a more challenging exercise or when working with a more highly empathetic group (e.g., when training resident advisors), a more open-ended, less structured set of questions or directions could be used. An example would be: "Talk to your partner for ten minutes and learn all you can about them in this time period."

REHABILITATION OF PERPETRATORS

When presenting on comprehensive prevention strategies for sexual violence on college campuses, we often get asked about resources and tools for the rehabilitation of perpetrators following a lower-level sexual misconduct offense, especially non–contact-related incidents. While not a primary prevention strategy, it is a form of prevention and a strategy for decreasing the likelihood of repeat offenses in the community. There are a number of models available related to the treatment of sex offenders that can be used to draw information for educational modules for offenders. According to one literature review focused on child sexual abuse treatment programs (Kaufman 2010), program content typically includes the reduction of factors related to sexual offenses, the development of prosocial skills, and the establishment of support networks.

This framework can be used to build content as part of an educational sanction for a student found responsible for lower-level sexual misconduct. The risk factors identified throughout the book can be used in structured interviews with students to assess problematic attitudes and behaviors and to determine the nature of their impairment. Pairing this with motivational interviewing strategies, these meetings can help students better understand how to change and how their actions affect the world around them.

We'd like to offer you an example of a program that could be used as a starting place to educate those exhibiting some of the risk factors explored to this point. The following ten meetings could be seen as progressive educational sessions useful for a group or individual to gain awareness of problems related to relationship violence. While not counseling sessions, the educational sessions do borrow heavily from the counseling field to discuss potential causes and solutions to these risk factors. The goal for these sessions is improving perspective taking, critical thinking, and behavioral change.

MEETING 1: BASICS OF COMMUNICATION

The central goal of the first meeting is to explain the process and help the student feel a connection with the staff member. Without a rapport, it is unlikely the material will sink in for the student. This is particularly important as the student may already have a low frustration tolerance for being assigned to this meeting and be frustrated with the school authorities for giving this sanction. Staff should allow students to express their frustrations with the process and identify obstacles to them attending future meetings. This should be allowed as long as they are expressing themselves appropriately and verbally; threatening behaviors or gestures should be addressed immediately.

The staff member should discuss the basics of communication— the give-and-take of conversation and how communication can become difficult when there is not mutual respect.

One approach to positive, effective communication is outlined by Stephen Covey (1990). These seven habits of highly effective people outline ways to improve communication.

Be proactive: Here the goal is to get out ahead of problems with improved communication. Staff should encourage the student to find ways to create an environment where communication can be successful. Successful communication involves thinking about how to respond prior to problems starting—getting out ahead of problematic communication. Before starting a conversation, consider the environment where it occurs and what hidden issues may push the conversation in a negative direction. For instance, if a student waits to confront his girlfriend while she is on the way to an exam and says, "I know what you did—I'm really pissed at you," this is not a proactive stance.

Begin with the end in mind: Good communication focuses on the end goal of the conversation. The students should learn to ask themselves what the goal and vision are for the future and what habit will be reinforced. Conversations that start with accusations, shouting, or demands are likely to have negative ends.

Put first things first: The student should learn to have the right mind-set before engaging in a conversation. Short-term goals should be designed to be successful and build upon future successes. What are the goals of the conversation in question? If the student could have anything he or she wanted, what would the outcome look like?

Think win-win: Any successful communication depends on a mutual agreement to cooperate toward a goal. Students should look for ways to work together with the person they are communicating with. Is the student looking for creative, novel solutions that lead to win-win scenarios? Or are they looking to win, regardless of the person they are talking to?

Understand, then be understood: Before trying to have your goals met in a difficult conversation, students should look for ways to actively listen to the person they are trying to communicate with before trying to have their needs or desires understood. Can students come up with an example where they listened actively, trying to understand another person's point of view regardless of how they wanted the conversation to go?

Synergize: Help the student understand that successful communication can bring two people together to create novel solutions and interactions that can take the relationship to the next level.

Sharpen the saw: It is not enough to begin creating positive communication, but the process is one that needs to be maintained and renewed over time.

MEETING 2: HOSTILITY AND VIOLENCE

Staff will discuss the various stages of hostility that a person goes through, from the initial trigger event (a girlfriend not calling them back, fears that boyfriend is cheating, an argument that involved campus safety or RA staff) through the escalation phase and toward crisis.

As a person becomes more anxious and frustrated there are biological changes that occur. Heart rate increases, breathing becomes faster, adrenaline is produced, and there is a diminished capacity for creative and rational thought. Dr. Nay (2004) also highlights how the stomach and GI systems empty of blood as digestion slows or holds to free up blood for the brain and muscles. This may cause shallow breathing, chest heaviness, and feelings of suffocation. Senses may become more sensitive and magnified; movements toward you may seem more threatening. Muscles begin to tighten, particularly around the shoulders, neck, forehead, and jaw.

It is helpful for the student to practice "catching oneself" prior to these escalations reaching a crisis phase and thus a loss of control and violence.

Staff will teach the student the process of "cycle breathing," which is useful in reducing the biological changes that overcome a person when he or she climbs through the escalation toward crisis. The process of cycle breathing involves breathing in to a slow count of 4, holding breath for a slow count of 4, breathing out for a slow count of 4, and then repeating. This process lowers blood pressure and heart rate, allowing the student to regain calm and move down the escalation phase rather than up it.

MEETING 3: TRIGGER AWARENESS

A key aspect of addressing aggression in relationships is being aware of trigger events. In this meeting, staff will teach students the importance of identifying trigger events that can begin the process of frustrating and escalate them.

Trigger events can occur in a variety of settings. These could occur through daily hassles that students encounter in their environment (daily work stress, financial worries, self-esteem), life changes (graduation worries, family divorce or conflict, being away from home the first time), environmental stresses (construction noises outside dorm, heating or cooling problems in the residence hall, frustration from living in close quarters with other college students), chronic pain (from past surgery, illness, or injury), or acculturation stress (moving from another country or geographic region, living in a religiously different area).

Staff help the student identify some of these trigger events that lead to potential escalation. Once the trigger events are identified, focus can be placed on applying cycle breathing techniques to counter these stress events.

MEETING 4: INTRODUCTION TO ELLIS AND REBT

Rational emotive behavioral therapy was developed by Albert Ellis (2007) and is useful to assist students in identifying irrational thoughts that they have in reaction to activating (or trigger) events.

The REBT approach can be described in terms of A-B-C's. These are Activating events, Beliefs about these events, and the Consequences of these beliefs.

Activating events can be anything from a relationship argument, getting cut off in traffic, spilling coffee on your favorite shirt, or having your computer crash. These events cannot be prevented; they just occur throughout our lives. It is our *beliefs* about the activating events that lead to aggressive actions and negative *consequences*. We cannot change the activating events in our lives, but we can change our beliefs about the activating events and the resulting consequences of our behavior.

Staff should discuss several A-B-C examples and have students come up with some of their own examples. Highlight both negative and positive outcomes from the beliefs we choose to have.

Negative Example 1

A: You wake up late and don't have enough time to get to class on time.

B: You have to rush to class and believe you will fail because of being late.

C: You skip class altogether and dig yourself into a hole.

Positive Example 1

A: You wake up late and don't have enough time to get to class on time.

B: You gather yourself and go to class late and take a tardy for the class. You stay afterward and apologize to the professor.

C: You have a tardy mark, but the professor respects you taking responsibility for your action.

Negative Example 2

A: You text your girlfriend, who doesn't respond back after several attempts.

B: You become more and more angry and begin to fume about her ignoring you.

C: You leave several angry voice mails and go to the place where she works and yell at her.

Positive Example 2

A: You text your girlfriend, who doesn't respond back after several attempts.

B: You think of some other reasons she might not be texting back, like her phone is off, broken, or in her purse.

C: You find something else to occupy your time and your girlfriend text messages back later—apologizing for not getting back to you and explaining an emergency at work.

MEETING 5: SUBSTANCE ABUSE AND RELATIONSHIPS

Many studies have discussed the causal nature of aggressive behavior correlated with substance abuse. Staff should explore students' own relationship with substance use, abuse, and dependence and discuss how these may correlate with aggressive behaviors. If your college has the ability, consider using a brief substance abuse screening measure, such as the DQ30, SASSI, or CORE. This may help students put their own substance use in perspective with other students.

Staff should discuss previous examples in which the student's drug/alcohol use contributed to aggressive behaviors. These can be explored through simple storying of the student's past experiences, with the staff person asking questions to clarify and expand the narrative (White and Epston 1990). Likewise, the cognitive behavioral approach may be useful to identify trigger events that lead to excess use or patterns of behavior that lead to destructive decisions. An example here might be a student who drinks excessively and gets into fights with other students on the floor or a student who uses marijuana and gets into frequent arguments about his or her drug use with the person he or she is dating.

It may also be helpful to encourage the students to talk about the positive impact alcohol and drug use may have in reducing their aggressive tendencies. These may include reducing social anxiety, a brief escape from overwhelming feelings, or an increase in their social/dating relationships. Staff could then explore ways to achieve these ends without the use of substances and help the student brainstorm more positive choices.

Some staff may struggle with putting substance use in a more positive light, yet honest identification and exploration of the student's substance abuse are the first step toward behavioral change.

MEETING 6: FAMILY MESSAGES ABOUT VIOLENCE

The relationship between past trauma and negative experiences in childhood creating a negative impact on future healthy relationships and self-image dates back to Sigmund Freud. While the goal here is not Freudian analysis, staff should discuss the role of family of origin issues as related to anger, aggression, and violence. Students can be asked to explore early messages they received in their family related to gender roles, expression of emotions, conflict resolution, and negative self-image with the understanding that these experiences may contribute as causal factors to current hostility.

It may be helpful to create a genogram at the start of this meeting to help students understand who exactly makes up their direct and more distant family influences. A basic genogram consists of boxes for males (with their name in the center) and circles for females. Straight lines between boxes indicate a relationship; a line with a slash through it indicates a separation, as in Figure 12.1.

It is important to identify positive family interactions and childhood experiences that would serve to strengthen the student's self-image and positive, nonaggressive communication. The staff should assist the student in identifying positive experiences, messages, and

173

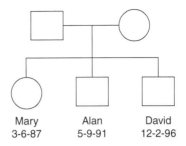

Mary 3-6-87   Alan 5-9-91   David 12-2-96

FIGURE 12.1 Sample Genogram

lessons that may help strengthen the student's overall view of self and nonaggressive actions.

Staff should also encourage a discussion of how males and females communicate in the family. How is authority seen within the family? What role did punishment have in the family? How was marriage seen by the student at a young age?

MEETING 7: CHANGE THEORY

Change theory was introduced by Prochaska, Norcross, and Diclemente (1994) as an approach that outlines how people move through various stages before becoming ready to make change in their lives. It is useful for students to understand this model and how it impacts how they view change.

Precontemplation: The student here is unaware that there is a problem and hasn't thought about change. This stage would be rare for students struggling with a lack of empathy or resulting aggressive behavior in relationship violence. It is likely they have had some experiences where their unwillingness to view things from a different perspective has gotten them into difficult situations, fights, or arguments with their boyfriend/girlfriend. In fact, the very idea that they are in this course would indicate they have experienced some discomfort.

Staff should help students increase their awareness of their need for change through discussion and helping them understand how their anger and aggressive behavior may be impacting their life.

Contemplation: This is the most common stage of change for students to be in. They have thought about change and are thinking about it in the near future. Here students realize their current behavior is not in their best interest, but they are not yet ready to begin their plan to change. Students aren't happy about their current state, want things to be different, but have not yet explored how to do things differently or take action to make change in their lives. They may struggle with feeling like an outsider or that no one understands their perspective. One common issue with those who express a lack of empathy is they rarely get empathy from others. The resulting feelings of being misunderstood are common for them.

Staff should motivate students and encourage them to think about how their anger and aggressive behavior make their life more difficult. They should explore the ideas of planning and what possible resources could be helpful in implementing change.

Preparation for action: Here students are aware of a problem and ready to actively create goals and plans to address the problem of their lack of understanding, anger, frustration, and aggressive behavior in their lives. Plans and goals should be focused, short-term, and designed to be updated and altered to ensure their success. Plans should be measureable and something students can monitor and understand if they are moving forward, static, or moving backward (Glasser 1975, 2001). Staff should help students brainstorm and update their plans to ensure a better chance of success.

Action: This stage of change is where students put into action their plans to change behavior. Students will attempt to alter their perspective, triggering events, and beliefs associated with negative consequences. Staff should support students in trying out these action steps and encourage them to keep trying, despite setbacks and the potential failures they may encounter.

Maintenance and relapse prevention: The goal for this stage is to continue successful plans and repeat those that work, adapting those that don't. Students have experienced change, and there has been a reduction in their myopic and limited worldview and feelings of isolation and anger. Students need to maintain their successful change and reduce the risk of falling back into bad habits.

Staff should help bolster students in their success and develop awareness of potential obstacles that could lead to relapse (allowing angry feelings to fester and become magnified, a single aggressive outburst occurs, they don't respond exactly the way they want in a difficult situation).

MEETING 8: CYBERNETIC AND FEEDBACK LOOPS

Family systems therapy introduces the concepts of cybernetic systems—those complex sets of human interactions that create feedback loops that build upon themselves.

These feedback loops occur often in couples' communication. They can be negative or positive. Negative feedback loops occur when a problem happens in a relationship (jealous boyfriend, girlfriend who flirts with boyfriend's friends at parties) that leads to future behavior being seen as "making everything worse." The cycle continues and spins with new behavior caught up in the negative loop.

Staff should ask students to discuss some examples of negative feedback loops that occur (or occurred) in their relationship. What common arguments occurred? Are there certain themes that occur over and over again? Are there arguments that tend to recycle themselves until the student loses track of why they even began?

There are two ways to address negative feedback loops in cybernetic systems (e.g., families or relationships). The first is creating positive feedback loops. Positive feedback loops operate the same as negative ones, but instead center on positive experiences and healthy relationship concepts.

For example: a girlfriend comes home to see the apartment cleaned and the dishes done after a long day of work. She then takes some time to iron the boyfriend's clothes for work the next day. The boyfriend sees this and gets her flowers. She appreciates the flowers and sets up poker night for her boyfriend and his friends. He then plans a romantic weekend away for the two of them. Positive behavior creates new positive behavior.

In the same way negative loops can spin with their own velocity and pull new behaviors into the vortex, positive feedback loops operate under the same principle. Staff should have students discuss some behaviors that could "jump start" a positive feedback loop in their relationships.

The second way to address negative feedback loops is to "do something different." This commonsense tenet of couples and family therapy can be applied when negative communication patterns and behavior repeat themselves and pull in new behavior. Here, the staff can talk to students about catching themselves when a negative loop is occurring and to choose a behavior that does not perpetuate the negative loop.

The use of a visual metaphor may be helpful to drive this point home. Imagine a spinning black tire on a red ten-speed bike. Watch the tire spin and spin, picking up momentum as pedals are worked over and over again. Now imagine taking a big wooden stick and shoving it between the spokes. This wooden stick is a new communication or approach that goes drastically against adding to the feedback loop.

MEETING 9: ROLE OF THERAPY AND COMMUNICATION

There is a connection between introspection, therapy, and the ability to communicate with others. By understanding ourselves, we become closer to understanding others.

This session is designed to cover the basics of what is involved in going to psychotherapy.

- Therapy is not just for those who have mental illness; therapy is helpful in learning about yourself and learning how to better communicate with others.
- On-campus treatment may allow for a number of free sessions where anything shared with the therapist is kept confidential.
- Couples counseling is a chance to examine a relationship and find ways to improve how each person communicates with each other. The counselor takes a neutral role and helps each person express him- or herself and learn active listening skills.

MEETING 10: PERSONALITY TYPES AND CONFLICT

We all have different preferences when it comes to how we communicate with others. Some of us are extroverted in our interactions, and others tend toward introversion. Some of us focus on our feelings when making a decision, and others think through things based on facts and figures.

There are several brief measures useful to determine people's preferences when it comes to their personality style and how they communicate. These include the Myers-Briggs Type Indicator (http://www.myersbriggs.org/) and the Keirsey Temperament Sorter (http://www.keirsey.com/). Staff may have additional training in other surveys that look at personality and communication preferences. These may be helpful to better identify preferences. It may be that a university's career counseling unit has access to these tests.

If possible, it would be useful to have scores for each person involved in the relationship conflict. It is understood that if the relationship has ended or judicial affairs requires a separation order between the two, this would not be advised.

DISCUSSION QUESTIONS

1. Discuss a scenario where the fundamental lack of empathy for another person or group's perspective has led to violence or threats of violence.

2. Is a lack of empathy or the experience of others a generational problem? Why or why not? How do you think social media and smart phones impact our ability to empathize and see things from another's perspective? Does it make it worse or better?

3. What groups on your campus excel at being empathic? Think about student organizations, faculty, and staff. What is unique about these groups that make empathy more easily expressed?

4. What is the relationship, in your mind, between punishment and education? Give some examples of behaviors or actions where punishments such as removal from school or revoking of a charter would be appropriate. What are some examples where education and attempting to teach new ways of acting would be appropriate? How do you differentiate between these two?

5. The authors discuss some approaches to teaching empathy as a skill. What are your thoughts on teaching empathy skills, such as perspective taking and active listening? Can you teach someone or a group to be more empathetic? What conditions make this teaching more effective? Less effective?

Chapter 13

Sensation-Seeking Behaviors

> Then one day the boy came to the tree and the tree said, "Come, Boy, come and climb up my trunk and swing from my branches and eat apples and play in my shade and be happy."
>
> "I am too big to climb and play," said the boy. "I want to buy things and have fun. I want some money . . ."
>
> —*Shel Silverstein*, The Giving Tree

KEY TAKE-AWAYS

1. Sensation-seeking behaviors occur when individuals or groups seek to find the next high, rush, or excitement. Those who chase pleasure and experience find the search for the next thing often can be addictive and an ultimately self-destructive process.

2. Individuals who exhibit these behaviors may also have a negative impact on those who care for them. The pursuit of pleasure and sensation seeking often comes at the cost of a relationship or other healthy, prosocial activities.

3. Two approaches to addressing sensation-seeking behaviors include motivational interviewing (MI) and redefining failure and self-worth. Changing entrenched behavior or addictive behavior can be a difficult, uphill battle.

In this chapter, we want to capture the idea that some who engage in gender-based violence do so as they seek pleasurable activity. There is the need to chase the desire to possess something new. These cravings fuel previously mentioned risk factors, such as objectification, addiction, grooming behaviors, and misogyny. Women are seen as objects along the journey for pleasure or to control and dominate them.

Grooming and controlling behaviors, in and of themselves, may provide the individual or group with a rush of dominance and control. Nonconsensual BDSM sexual activities are an example of where domineering and degrading behavior provides a brief adrenaline rush and excitement. The thrill of controlling another person, acting as predator chasing prey, becomes a chance for fresh and unique experiences. In abusive relationships, the domestic/dating violence or IPV can be a rush of excitement at the thought of controlling or subjugating another person. While the cycle seems chaotic to those on the outside, the abuser and victim often acclimate to this new sense of normal.

Sensation seeking, in moderation, isn't inherently a problem, but rather how most people go through life. We find excitement in new experiences, exerting control and enjoying pleasurable experiences. As most people learn, the problem is hedonism—seeking pleasure for pleasure's sake. The problem here is pleasure and hedonistic pursuits habituate. What previously was sufficient for excitement and a rush fades with multiple exposures, as there is a desire for novelty and new highs. These individuals and groups chasing new pleasures at the expense of logic, health, and moral behavior are the focus of this risk factor. There is often impulsivity and risk taking that escalate and create a risk for the person and/or the community.

DEFINING THE FACTOR

As mentioned, the individual or group in question is focused on achieving pleasure and sensation as a central goal. Their outlook resists discussion and change, and their central desire is experiencing something pleasurable in the here and now. There is an addictive nature to this pursuit, often at the expense of social standing, finances, and moral code (Zuckerman 2007)—a hedonistic pursuit of pleasure that is never quite enough. Zuckerman (1994, p. 27) describes this trait this way: "the seeking of varied, novel, complex, and intense sensations and experiences, and the willingness to take physical, social, legal, and financial risks for the sake of such experience."

This behavior may also coincide with impulsivity and risk taking. Research suggests sexually aggressive behaviors are most common when the perpetrator is experiencing intense emotions and a corresponding lack of forethought and planning with his or her actions (Mouilso et al. 2013). There is little focus on the consequences of behavior beyond the immediacy of the act. It would be fair to surmise that this sensation-seeking behavior often coincides with Factor 9 (lack of empathy) and their inability to see their beliefs or behaviors from the perspectives of others. The concept of others' perspectives, to the extent that the others are not giving them pleasure or sensation, is not a consideration for the individual or group.

There are indications that those found responsible for sexual violence on a college campus may see violence and danger as masculine and exciting (Schwartz and DeKeseredy 1997, p. 52). This has led to some discussions that the motivations for sexual violence include the idea that it is criminalized and some offenders will commit crime just for that reason (Clarke and Felson 1993). While this may be seen as counterintuitive to many college students, the excitement and illicit nature of the behavior become a driving force motivating some individuals forward.

ADDRESSING THE INDIVIDUAL

An example of this could be a male college student who is obsessively using pornography who then begins to look for increased sensation-seeking behaviors in terms of sexual behaviors with others (Carr and VanDeusen 2004; Sinkovic et al. 2013). The idea that pornography becomes insufficient to satisfy desires results in potentially more violent or depersonalized pornography consumption or an expansion to acting out at parties or on campus. The behavior then escalates and the resulting rush becomes more elusive to achieve. Further risk taking, expenditure of finances, and objectification of the individual or group become the new normal.

Let's look at an example:

Jeff is in a stable relationship with his long-term boyfriend, Craig. The two have been monogamous with each other and live off campus in a small apartment. Craig is content with the relationship and has no complaints. The two don't have sex as often as they did when they first met, but they have drifted into a calm and peaceful routine that seems to have been working well for the past six months.

Jeff is not as happy in the relationship. He isn't sure what he wants and ends up going out late at night to parties without Craig. Jeff hooks up with several men at the parties and finds himself turned on by the excitement and the unknown of these encounters. Craig becomes suspicious of Jeff's late nights and confronts him about this. Jeff is angry to be accused by Craig and the two of them get into several days of nasty arguments and physical fights. The fights end with the two of them feeling more passionately connected and they have sex reminiscent of when they first met.

Jeff continues his late nights out and begins coming home high or altered on party drugs. Craig continues to be frustrated by Jeff's behavior. He talks about Jeff needing to get some help for his drinking and drug problem. Craig does not know about the cheating, but has some suspicions. When he accuses Jeff, they fight again and their sex becomes more aggressive and dominant.

Jeff continues to use and drink and begins to have trouble keeping up in his classes and internship. As Jeff gets more depressed about falling behind in his responsibilities, he ends up using more and getting into higher-risk sexual situations when he stays out late at night (unprotected sex with several other men, drinking and using drugs to the point of blackout).

The relationship that develops between Craig and Jeff has many of the hallmarks of abusive dating/domestic violence relationships. The emotions have an up-and-down quality, with things sometimes being exciting and dangerous and other times frustrating and angry. Jeff engages in additional sensation-seeking behaviors with Craig, drugs, alcohol, and other partners. As school work and obligations begin to fall behind, Jeff doubles down on his risky behavior and increasingly looks for a new high or way to tune out.

ADDRESSING THE GROUP

An example of this behavior in a group setting would be men who see sexual activity as conquests. They may keep individual numbers and enter into competition with each other to see who can reach the highest score. Women are reduced to objects of pleasure or marks on a scorecard. Once again, this resonates with previous factors, such as a lack of empathy and objectification of others.

Another problem that develops is the tendency toward habitualization. This is the propensity for a pleasurable or risky behavior to have a quick and powerful attraction or rush at the start, but as time passes the attraction or high fades. What once used to be sufficient is no longer enough. More sexual conquests, pleasure, or experiences become a driving force. Another group example might be an athletic team that previously traveled to strip clubs together hiring an escort or prostitute to come to their party and have sex with multiple members of the team.

As mentioned in earlier factors, Kanin's reference group theory indicates that:

there exist on most campuses men who are socialized by their friends or groups into a "hypererotic" subculture that produces

SENSATION-SEEKING BEHAVIORS

extremely high or exaggerated levels of sexual aspiration. They *expect* to engage in a very high level of consensual sexual intercourse, or what is to them sexual conquest.

He continues, saying that "these men are highly frustrated, not because they are deprived of sex in some objective sense, but because they feel inadequate in engaging in what they have defined as the proper amount of sex" (cited in Schwartz and DeKeseredy 1997, p. 34).

Athletic and Greek life parties are two common locations for high-risk behaviors and sensation seeking to occur. The environment is often primed for this kind of predatory interaction by generous distribution of alcohol and groups that are supportive of objectification and depersonalization. And always the concern is the escalation in the behavior. What first satisfies then seeds the craving for the next. The process is circular and self-destructive while harmful to individuals and the community.

It can become problematic looking at the examples in all the risk factors and finding yourself placing blame on the college environment or the fraternity environment. Certainly, these are contributing elements, but I want to pause a moment to share this story.

I was working with fraternity recruitment activities last fall and observed some disturbing behavior from the men participating. Fraternity recruitment (rush) occurs during the week prior to school during the fall semester and is the process to become a new member in an organization. In this case, the majority of the participants were new freshmen just arriving to campus. It was early in the week, and there were about 500 men participating in the process. One of the activities each day is that the men have to take turns in computer labs making selections about the organizations they are most interested in joining. It was taking a while to work all the students through the process, and a line of men had formed outside the campus library. The men became agitated and impatient very quickly. Instead of just complaining to one another or asking how much longer the process would take, large groups of the men began chanting and shouting loudly, "We want beer!" and some even began banging their hands and fists against the doors and windows to the library while shouting curse words at staff.

Now, we were able to calm the group down by bringing out some of the fraternity student leaders to walk amidst the group and by speeding up the movement of the line, but my staff and I were disheartened by the incivility of the behavior, especially from a group of students that had been on campus for only one day. These students had barely interacted with any current college students. The problematic behavior with the new students continued throughout the semester in some other telling incidents.

The institution had reinvigorated leadership development activities for the officers of the fraternities and spent time emphasizing that organizations needed to utilize self-accountability structures to identify problematic behaviors early in their organizations. We were seeing some success in officers reporting concerns to the staff before they escalated. What we also saw were a few incidents, not of current fraternity members hazing new members, but of new member classes hazing one another. What we were being told is that while the active chapter members were holding the line about the elimination of any form of hazing from chapter activities, some of the new member classes were deciding to haze one another in order to be considered "real brothers." The perception was that if they did not experience the ritual of hazing they had not experienced what those before them had.

There are probably a variety of reasons this behavior was occurring. The staff who work daily with Greek Life shared that fraternity recruitment actually starts much earlier than the week that I described. Many high school students travel to college campuses to stay with older siblings and experience the social environment, or some high school students living nearby college campuses party at college events on the weekends. Also, many fraternity chapters host summer recruitment gatherings off campus (often in the form of weekend trips to lakes, sporting events, or outdoor activities) before a new freshman ever arrives to campus. It reinforces the need for education beyond the campus community to our alumni, organization advisory boards, and parents because these first interactions with students are important in helping frame what a student expects from the college experience.

My other conclusion was that it confirmed that students are entering the college environment with preconceived notions of what to expect here, and some are seeking out high-risk and sensation-filled activities. In this situation, regardless of the nature of the current Greek environment, many of its newest members were arriving to campus with predispositions about what to expect from fraternity life.

Dr. Amy Murphy
Assistant Professor, Curriculum and Instruction
Angelo State University

FROM THE FRONT LINES

Couples Counseling With Ron and Sylvia

We will use this case as an example through the Reducing the Risk section in this chapter.

I recall working with a couple named Ron and Sylvia. Sylvia made the initial request for them to come into therapy. They had been dating on and off for two years and Sylvia was at her wit's end with Ron.

Ron was a successful athlete and well liked on campus. He is an African American student and Sylvia is Caucasian. They had a number of fights with Sylvia's parents about her dating Ron. Ron's family had a similar problem with Sylvia as they felt he should date "a woman like him" and that he was disrespecting the family by dating a white girl.

Ron was very outgoing and extroverted. Sylvia was very introverted and her idea of a perfect night was staying at home, ordering in, and watching a movie. Ron's perfect night was going clubbing and to bars with friends. To complicate matters further, Ron was 24 and Sylvia was 20 with another six months until her 21st birthday.

Sylvia was frustrated at Ron because he had been going out once or twice a week with his friends to blow off some steam. She found out that he had been dancing with an ex-girlfriend and Sylvia didn't want him going out to clubs anymore. Ron admitted to dancing with the ex, but denied any feelings between the two of them.

Sylvia had taken to monitoring Ron's phone and found several questionable text messages from his ex-girlfriend and several other women. Ron said they are just platonic conversations and Sylvia disagreed.

I met with Ron and Sylvia separately after the first couple's session. Sylvia was wondering why they were still together and having panic attacks and anxiety each night when they were not together. This is an old problem she had with anxiety and she was angry at Ron for making this come back. Ron was frustrated with the entire situation and felt that she was overreacting. Ron did admit to being a big flirt and that many of the phone messages and emails with other women were indeed sexual in nature. Ron liked his time with Sylvia and felt as if they had overcome so much with their families that it would be silly to break up.

Ron was unwilling to stop going to the clubs and began escalating the arguments between the two of them when he shared with her one night that he had gotten drunk and ended up having sex with two women at the party. Sylvia hit him several times when he told her about this during the week, and Ron was somewhat apologetic about his behavior. However, he showed little insight and also said things like, "Well, I had been drinking, so I'm not even sure what happened." Sylvia was upset that he can't remember if he used protection when he had sex with the women and refused to be physical with him until he was tested. Her anxiety and panic attacks had become quite severe.

Ron continued to drink and flirt at parties and refused to stay at home. Sylvia was ready to break up with him, but had the same hesitancy at throwing away something they both had worked so hard on between their families.

Brian Van Brunt, EdD
Author
A Guide to Leadership and Management: Managing Across the Generations
Harm to Others: The Assessment and Treatment of Dangerousness
A Faculty Guide to Addressing Disruptive and Dangerous Behavior

REDUCING THE RISK

The challenge in working with individuals or groups with sensation-seeking behaviors is the same challenge in working with an addict. While there may be part of them that desires change, that part often is a quiet whisper in comparison to wanting the next experience or rush. In this section, we will offer several theories that may be useful in working with students or groups who are on a path escalation by seeking new and increasingly risky and dangerous experiences to titillate and excite.

One approach to addressing irrational thoughts such as those with individuals who chase increasingly sensational pleasure is rational emotive behavior therapy. This approach was developed by Albert Ellis (2007) and can help individuals identify irrational thoughts that are reactions to activating events. This treatment approach can be described in terms of ABCs: activating events, beliefs about these events, and the consequences of these beliefs. Assisting students and groups to see their irrational thoughts is the first step to helping them find alternative ways to process the world around them. One way to do this is to see the upsetting things that they find themselves thinking about as activating events and to adjust their beliefs about the events. (See chapter 12 for more details.)

Escape from pain or feelings of failure or the daily hassles of life may be one of the reasons people seek increasing sensations. If life isn't going as well, the comfort of the feelings and pleasured offered, even if harmful in terms of finances, legality, or morality, drives the individual forward. Long-term consequences are placed on the back burner when there is the initial feeling of pleasure waiting.

A student may know that the girl he is talking to has been drinking heavily and may have crossed the line from intoxication to inebriation.

There is a cost-benefit analysis that balances the unlikely outcome of her filing rape charges or making a scene against the pleasure of getting off with her. He says to himself, "Hell, we are both drinking and she has been coming on to me all night." The consent education he received at orientation several months ago is far from his mind. What he thinks about now is finding a bed to take off her shirt and bra. What he thinks about is being inside of her and the pleasure that will give him. Neither the consequences for his behavior nor taking the time to think about how she feels about this encounter is anywhere on his mind.

When described graphically like this, we hope you see the connection between sensation-seeking behaviors and the way an addict behaves. The allure of the rush drives the behavior.

Another approach to helping a student or group is helping them to empathize (i.e., see things from another perspective) in order to make better choices about their behavior. For example, we are less likely to be aggressive toward the driver of a car that cuts us off when we understand that the other driver may be rushing his pregnant wife to the hospital. Our aggression is dissipated because we acknowledge that we might act in the same manner if we faced a comparable situation. A student who is frustrated by a professor for receiving a failing grade on an exam is likely to be less aggressive if the reason for the grade is clear and the student can acknowledge that the quality of work merits the grade that was given.

In our case example, we learn that Ron's behavior while clubbing and sleeping with other women comes at the expense of Sylvia's peace of mind and the stability of their relationship. The desire for novelty and excitement trumps his commitment to Sylvia and keeping their relationship together. Helping Ron better identify his behavior as problematic to Sylvia and their relationship would be more possible if he took a moment to consider how his behavior is affecting her. Ron is focused on his sensation seeking rather than making any attempt to understand how Sylvia feels about this. In the next section, we discuss the motivational interviewing approach, which may prove helpful in addressing Ron's behavior.

MOTIVATIONAL INTERVIEWING

In addressing many of the risk factors identified in this book, we encourage faculty and staff to encourage students to see the "why" behind behavior and better understand the motivations for their behavior. One approach to working with students or groups who may have a hardened and inflexible perspective (this is how I am going to behave and you cannot change me) is motivational interviewing. Motivational interviewing (or motivational enhancement therapy; MET) was developed by Miller and Rollnick (1991). The approach was initially used for mandated alcohol treatment to help students change addictive behavior. In more recent years, the MI approach has been applied to working with difficult, reluctant, or entrenched attitudes.

We've used their approach in the higher education setting in various applications and have found it helpful in working with mandated students in ongoing treatment and connecting with those who are initially unwilling to explore a change in the way they behave. It is a proactive approach to working with those who don't yet see they have a problem or aren't yet ready to tackle it or head in a new direction. The heart of Miller and Rollnick's approach centers on five key concepts that can be applied well to working with students who are mandated to treatment.

Expression of empathy: This involves a conversation with the student that attempts to both understand the student perspective (empathy) and communicate an understanding of that perspective (expression of empathy). This expression of empathy respects students' point of view, freedom of choice, and ability to determine their own self-direction. Suggestions from the staff for change are subtle, and the ultimate change is left in the hands of the student.

In meeting with Ron and Sylvia, having the ability to empathize with them is akin to putting money in the bank to be withdrawn during later conversations. If Sylvia doesn't think the person she is talking to will understand panic attacks or not wanting to go out socially to clubs, it will be less likely she will share this. Likewise, if Ron feels the person talking to him is judgmental of his choices, he will be less likely to share. Expressing empathy here is about appreciating their perspectives while connecting to similar experiences you have had. There is the caution to avoid taking sides with students such as Ron or Sylvia or oversharing your personal experiences in order to connect with the students.

Avoidance of argumentation: This one of the easier techniques to understand, but one of the most difficult to put into practice. When you argue with the student who is arguing with you, neither of you is listening. While indeed, the other person may be completely wrong, simply telling the person that isn't sufficient to change his or her point of view. Arguments should be avoided, even nonverbal ones. When students tune out, look down and away, fidget, or roll their eyes, the argument might not be a verbal one; instead it is communicated more subtly through a slow distancing of students from the staff. In some ways, this can be even more destructive to the change process. Students become disillusioned with the process, disengage, and lose faith in the person talking to them or their ability to understand and relate.

Being agreeable with the student, at least at the outset of the conversation, is one of the best ways to build rapport and establish a connection. As the meeting progresses, the staff typically has established some credibility and trust, which allows them to challenge the student's established harmful thoughts or behaviors. Direct argumentation rarely addresses any underlying change but rather becomes caught up in the process of exchanging opinions back and forth without any kind of empathic consideration.

While Ron's behavior could clearly be argued to be escalating, dangerous, and not conducive to the relationship, taking a hard or judgmental stance against his behaviors will reduce his willingness to share with staff. Open-ended questions that are designed to explore the thinking behind Ron's behavior will be a more productive course of action. If Ron is able to understand his behavior is sensation-seeking in nature, he may be more willing to understand the danger in this behavior never reaching satisfaction or resolution. If he chooses to continue his behavior, then he can be encouraged to have a more responsible discussion with Sylvia about how his choices impact their relationship.

Rolling with resistance: Staff are encouraged to avoid meeting a student's resistance to change head on. Instead, they should try to engage the student in new ways of thinking about the situation, perhaps trying to evoke from the student new solutions to the conflict. Lack of motivation or an unwillingness to change and be positive is understood as a normal developmental response, and interventions are designed to avoid becoming mired down in the student's lack of developmental growth and personal responsibility for change.

As Ron is engaged in conversations, it is likely he will have moments when he becomes upset or feels trapped in his choices. Rolling with resistance teaches the importance of not being caught up in arguments that lead to unproductive ends. For example, a staff person talking with Ron or Sylvia would have to be careful about adopting Sylvia's viewpoint, which is, arguably, one that many of us would be more drawn to defending.

Likewise, Sylvia may take an aggressive and argumentative stance when discussing her frustration with Ron's behavior. While there may be a temptation to argue with her about this and hold her accountable to staying in a relationship that is abusive, fighting with her about this will be counterproductive. A subtler approach, designed to help her explore her thoughts and wrestle with some of her inconsistencies (e.g., being upset about Ron's behavior but staying with him in the relationship), would be advisable.

Development of discrepancy: This is the process by which the staff helps students understand that their current behavior won't help them achieve the desired goal. The staff explores the consequences of the student's actions in a neutral manner, avoiding sarcasm or a condescending tone. Students then become aware of their choices and start to explore the advantages to choosing a different way to behave.

This skill is better applied when some trust is already established with students. A common mistake is attempting to develop discrepancy with a student early on, as the student then sees the staff as overintellectualizing the problem and becomes upset with them for ignoring the emotional component of his or her frustrations.

Here, the staff can help Ron explore in a bit more detail what he is looking to get out of the relationship. For example, what are his expectations around monogamy in the relationship and does Sylvia share those? What would his reaction be if the situation was reversed? Does Ron want to stay in the relationship or is his behavior a passive-aggressive way of ending things? All of these questions are designed to help Ron think more directly about his behavior and actions.

Support for self-efficacy: This involves helping the student or group understand that change is possible and that the future can be better than the present. The staff does this by encouraging and nurturing growth in students, finding times and opportunities to "catch them doing well," and praising this behavior with hopes of shaping future positive behavior.

Here, the staff may have the opportunity to find and highlight positive things that are occurring in the relationship. For example, Ron and Sylvia could be "caught" having a positive conversation without yelling or escalation. Ron could be praised for repeating back accurately Sylvia's concerns. If they reach a compromise, perhaps agreeing to go out to the movies on a date night, this middle-ground behavior between staying home and clubbing could be an opportunity to support both of them.

REDEFINING FAILURE

In relation to developing patience as students consider changing their behavior, it can be helpful to explore how the student or group defines failure in their lives. How they see failure can have an effect on how easily they are able to let go of their frustrations or established, problematic worldview. Having a grounding in preventive practices, such as guided imagery and in-the-moment techniques like cycle breathing, will help improve students' frustration tolerance and increase mindfulness; however, it remains important to challenge the underlying thoughts and emotions that students experience in their environment.

Ron may see the ending of his relationship with Sylvia as a failure in his life, rather than an opportunity to grow and define himself. Likewise, Sylvia may be holding onto the imagined safety of relationship with Ron when she would be far better off making a clean break of the relationship.

Sylvia might see her failure at her relationship with Ron as larger failure with any relationship. An underlying assumption for Sylvia might be her internalization of the negative beliefs that she is unworthy of love or monogamy, has nothing to offer, and is worthless. Staff may challenge Sylvia and help her appreciate that even though things didn't work out with Ron, this does not automatically reinforce her belief that she is bad at relationships. Instead, the relationship with Ron is a bad and unhealthy one.

People often internalize negative messages about their worth, the quality of their abilities, their physical features, or their place in the world. When they see these as absolute failures rather than temporary obstacles, they overemphasize the importance of the event and become reactive rather than thoughtful about their response. Students who are successful in their ventures have a rather open and flexible view of success. They see achievement as more of a marathon than a sprint. They see obstacles to their success as temporary setbacks rather than permanent roadblocks.

DISCUSSION QUESTIONS

1. What are some ways we can seek pleasure and pleasurable activities without having this pursuit cross over into an obsessive or addictive pursuit that hurt our relationships or creates other negative outcomes?

2. Is there something inherently problematic in the pursuit of pleasure or adopting a hedonistic lifestyle? What are the benefits and limitations of these choices?

3. What are some of warning signs of Jeff's problematic behavior in his scenario with Craig? How might you intervene with this scenario if it was raised to the attention of the student conduct office, behavioral intervention team (BIT), or counseling office?

4. Discuss how you might apply some of the concepts of motivational interviewing (MI) in attempting to change an individual engaging in sensation-seeking behaviors.

5. How does a person's self-worth impact his or her tendency for sensation-seeking behaviors? What motivates this desire for seeking these behaviors? In your opinion, is it a learned process or something that is inherent in our biology and heredity?

Chapter 14

Obsessive and/or Addictive Thoughts or Behaviors

But those trees! Those trees! Those Truffula Trees!
All my life I'd been searching for trees such as these.

—*Dr. Seuss*, The Lorax

KEY TAKE-AWAYS

1. Students can find themselves caught up in the addictive and obsessive web of thoughts and behaviors related to achieving sexual gratification. While this factor overlaps with several others, such as sensation seeking, pornography addiction, and objectification, there is a unique risk here as students escalate in their dependencies.

2. The authors discuss paraphilic sexual behaviors that involve urges, fantasies, and behaviors directed at nonhuman objects or children or involve sexual humiliation. They also discuss hypersexuality and process addicts who seek pleasure in the short-term despite negative long-term consequences.

3. Identifying and teaching the community to be aware and watch for these escalations in behaviors are one important way to be proactive in bringing about intervention. These addictive thoughts and behaviors can manifest in secret or be glaringly public in their expression. Identifying and managing these behaviors often require involvement from multiple departments, including campus police, student conduct, counseling, BIT, and off-campus police.

It has been said that sexual assault and rape are about power and control. But sometimes, with our students, the goal of sex is the physical pleasure. When anything gives a euphoric high, such as drugs, alcohol, or sexual pleasure, there is the risk that this high, this pleasure, becomes the goal for the individual or group.

We have spent most of this book looking at some of the other reasons individuals move forward with sexual violence in our college communities, such as a lack of respect for women, a tendency toward objectification and depersonalization, or achieving dominance or power and control over another. Yet, some pursue sex for the sake of sex. They take the path of least resistance to obtain their particular drug of choice. Asking heroin addicts why they shoot up or alcoholics why they take their next drink may be an interesting philosophical question; however, the true answer is because they are addicts.

We bring up this risk factor not to take away from earlier conversations about the other behaviors, thoughts, and beliefs that we should be concerned about when preventing gender-based violence, but instead to highlight that a driving factor for some may just be the pursuit of their own sexual gratification. We have seen these addictive and obsessive thoughts drive sexual addicts and pedophiles; we also see these traits in some of those who are on our campus and seek their next fix, no matter what stands in their way.

DEFINING THE FACTOR

Addiction, and specifically sexual addiction, is increasing on college campuses (Seegers 2010). This factor describes a tendency to focus intensely on a particular goal at the cost of other reasonable alternative behaviors. This factor overlaps with sensation-seeking behaviors as well as the earlier factor involving obsessive pornography addiction. The hardening of a point of view through inflexible thoughts relates here in terms of the intensity and focus of the desires. The uniqueness of this factor, differentiated from the others, lies in the driven or focused pursuit on thoughts related to sexually aggressive or violent behaviors. Sussman et al. (2011) describe a process addiction as a series of potentially pathological behaviors that expose individuals to "mood-altering events" by which they achieve pleasure and become dependent.

While this group of sexual "process addicts" is estimated to include only 3%–6% of the population, those experiencing addictive tendencies or pleasure seeking would be considerably higher. In either case, these individuals present a concern on campus. The thoughts they experience are repetitive in nature and the individual often ruminates on the topic with little success in redirecting focus

OBSESSIVE AND/OR ADDICTIVE THOUGHTS

onto other topics. There may also be an underlying insecurity and clinging to the desperate shortsighted "need" for something and great fear at the prospect of not getting it.

These sexual thoughts may have a mental health basis in addictive and repetitive thoughts as found in obsessive-compulsive disorder (Gordon 2002; Grant et al. 2006; American Psychiatric Association 2013) or within sexual paraphilia. There may be past thoughts or behaviors that manifested in previous relationships. There may be a history of early childhood or teenage sexually addictive or impulsive behaviors. These thoughts and behaviors are often perceived as outside of the control of the person experiencing the impulses. There may be a history of hypersexuality or a series of impersonal sexual encounters that are more about fulfilling some sense of quota rather than fueling a healthy sense of satisfaction. In fact, the lack of satisfaction—the pursuit for some new habitual experience—is another way to consider this factor. While the newest *DSM* did not include a proposed diagnosis by Kafka (2010) on hypersexuality disorder, more research is being conducted (Reid 2013).

Paraphilic behaviors must be considered when any risk assessment for sexual violence is made. "Paraphilias are mental disorders that are defined as involving sexual urges, fantasies, and behaviors that fall into three categories: (1) nonhuman objects; (2) children or other nonconsenting persons; and (3) suffering and/or humiliation" (O'Toole and Bowman 2011, p. 76). The range of paraphilic behaviors is broad, from voyeurism to exhibitionism to partialism to sexual sadism, an extremely aggressive paraphilic behavior. In her book *The Biology of Violence*, neuroscientist Dr. Debra Niehoff poses these questions: "But what if sex and aggression can't be disentangled?" and "What if the deviant fantasies require suffering, or a dead body?" Her answer: "When a paraphilia takes a violent or homicidal turn, aggression engulfs sex, testosterone becomes irrelevant, and turning back is no longer possible" (Niehoff 1999, p. 165). When assessing for risk factors of sexual violence, the presence of paraphilic behaviors must be determined. Depending on the specific paraphilic behavior, as well as the individual's sexual fantasies and urges, his or her risk for violence can increase exponentially.

ADDRESSING THE INDIVIDUAL

One example would be a student who remains obsessive with someone he dated in the past or recently met at a party despite clear messages from the woman that she does not want the attention or pursuit. Meloy and Fisher (2005) write,

> An addiction model may also shed light on the neurobiology of stalking. This is hypothesized because normal men and women who are in love show all of the basic symptoms of addiction, including tolerance, dependency/craving, withdrawal and relapse. The spurned or unrequited stalker simply goes to far greater lengths to procure his/her drug, the victim.
>
> (p. 6)

We offer the following two examples of sexually addictive behaviors:

Phillip spends several hours each day watching pornography. He has vast collections stored on several large portable hard drives. Growing up as the only child in his family, Phillip spent a good amount of time by himself on his computer and became increasingly interested in pornography. Over time, he has found himself looking for more and more novel and graphic depictions of sexual acts.

Lately, Phillip has been collecting pornography that involves voyeurism and public sex. These images and videos depict up-skirt pictures of women, exposed public cleavage, and acts of public sex in bathrooms, parks, and office buildings. Phillip has also spent a lot of time researching hidden cameras and ways he could potentially record his own pictures or videos of people who are unaware of his observations.

Phillip also has downloaded a camera app and purchased a device that allows him to take pictures with a small triggering device attached to his phone. Phillip has used this some around campus to take pictures of women on the stairs and leaning over and exposing their cleavage.

Other students begin to notice his isolation and oddness around campus and in the residence halls. Many women give Phillip a wide berth and often describe him as creepy when they do interact with him in class. One student filled out an anonymous report on the behavioral intervention team website saying she worried Phillip was "going to rape someone one of these days if the school doesn't do something."

Contrast Phillip's case to that of Cal.

Cal is well liked and popular on campus and has a reputation for having sex with many women. He attends athletic and Greek parties frequently on campus and has little problem finding new women, often intoxicated, at these parties, with whom he engages in sex.

> Cal keeps a collection of videos of women giving him oral sex on his cell phone. For most of the short video clips he has saved, Cal recorded the drunk women giving some form of agreement that it was okay to film them. The consent is often dubious, however, as many of the women slur their words and some say it is okay as long as he deletes it right away. Cal has over 50 of these videos saved, some dating back to his time in high school. He often brags about his collection and has been known to show the videos to some male friends. He is usually cautious about this and lets only close friends watch them on his phone.
>
> The rumor makes its way to the dean of student's office about Cal's behavior. The womyn's group on campus also learns of Cal's collection and makes a report to the school's Title IX office.

Both students have developed some degree of addictive, high-risk sexual behaviors that are in need of intervention. In both cases, the details are complicated. The issue of freedom to possess images and videos is central, though other issues of consent, filming of a minor, or hidden cameras also are raised. Intervention techniques with both Phillip and Cal are multifaceted and complex, likely having to address their resistance to changing a well-established habit, if not full-on addictive behavior. We offer some guidance moving forward with cases like these in the Reducing the Risk section at the end of this chapter.

ADDRESSING THE GROUP

For a group example, we may see a driven focus to continue a socially unacceptable behavior, such as underage drinking, making pornography available publically, sending an e-mail to the group educating new members on how to have sex with women by getting them drunk, and so on.

Consider the following example:

> Jessica and Ellie have been drinking all evening at a forensic debate team party following a win. The party features "blowjob shots," a mixture of Kahlúa and Amaretto with whipped cream on top. They each have six of these shots during the party by 10:00 p.m. Their friend Tim, one of the leaders on the team, comes over and starts talking to them.
>
> The three of them joke about the blowjob shots and Tim takes a long drink from the bottle of Kahlúa. The three of them flirt and Tim tells them how hot

they look in their outfits. Tim had sex with Jessica about a month earlier after an away debate. He hasn't had any sexual contact with Ellie.

Tim grabs Jessica's buttocks and Ellie seductively runs her tongue over the blowjob shot before drinking one more. Tim licks the remaining whipped cream off Ellie's cheek before the three of them go to hang out in one of the back rooms. All three are laughing and having a good time.

Tim's friend Jake and his girlfriend Sara are seated on the couch across from them in the back room. It is dark and the music is loud. Tim, Jessica, and Ellie all pile onto a couch in the corner of the room. Tim sits in the middle. Both Jessica and Ellie are intoxicated and laughing with Tim about blowjobs and blowjob shots.

Tim frequently watches pornography that involves two women giving a man oral sex and discusses this with Jessica and Ellie. Jessica touches Tim's penis through his pants and kisses him. Tim puts his hand on Ellie's breast as Jessica begins to give him oral sex (mouth-to-genital contact). Tim kisses Ellie and puts his hand on the back of her head. Jessica and Ellie are both laughing and they both perform oral sex on him. Tim gives Jake and Sara a thumbs-up while this goes on. Everyone is laughing and continuing to drink.

Jessica and Ellie stop giving Tim oral sex and Jessica starts to dance by the table. Ellie begins to feel sick and goes to the bathroom to vomit. When she comes back, she is slurring her words and has trouble standing up. Jessica is also slurring her words and had fallen once over the table she is dancing next to in the back room. Sara walks them both upstairs to a quiet bedroom to let them sleep it off. Tim and Jake stay downstairs and drink more with some other debate team members. Many of them slap Tim on the back as the story of his oral sex with Jessica and Ellie comes up.

Around 2:00 a.m., Sara comes back downstairs and leaves Ellie passed out (lost consciousness) on her bed and Jessica lies down and feels the room spinning around her.

Around 3:00 a.m., Tim goes up into the room. Tim had been drinking heavily throughout the night and tells Jessica that he wants to finish what they started earlier. Tim undresses Jessica and begins having sex with her (genital-to-genital contact). Jessica has trouble focusing and falls asleep.

Tim stands up and goes over to Ellie and tells Jessica that he wants her to join in. Jessica remains in her bed and doesn't respond. Tim has sex with Ellie, who remains unconscious. Tim then leaves the room.

Jessica and Ellie wake up around 8:00 a.m. Ellie becomes very upset at the idea that she had sex last night. Ellie doesn't remember anything after leaving the party. Jessica remembers Tim coming into the room and having sex with him, but remembers nothing after that.

Jessica considers it a regrettable night, not a sexual assault. But Ellie feels violated and calls the police to make a report and be taken to the hospital for a rape kit.

The scenario is a complicated one, with many different aspects that draw from risk factors. Alcohol plays a significant role throughout the example with students who were both intoxicated and inebriated. It becomes increasingly clear that any attempt at obtaining consent was invalid due to Jessica's and Ellie's levels of inebriation. Someone who is unconscious cannot give consent. The sexually charged environment of the party and Tim's consumption of pornography related to oral sex served to push the night forward into the final sexual assaults that occur. While there are many opportunities in this case study for bystander intervention, it is also useful to explore what motivated Tim's behavior from the onset. In this case, the desire for sensation-seeking behavior, the novelty of the experience he witnessed over and over again, overtakes any hesitancy he has about his behavior.

This case, like many in the book, is drawn from actual scenarios that occur on campuses across the nation. In this case, Tim defended his actions of raping Jessica and Ellie by suggesting they (1) didn't say no and (2) gave him oral sex, so the sex later was assumed. While it is essential to train bystanders to intervene and teach students about obtaining affirmative consent, we would argue there is also a place to explore the obsessive and addictive thoughts a student like Tim has running in his head. We should also pause at how this action is seen as an event that gives Tim status and praise among the group. While not directly causal to the assault, Tim's obsession with getting two girls to do to him what he fantasized about in his mind and the accolades he received for having this occur at the party become a variable in this equation we must address.

FROM THE FRONT LINES

Reluctant Recollections

Early in my career, I worked with sexual offenders and survivors placed from the greater Philadelphia area to a group home facility near Boston, Massachusetts. The students in this locked, residential facility ranged from about 10 to 17, and all had lengthy and traumatic histories of sexual abuse, trauma, and/or sexual predation. These were children who had been ritually abused in satanic cults, raped repeatedly, and had experienced incest and group sex with their siblings and parents from a young age. Needless to say, these were extremely high-risk youth who, without exception, struggled with sexually addictive and obsessive thoughts and behaviors.

In working with these children, I observed their tendency between self-soothing behaviors (behaviors that allowed them to escape into their fantasies) and those fever-like pursuits of the next act of gratification. There was a tidal pull between these extremes. I'd come to learn that this was common among those addicted or obsessed. Students would attempt to sneak sexually explicit magazines past staff, form illicit relationships with each other, and disappear into whatever sexual gratification gave them some solace in their darkness. The teachers, therapists, and direct care staff worked to bring the students back to some degree of healthy growth, showing them how to participate in nonexploitive relationships and find some path back to well-being.

Thinking back to this time in my life is a reluctant process. There was daily violence in this work. I recall wrestling a razor away from a 14-year-old girl trying to kill herself following the trauma of being raped by a motorcycle gang when she was 12. Children who had been preyed upon then, in turn, preyed upon others. What brings this back into my mind is the idea of obsessive sexual thoughts as a precursor behavior to action. There is a fantasy rehearsal in this process, where the addictive, repetitive thoughts habitualize and, at the very least, create the ruts in the road toward action.

As I became a therapist and worked with college students, I treated a handful of patients who had similar obsessive thoughts they could not shake. I worked a statutory rape case in which a 20-year-old male student continued to send explicit text messages and photos to a willing, but not able to legally consent, 15-year-old. I provided therapy to a student who would bite his girlfriend repeatedly and left vicious teeth marks and large bruises. He told me about an escalating fantasy he had in which he would bite her hard enough to make her bleed and taste her blood while having sex. I've provided couples counseling for an abusive man who continued to humiliate and degrade his girlfriend in the bedroom and was unabashedly escalating his behavior.

The commonality with all of these examples, and those earlier recollections from the group home, is the presence of intense, repetitive, obsessive thoughts and fantasies that weren't quite yet behaviors, although they were headed in that direction. When I think of the central premise of this book, attending to risk factors with the hope of getting out in front of gender-based and sexual violence, this chapter holds a special place of importance. While it is not the easiest of the contributing factors to understand, it is one of the most important in terms of identifying opportunities to gain insight into the driving motivation behind these behaviors.

Brian Van Brunt, EdD
Author
A Guide to Leadership and Management: Managing Across the Generations
Harm to Others: The Assessment and Treatment of Dangerousness
A Faculty Guide to Addressing Disruptive and Dangerous Behavior

REDUCING THE RISK

When addressing addictive behaviors from students, the goal is twofold. First, the behaviors need to be identified and shared with the appropriate people within the campus community. Depending on the nature of the behavior, this may involve campus police, off-campus law enforcement, the behavioral intervention team (BIT), student conduct, or the campus counseling center.

The second part of this is educational efforts designed to help students realize they have a problem and move forward with change. Techniques such as motivational interviewing, mentioned in chapter 13, have proven effective at working with students who are reluctant to change their behavior.

With a student like Phillip, this will likely involve more close education and monitoring of at-risk behaviors in the community. Phillip is cautious about his addiction and the opportunity for intervention is more likely at the point his addiction escalates and he is less careful about his pornography use, or hidden camera filming of others. With Cal, the behavior is clearer and likely the challenge in his case will be focusing on how best to intervene to bring about a change in his behavior when he may be within his rights to capture and retain such videos.

Both scenarios will likely require multidepartmental involvement that may involve on-campus law enforcement, student conduct, counseling, risk assessment, coordination with residential life, campus Internet technologies, and potential off-campus criminal charges. Each will potentially have an effect on the student population and may involve Title IX offices and how the media relations department chooses to handle details released and the resulting public image damage to the school.

Teaching the campus community, and specifically residential life staff, some of the signs and behaviors to watch for can be an effective first step in monitoring the community. Some sample clues to look for are included in Table 14.1. This list of behaviors is designed to be a starting place for awareness and discussion. It is not advised to take this list and use it as type of "wanted poster" around campus. Many of the items on the list may have other causes besides sexual addiction.

Sexually obsessive thoughts may also be the topic of the conversation of students with their friends or associates. Does the student always seem to be talking about sex or sex-related ideas? Do other students feel uncomfortable around students because of their leering or constant gazing at other students' cleavage or buttocks? Do they seek to develop groups of close associates or friends who are "in the know" with whom they share their exploits?

When working with an individual who is experiencing an addictive level of sexual thoughts and behaviors, it can be helpful to

Table 14.1 Clues to Sexual Addiction

Isolating self for long periods of time away from other students in room with computer	Spending money on Internet pornography sites the student cannot afford
Locking of phone or computer in a paranoid to scared manner	Attempting to copy credit card numbers or stealing these numbers to support habit
Collecting or studying surveillance equipment, cameras, or recording devices	Joining online groups that share a common interest in the pornography
Missing classes or other responsibilities	High Internet download usage noticed by IT department (also peer-to-peer sites)
Explosive or unexpected anger	Locking self away in office or dorm room
Hanging around stairwells, locker rooms, laundry rooms, bathrooms, or other places people may expose themselves	Escalating behaviors exploring strip clubs, escort sites, and Craig's List–type sites for encounters
Spending much time looking to obtain sex or engaging in a sexual activity for much longer periods than intended	Frequent distraction or thinking about sex, fantasizing, or losing track of time
Continuing to seek increased sexual gratification despite negative financial, physical, or emotional cost	Escalation in the sexual behavior to reach similar levels of satisfaction

OBSESSIVE AND/OR ADDICTIVE THOUGHTS

understand how individuals with addictive, obsessional, or repetitive thoughts or habits make attempts at changing these habits. To this end, we introduce the concept of change theory.

CHANGE THEORY

Miller and Rollnick (1991) offered a useful set of practical techniques when working with unmotivated or defensive students, and we refer the readers back to the previous chapter, where this technique is described in more detail. We have also found it helpful for faculty and staff to understand the framework of transtheoretical change theory, developed by Prochaska et al. (1994).

Their powerful book, *Changing for Good*, is useful when attempting to help a student who becomes entrenched or obsessed with a particular behavior that becomes addictive. This approach is useful for students who are struggling with alcohol, drugs, or eating disorders, as well as sexual addictions. As with these more serious addictions, it is also recommended to refer the student to the counseling office for more in-depth treatment. The reality in higher education, however, is we are all called to work with students with these kind of challenges and having a grounding in change theory can be helpful. The approach is useful, in particular with students who seem to be stuck or incapable of changing their behavior. The concepts are universally helpful when looking to answer the question "Why is it so hard for this student to make different choices?"

As we move forward, keep in mind that this approach may be reasonable for a staff member to attempt with students who are isolating themselves from their friends and locking themselves away watching pornography on the Internet for six hours a night. The approach should not be used by paraprofessional, unlicensed staff to address more concerning behaviors, like stalking, possessing torture or child pornography, or taking up-skirt pictures of students on the student center stairs. As mentioned earlier, these behaviors will typically involve law enforcement, student conduct, or psychological counseling.

Prochaska et al. (1994) outlined how individuals move through various stages before achieving lasting change in their lives. They offered a unique perspective for students who repeat difficult or frustrating behaviors. When we teach these concepts to colleagues, we ask them to pause and consider a behavior they have tried to change in their life. This can be either something they are currently struggling with (smoking, watching too much TV, not getting enough exercise) or something they have tried to change in the past.

As we review the five stages of change, it can be helpful to think about a behavior you have tried to change before in your life.

Precontemplation: At this stage, the student is unaware that there is a problem and hasn't thought much about change. The staff's main goal is to help the student gain increased awareness of the need for change. This is done primarily through nonjudgmental, nondirective open discussion. The staff helps students understand how their behaviors may be affecting their life.

For Phillip, the student mentioned earlier with the pornography addiction and escalating desire to take sexual photos of women without their knowledge, he may or may not be aware that this is a behavior in need of change. Conversations with Phillip may reveal that he knows his current behavior is out of control and in need of change. He may lack the ability at this time to commit to such a change.

For Cal, it is unlikely he feels much guilt or concern about his behavior. In fact, it may be the opposite, as he takes pride in his collection of women performing oral sex on him and sharing this with others. Any change in Cal's behavior will likely start here at this stage, helping him further explore the negative implications of continuing this behavior (e.g., losing his popularity, impacting future job opportunities, legal difficulties related to age or consent).

Contemplation: This is the most common stage of change for most students. The student has thought about change and is getting ready for movement in the near future. He or she realizes that the current behavior is not productive but is not yet ready to begin a plan to change. The student isn't happy about the current state and wants things to be different but has not yet explored how to do things differently or take action to make change in his or her life.

In this stage, the staff continues to motivate students and encourage them to think in more detail about the negative impact of a specific behavior on their life. Together they should explore ways the student might plan for change and what resources could be helpful in implementing change. The staff's role here is to continue to explore and push the student closer to a plan for action. The focus is less on the specifics of how this plan would be implemented, but instead a further exploration of why the student wants to behave differently.

For Phillip, it is likely he is in this stage. He is aware that his behavior is out of control and not particularly healthy for him. He senses his difference and isolation from the larger community, and while he is driven to obtain these images and collect the pornography on his hard drives, he feels stuck and powerless to make a change. The goal here becomes discussion about what change might look like in his behavior. Given he is not quite ready to act and change, what might his change look like down the road? This is more of an exploratory process at this stage, with the staff avoiding pushing Phillip toward action.

For Cal, he may be more willing to explore and consider behavioral change as the pressure increases through his collection becoming more known publicly on campus. While he may not have an internal desire to change, there may be some pressure from the loss of social standing, a student conduct action, or off-campus criminal charges that begin to have Cal thinking more that he should behave differently. Staff should look to expand this idea, almost as if nurturing a small ember until it grows into the flame of a fire. Progress should be slow and steady, encouraging him to think more about the impact of his choices—perhaps looking at opportunities to develop empathy for the women he filmed and ways to avoid further objectification.

Preparation for action: In this stage, students are aware of a problem and are ready to actively create goals to address the problem behavior in their life. Plans and goals should be focused, short-term, and designed to be modified as needed to ensure student success. Plans should be measureable and easy to monitor to see if they are moving forward, staying in place, or moving backward. The staff can help the student brainstorm and update plans to ensure a better chance of success.

To this end, Glasser (1975, 2001) outlined a process of change based on understanding of and assessing the client's WDEP: Wants and needs, Direction and what they are doing, an Evaluation of their behavior, and Planning and commitment to change. Glasser advised therapists who are reviewing plans with clients to make sure that the plans are simple, attainable, measureable, immediate, consistent, controlled by the client, committed to by the client, and timely.

The preparation stage for Phillip is an important one, helping him explore his goals, discuss potential obstacles to reaching those goals, and develop a plan moving forward. While there are some behaviors that would be required to avoid completely (setting video cameras up around campus, taking pictures of unsuspecting people), there would be a larger discussion around the collecting or viewing of the pornography. It would be helpful to consult with counseling to determine if this behavior could be continued in a more measured way or if any viewing or collecting of pornography would be seen as potentially exacerbating the risk of higher-risk behaviors. Parsing out the different types of pornography viewed and/or collected should also be part of this consultation.

Cal will likely spend most of his time in the two previous stages. If Cal would consider reducing or erasing his collection or avoiding future filming, we could then discuss with him the various options he could consider. These options may involve enforcement and consolation with student conduct along with on/off-campus police. There may also be state laws that impact his collection in terms of revenge pornography or sexual exploitation. These areas are currently expanding and developing in the field.

Action: In the action stage of change, students put their plans into action in order to change behavior. They attempt to alter their negative behaviors and develop new positive behaviors to replace them. The staff can support students as they try out these action steps and encourage them to persist despite setbacks.

For Phillip, action goes hand and hand with monitoring. One challenge for the action stage for Phillip is compliance with external sanctions or restrictions on his Internet usage. Again, there are some behaviors, such as taking sexual pictures without someone's permission or downloading material on the campus Internet that violates its usage policy, that will likely have a zero-tolerance response from the institution. Other behaviors, such as collecting hidden video pornography or isolating himself from others in the hall, could be seen on a spectrum of harm reduction. Perfection in these areas would not be the goal, but instead helping Phillip move forward in changing his behavior. It should go without saying that this process would work better with a campus partner, like a counselor, psychologist, or case manager.

In Cal's case, it would be likely that any misstep would result in further conduct action if he records sexual acts with underage women or films sexual acts without proper consent.

Maintenance and relapse prevention: The goal of the maintenance and relapse prevention stage is to continue successful plans and repeat those action steps that work and adjust things that don't. The student has experienced change and a reduction in problem behavior and now needs to maintain the successful change and reduce the risk of falling back into bad habits. The staff can help bolster the student's success and develop awareness of potential obstacles that could lead to relapse.

For Phillip, there is likely some room here as he develops some new ways to behave and reduces his addictive and obsessive sexual behavior. Growth should be supported as he gradually moves away from at-risk behaviors and toward more adaptive ones. This will be more likely to occur with the presence of a supportive relationship.

With Cal, part of his goal moving forward may be reducing the volume of sexual partners, or at least exploring ways to maintain those experiences in a safer way to avoid future employment, student conduct, or law enforcement problems. If filming and collecting remain in Cal's desired sexual activities, he could also potentially explore this through fewer, more consistent relationships with fully consenting partners.

DISCUSSION QUESTIONS

1. Discuss some examples of students you have encountered with addictive sexual thoughts or behaviors. How do we define the line between obsessive and addictive thoughts when compared with normal sexuality?

2. What are some signs or symptoms that may indicate a student has a problem with his or her sexual thoughts or behavior?

3. In Phillip's case, how might you intervene given the BIT report and the rumors of his isolation and odd behaviors on campus? Is there a concern that students may begin to bully Phillip if news gets out about the details of his behavior? How might you balance this risk? What are some different departments that would be involved in his case?

4. Cal's case is a different one in that there is a very public side of his behavior and he is likely going to be unwilling to stop. Share your thoughts on Cal's collection. Is Cal within his rights to keep these? How would your campus handle the potential fallout from a case like this?

5. What role do educational programs have on your campus to address the issue of addictive or obsessive sexual thoughts or actions? What groups would assist with programming related to healthy relationships, at-risk behaviors, and nontraditional sexual activity (e.g., kink, BDSM)?

Chapter 15

Past Experiences

Count the dark rings, and you know the tree's age. Study the rings, and you can learn much more. Many things affect the way the tree grows, and thus alter the shape, thickness, color and uniformity of the rings.

"What Tree Rings Tell Us About the Life of a Tree," Arborday.org

---

KEY TAKE-AWAYS

1. There are a number of risk factors in the literature that create a higher likelihood of violence. These include substance abuse, being the victim of or witnessing past emotional, physical, or sexual abuse, and growing up in a family with negative views toward women or one that fostered a rape, assault, or violent culture.

2. Campus units and student organizations can be trained on how to best support those with histories of trauma or violence in addition to how to watch for early signs that concerns are arising. These same units should be active in supporting a student's healthy transition to the college or university.

3. Conduct boards and officers should be trained in evaluating incidents for the potential of repeat perpetration as well as comprehensive Title IX training to support equitable and effective accountability processes.

We all come from somewhere. Freud taught us in his early work that the experiences that happen to us as children impact the kinds of adults that we become later in life. In the same way, our experiences related to relationships, how men should treat women, with pornography, and sensation-seeking behaviors don't suddenly begin when we enter college. Instead, these experiences are layered and multidimensional, weaving together like the roots of the cypress trees in the swamps and bayous of Louisiana.

In the same way, this chapter weaves and interacts with many of the other chapters in the book as it explores how past experiences impact current behaviors and attitudes. In chapter 5, we identified the risk factor of obsessive or addictive pornography use or sex focus. We suggested a relationship between pornography and sexual violence developed from the idea that sexual learning is based on past experiences and what we are taught by friends, family, educators, and the media. If pornography is the only source of information on sex or sexual health, then behaviors and attitudes will be skewed in those ways. This risk factor is explained in a similar manner: if experiences related to sex have been abusive or violent, there is a possibility that behaviors will be abusive and violent as a reflection of past experience.

Another area of overlap is substance abuse and addictive sexual behaviors that are, in and of themselves, connected to other risk factors for sexual violence. If an individual's past experience includes these things, it increases the likelihood of a connection to sexually violent behaviors. Individuals who abuse substances or participate in sensation-seeking sexually are often at greater risk because perpetrators are able to excuse their behaviors through additional objectification of the victim. The victim was drinking or taking drugs or coming on to the perpetrator and asking for sex.

Experiences with families and in the social environment impact future sexual behavior in a similar way to how group social norms impact other member behaviors. If family and social environments have been filled with supportive attitudes related to sexual violence, then a person's concept of normative sexual behaviors and attitudes will reflect the understanding of that social environment.

This chapter, unlike many of the others that are more clearly defined, serves to catch the central idea that our early negative experiences shape our worldview and can increase the risk of gender-based violence and sexual assault. Early experiences of seeing women mistreated, falling into the addiction cycle of pornography and sensation-seeking behaviors, or witnessing those around you being physically, emotionally, or sexually abused carries with it a toll. Our aim in this chapter is to survey the ways these experiences can contribute to the current problems we face in higher education.

DEFINING THE FACTOR

"Sexual violence is a learned behavior" (American College Health Association 2008). Past experiences have the potential to increase the risk of perpetration and future abuse. The grouping includes past behaviors and experiences that may contribute to a predisposition for sexual violence. These also include mitigating items that decrease inhibition, making the individual or group more likely to act out in the future.

These include the following:

- Past physical abuse (O'Hearn and Margolin 2000; Reitzel-Jaffe and Wolfe 2001; Ehrensaft et al. 2003; White and Smith 2004)
- Past sexual abuse (Kanin 1985; Craissati et al. 2002; Jewkes et al. 2002; White and Smith 2004; Hines 2007)
- Past violation of "no-contact" (Kropp et al. 1994, 1995, 1998; Harris et al. 2003; Helmus and Hanson 2007)
- Victim or witness of violence or sexual assault (Jewkes et al. 2002; Morrison et al. 2004)
- Substance abuse (Koss and Gaines 1993; Larimer et al. 1999; Carr and VanDeusen 2004)
- Sexual-addictive behaviors or impulses (Harris et al. 2003; Helmus and Hanson 2007)
- Family or societal support for rape or assault culture (Jewkes et al. 2002; Resnick et al. 2004; Loh et al. 2005)
- Negative masculine attitudes (Kilmartin 2000; Rozee and Koss 2001; Carr and VanDeusen 2004)
- Past relational experiences as predictor for IPV (Knight and Sims-Knight 2009; Teranishi-Martinez 2014)

Past behaviors as indicators of future behaviors have a long history in the literature about sexual violence. As with any of the risk factors, caution should be taken when making blanket assumptions based on singular or small data sets. These risk factors, like the previous ones, should be taken in the larger context of how concerning behavior is heightened as multiple factors overlap with one another, rather than a singular attention on any given factor.

As with examining the rings of a tree once it has been cut down, looking to the past helps us understand where our students have been and what factors contribute to their behavior. If our goal is to identify these risk factors and get out in front of these problems before they start, an accurate understanding of the potential contributing factors to this kind of violence is key.

ADDRESSING THE INDIVIDUAL

Our past, to some extent, defines our present. While we are not locked into a set of actions that are predestined by our past experiences, the worn, deep wheel ruts carved out in the dirt road of our past create a challenge of inertia to jump beyond and find a new path. A young boy who has grown up watching his mother being beaten by his father after he comes home from work drunk each night has certainly experienced behaviors that inform his future choices. This may be avoidance of relationships because they might turn out like his parent's relationship. He may walk in his father's footsteps when it comes to alcohol and managing his frustration tolerance and impulse control. Or he may grow up with a profound respect for women and find ways to advocate and care for them in his relationships. Past behavior has an impact on future behavior. The exact impact requires a more careful analysis.

Imagine a male high school student has a series of relationships in which he is aggressive and controlling with his girlfriends. He has negative attitudes toward women and how he treats them. He was taught growing up that real men take control of their women and take what is owed to them. The last of these relationships ended with a no-contact restraining order and criminal charges. These past experiences should be seen as creating the likelihood of similar future behaviors. Addressing these potential risks within a student conduct process or counseling treatment could help the student develop new ways to behave.

In a different vein, a student may have past behavior related to consuming rape fantasy pornography. The student then is involved in a case of nonconsensual sexual touching on a bus that brings students from the parking lot to the main campus. While the current behavior would be difficult to predict based on his past behavior, hindsight following the bus incident allows us to connect the dots to better understand where the behavior was nurtured and developed. This points to the importance of providing opportunities for students who have past addictive behaviors to seek help. This can be useful in preventing future repetitions of the behavior or escalations in the behavior.

In the Reducing the Risk section at the end of the chapter, we will spend some time talking about transitioning students to college and offering access to prevention and support groups to address negative past experiences.

ADDRESSING THE GROUP

Past negative group behaviors contribute to future negative behavior. The most common manifestation we have seen on campus occurs in groups that nurture and support misogynistic and objectified views of women. What once was an individual thought or idea now becomes supported and nurtured through a group process. Think of an individual with a racist ideology. Now think of that individual connecting up on the Internet with a group that supports and nurtures these ideas. This results in the KKK and Westboro Baptist Church. Singular ideas find footing and leverage as they are reinforced by the crowd.

While bystander intervention and empowerment can be used to fight gender-based violence and sexual assault, the group effect can have a dark side. Instead of students rallying together to confront problematic behavior on campus, groups can develop a mob mentality, foster a diffusion of responsibility, and ultimately create a fertile soil for some very bad plants to grow.

Consider the following scenario:

> The majority of the incoming first-year class at a small, southern college is made up of first-generation college students who come from farming and agriculture communities. To comply with VAWA recommendations, the Title IX office has invested heavily in orientation programming designed to educate students about consent, sexual assault, and gender-based violence.
>
> During the first orientation event, several students, part of an on-campus church-affiliated club, protest and walk out of a showing of the "tea and consent" video popular on campuses across the country (this is easily searchable under the key words "tea and consent"). The group doesn't like the cursing in the video, feel it is encouraging premarital sex, and refuse to watch it.
>
> Many of the students hold religious beliefs that women are on earth primarily to be the helpmate to men and to have children. Many believe that any form of homosexuality is a sin against God. They are planning a protest again about an on-campus drag show scheduled later in the semester. The women's group and GLBT resource center share that they have been receiving many hate-filled messages on their answering machines and threatening notes in the campus mail. Student health services has also gotten similar threatening messages about providing condoms to students. The threats are concerning, but non-specific. An example is "If you keep handing out condoms you will burn in hell."

This example looks at a group of students likely coming from a more conservative background, having some major adjustment problems to the more liberal campus environment. While everyone is entitled to their opinions, politically or otherwise, these behaviors begin to cross the threshold to threatening and limiting other students' right to self-expression. The example here is a useful one, as there is a clear preexisting mind-set that exacerbates and escalates when it comes onto campus.

In addressing a scenario like this, the potential threats and unorganized protests must first be addressed through the campus conduct, BIT, and potentially off-campus law enforcement departments. While it is not clear from the example that students will act on their threats, there is the creation of a hostile environment, clear Title IX and gender-based threats, and the potential for more dangerous escalations. Health centers are particularly sensitive to fire threats related to birth control offerings.

Once the immediate threats are addressed and the group is better identified, it might be helpful to find a way for the group to work within the college's existing systems and policies for education, protests, and sharing their ideas with the community in appropriate ways. This might involve organizing a club or student group and/or working with student activities to ensure there is equal time for entertainment and presentations that represent both conservative and liberal perspectives. In essence, it is important to harness this group's frustrations and give them a socially appropriate way to share their ideas, even if these ideas are distasteful to many. What cannot be tolerated is threats and unchecked escalation and intimidation to student groups.

More commonly, what we see on campus are groups that are already in existence that propagate negative messages to those who join. This is most commonly seen through the Greek and athletic systems, but certainly are not limited to these areas. The concern is the normalizing of ways of thinking to younger members that then become seen as the new and correct way of thinking.

An example may be a room in a fraternity house that contains bras and underwear that become trophies for new members to ogle over. This is problematic for several reasons. First, we have the objectification of women, who go from individuals with agency and depth to being reduced to cup size and thongs. Second, there is the establishment of sensation-seeking behaviors and escalation of these behaviors. What follows the collection of underwear trophies? Video or picture walls? Naked Polaroid pictures in a scrapbook? The trophy room becomes the new normal, the starting place, or a line in the sand to think of what else can be created. Third, it is more than likely consent issues for the trophy room are blurry at best. Were these items stolen? Were the women drunk when they were taken? Was consent obtained? Likely not.

The days of panty raids and campus streaking are over. Both of these activities now carry with them the potential for sex offender registry enrollment. Our call to our male athletes and brothers in the fraternity system is a passionate one. Step up and do better. The old way of doing things is over. If you continue, your team will be suspended and your charter lost. What we want is a safe place for everyone on campus. Fraternity members and athletes should be leading the charge in addressing these group behaviors. To this end, we have asked a colleague of ours, Dr. Gentry McCreary, to take some space in this book's afterword to address these issues.

FROM THE FRONT LINES

The Impact of Culture in Our Work

I have worked in higher education for many years, more than I care to count now that I think about it. Over the years I have learned many lessons, quite often the hard way. One of the most important of these lessons was to not take anything for granted. By this, I mean don't take for granted that our willingness to be open, caring, and compassionate will always equate to students coming forward to openly share their challenges with us and seek the help and support we are so eager to provide. Quite often, cultural and familial norms and pressures can trump what many of us would usually consider to be in the student's and/or student's family's own best self-interest. I will share the experience that made this fact crystal clear to me.

In the winter of 2006, I had just begun my tenure as dean of students at an urban community college in California. The campus serves a very high-needs population and the majority of students were first-generation college students. A student had come to my office to report that her best friend had shared that her grandfather had molested her several times, going back to when she was in junior high school. The student told me that she did inform her friend that she would be coming to my office to report what she had been told, and her friend was seeking help but didn't know how to come forward.

I immediately made arrangements to meet with the student. At her request, I also invited her mother, aunt, and her best friend. On the campus side, I invited one of my best counselors, my assistant dean, and an investigator from our campus police department, all of whom were female, and two of the three were from the same ethnic background as the student. When we met a day later, I opened the meeting and because of my maleness, offered to step out of the room because of the sensitive nature of what would be discussed. I thought the student would be more comfortable with me out of the room, but she insisted that I stay.

What I thought would be a confession from the student about how she had been taken advantage of turned out to be more of a confrontation. The student told her mother, aunt, and the rest of us what had happened, and asked or rather demanded to know from her family why they hadn't done more to stop it. The family's tearful response was that they tried to make sure the girls in the family stayed away from the grandfather as much as possible. It took a minute to sink in, but I finally got it . . . *they knew*. This was not new information; it was an attempt for my student to find out why her family did not do more to protect her.

We finished the meeting and the counselor made follow-up arrangements with the student and her family. I asked my staff to stay so we could debrief. My concern for the student was ever-present, but to be truthful, I was having a hard time containing my anger and confusion. I just did not understand how the mother and aunt could have known what was happening and not do anything about it. Apparently the grandfather had quite a reputation for this type of behavior. What my staff told me was that situations like this were unfortunately very common in their community. In fact, they told story after story from their own lives and what they had heard from students and community members about the same thing.

Sexual abuse and molestation were taboo subjects and something that was just not brought up. It was expected to be kept a secret, and "outing" the perpetrator would be a huge embarrassment to the family. Familial and cultural influences and norms were so strong that a mother could sacrifice her daughter's safety and well-being to not bring shame upon the family.

I remember that conversation like it happened yesterday. I still remember the anger, confusion, and an almost overwhelming sadness. This taught me that being well-intentioned was just not enough. I need to understand the communities in which I serve. Some lessons will depend on my being invited into the trust of those around me, and others will come from me asking questions and being open to learning. But perhaps the hardest lesson for me was not to judge. How could this mother let this happen? How could I not look down on her? There was obviously something wrong there, but I learned that it is not my place to judge. I definitely do not condone the behavior and to the core of my being I hate that this happens to any person anywhere, but I cannot be in the right space of mind and intention to help in these types of situations if I am judging those involved.

This is just one example of how challenging our service to others can be. Ten years and several positions later, I am still learning these lessons. When in doubt, I fall back on my fundamental belief that I am here to serve, and know that I am helping to change lives. My student's thank-you as she walked out of that meeting confirmed that for me.

Patrick D. Jefferson, EdD
Assistant Vice President
Student Services/Dean of Students
University of Houston–Downtown

REDUCING THE RISK

In most cases of sexual violence, it is likely that you will see multiple risk factors influencing the risk level for perpetration or victimization. This factor shows the intermingling of a number of factors and emphasizes the need to identify behaviors of concern early in order to provide education, intervention, and accountability. It also points to the importance of screening for sexual abuse in counseling and medical services sessions. It requires that Title IX administrators utilize systems that track the various incidents of concern occurring on campus, even those that do not rise to the level of a hostile environment by themselves, in order to scan for patterns and previous experiences that may be problematic. Similar to the BIT-related tips in chapter 11, BITs and conduct staff are essential in considering information related to past experiences when considering individual cases and the likelihood of future threats. Conduct boards and officers should also have comprehensive training in order to understand the complexities of sexual violence. Finally, in the following sections, we explore the importance of the transition to college in either maintaining healthy patterns or moving away from problematic environments.

CONTINUING THREAT DETERMINATIONS

In many ways, this factor highlights one of the main struggles for Title IX administrators. It is common for victims to be reluctant about pursuing university conduct or criminal proceedings when reporting sexual violence. Some victims are not emotionally ready to pursue charges against the perpetrator. Others may have other priorities, such as school, work, or family, and choose to focus on those responsibilities. Some may worry that they do not have enough evidence to result in an outcome in their favor, and others may be concerned about retaliation or their safety. Higher education administrators have to make a decision when receiving a report of sexual violence that involves a student, faculty, or staff member as the accused. Do you prioritize the request of the victim for confidentiality and not proceed with conduct proceedings, or do you proceed with conduct proceedings because of concerns about the safety and welfare of the campus community?

This question is particularly concerning when you consider the risk factor of past experiences. Think about a situation in which someone reports seeing a student masturbating in the library. It is unlikely the student started his or her public sexual activity with this act. It is more likely the student worked up to this behavior by first masturbating in the residence hall room, then a public restroom, and then a more public location, like the library. Other sexual behaviors often escalate in a similar fashion, so the likelihood of repeat perpetration is concerning.

This is where the risk factors give a nod to individual psychologies related to perpetration, in addition to larger social factors. David Lisak's (Lisak and Miller 2002) work on repeat offenders is often cited because he identified, by studying convicted rapists, that the average number of rape victims was seven for each offender. Despite recent criticism of one study, the idea of repeat perpetration is an area of concern. Thus, conduct officers and Title IX administrators must consider previous behaviors related to sexual violence and the likelihood of repeat perpetration. It is our hope that the DD-12 gives people a place to start thinking more about these issues in the higher education setting.

TRAINING CONDUCT STAFF, BOARDS, AND TITLE IX STAFF

Training those involved in Title IX investigations and coordination of university compliance is essential. The Association of Title IX Coordinators and Administrators (ATIXA) is one place where training can be provided for colleges and universities. Sokolow (2001, p. 18), the CEO of the NCHERM Group, shares his thoughts about training hearing boards:

NCHERM has established a minimum competence for our clients of 2 days for training judicial decision-makers each semester. It is rare to see a board operate truly competently without at least

2 days of training. The hearing board must be familiar with basic rules of evidence regarding relevance, credibility and rape shield rules. It must be thoroughly versed in an analytical approach to determining if a policy was violated. It must be instructed on questioning and deliberation techniques. It should understand Rape Trauma Syndrome and common rape myths. Furthermore, hearing board members need to be sensitized to what the alleged victim is experiencing. He or she may be traumatized by recounting the events of the incident.

Conduct administrators and boards trained in the continuum of sexual violence and related factors are better able to evaluate student and organization behaviors of concern. By understanding the root factors of sexual violence, such as misogynistic attitudes, staff can recognize concerns early and design educational sanctions to alter attitudes and behaviors in a positive way. Some conduct board trainings have been criticized for being tilted toward either a victim or respondent perspective; this is something to be avoided. The risk factors identified here provide objective behaviors and attitudes that can be described and observed in reports of sexual violence incidents, providing boards and administrators with a common language to discuss incidents of sexual violence.

In the 2016 ATIXA white paper titled *The 7 Deadly Sins of Title IX Investigation* (Henry, Lewis, Morris, Schuster, Sokolow, Swinton, and Van Brunt), the authors share the importance of conduct officers and Title IX investigators ensuring that their work is research-based in order to avoid common mistakes. They suggest those involved in Title IX investigations have an understanding of the impact of trauma on a neurobiological, physical, and emotional level and know positive ways to respond to avoid retraumatization.

Determining creditability is important as well. They write, "Credibility is the process of weighing the accuracy and veracity of evidence. To assess credibility, evaluate the source, content, and plausibility of what is offered in light of other evidence. When source, content, and plausibility are strong, credibility is strong" (Henry et al. 2016, p. 6). Likewise, they stress the importance of a balanced approach:

An investigator's duty is not to "believe one story over the other," but to assess each piece of evidence, independently, and as part of the bigger picture, to determine whether the preponderance of the evidence supports a finding of responsible or not responsible.

(Henry et al. 2016, p. 8)

Training on this will not reduce the number of sexual assaults on your campus; however, it will increase the chance for a fair process for those involved with student conduct, hearing boards, or Title IX staff.

SUPPORT HEALTHY TRANSITIONS TO COLLEGE

The transition to college includes new opportunities as well as new risks related to social experiences, relationships, sex, alcohol consumption, and other new stressors related to finances, academics, and wellness. The patterns students set during the first six weeks of college impact their behaviors and attitudes through their remaining time at the institution. Campuses have numerous opportunities to help students with a healthy transition into the college environment and to tailor programming to consider students coming from backgrounds with and without trauma and violence. Think for a minute about transplanting a tree from one location to another. Some trees do best when the roots are packed for transplant with the soil from their original location. Others do better when the roots are moved bare without soil from the previous environment. Either tree can experience transplant shock during the move, causing the growth and development of the tree to be impacted, or the transplant method can support its continued growth.

College students without traumatic past experiences or histories of violence who have supportive parental and family units may flourish in the college environment with more of a connection to their previous environment. In this case, prevention efforts need to include messaging to parent and family members about the expectations related to sexual violence, alcohol, and other related factors as well as the support resources available to assist students. Parents should be given tips and information for the types of conversations to have with students before they depart to college. Don't forget some of the examples in earlier chapters showing that some family units will be more open about issues related to sex than others, so messages need to be designed to work for either type of situation. For students who have been victims of abuse or violence, parents should be given prompts to consider the importance of establishing resource structures in the college environment that reflect some of the resources they had at home, such as the establishment of a counseling relationship.

For students who have had negative past experiences with violence or trauma involving parents or family members, one way to support a healthy transition to college is to provide support options and resources to support students in their transition. One example is helping students to navigate financial aid structures in order to establish themselves as independent from their parents and utilizing prompts in information that clearly indicate to students where they can find support and assistance on campus. This includes teaching the community to look for signs of abusive or controlling behavior, supporting those survivors of physical and sexual trauma, and teaching the skills of healthy relationships based on caring and support. We spent some time in chapter 3 outlining this approach through a review of several models and guidance on how to develop programming for different groups over a longer period of time, ensuring proper dosage and exposure. Counseling centers and medical providers can often integrate screenings in their practice to ask students about their histories in these areas and modify their treatment calls appropriately. Regardless of a student's history of past experiences, education must begin prior to a student's arrival on the college campus, which calls for college practitioners to engage with K-12 institutions and family educational organizations.

DISCUSSION QUESTIONS

1. What opportunities exist on campus to identify and engage with students with risk factors related to past experiences? What campus resources can be provided to these students?

2. What are your thoughts on engaging those in Greek life and athletes to be part of the solution to this problem on our campus? Are there opportunities for this? Are these groups unfairly targeted? Are they not targeted enough?

3. When might a student disclose information related to a past experience, as discussed earlier? How should faculty and staff be trained to respond and assist the student?

4. Victims of sexual violence are often reluctant to proceed with formal proceedings against the accused party. How can campus reporting systems help decrease victim reluctance? What elements should be considered when deciding to move forward with formal proceedings without the victim's participation?

5. How can the campus better support healthy transitions for new freshman, transfer, and graduate students? What about wellness strategies for faculty and staff?

Part III

Conclusion

Chapter 16

Consent

We smile at the ignorance of the savage who cuts down the tree in order to reach its fruit; but the same blunder is made by every person who is overeager and impatient in the pursuit of pleasure.

—*William Ellery Channing*

KEY TAKE-AWAYS

1. Consent should be ongoing and affirmative and can occur only when someone is not in an inebriated state, unconscious, or unable to give consent because of age or other legal issues.

2. Alcohol becomes a complicating factor for the consent conversations. It is imperative to address the differences between intoxication and inebriation as well as addressing group culture that fosters high-risk drinking on campus.

3. Teaching good consent is an excellent starting place, but cannot be the end of the education efforts we engage in. Healthy communication about sex and intimacy in relationships is essential.

While the main focus of this book has been on identifying the risk factors useful to mitigate sex- and gender-based violence on college campuses, we would be remiss if we let the conversation end here. Simply identifying the bad and developing a "Just Say No" type of program to reduce at-risk and concerning behaviors are not sufficient to stem the tide of sexual violence on our campuses. We also must teach sexual consent and relationship health in an ongoing, affirmative, and, quite frankly, engaging and entertaining format.

Students need to understand the satisfaction and pleasure that come from having consensual, willing sex. This ideally occurs with a partner or partners where communication is open, empathetic, and based on mutual trust. We cannot hope to reduce sexual violence on campus by simply telling students what not to do; rather, we must stress aspects of healthy sexuality, in all of its diverse forms, in sex-positive conversations.

WHAT DO WE MEAN BY "CONSENT"?

Consent has been in the news a lot lately, from California's and New York's recent affirmative consent legislation to sex educators across the Internet and on YouTube sharing their ideas. ATIXA, the Association of Title IX Administrators, has written extensively on the issue of consent as it relates to conduct policy at institutions of higher education. ATIXA (Sokolow, Swinton, et al. 2015) defines consent on page 16 of its *Investigation in a Box* this way:

"Consent is:

- Clear, and
- Knowing, and
- Voluntary (or affirmative, conscious, and voluntary),
- Words or actions,
- That give permission for specific sexual activity."

In addition to defining "consent," many policies take the discussion a step further and clearly identify situations where consent cannot be given. For example, the threat or use of force, or when a party overcomes the free will of another by coercing or intimating the other into sexual activity, is a barrier to consent. Other examples in which consent cannot be given include interactions between a minor and an adult and situations in which a power differential exists between the two parties (e.g., a therapist and their client or a clergy member and a parishioner). The degree to which the power presents a coercive or intimidating impact may be a point of distinction in a college's or university's policy (e.g., between a professor and a student). Some argue that this type of relationship prevents the individual in the subordinate role from being able to consent. Others argue that consent is possible, though these relationships are often fraught with additional challenges (e.g., the role of bias in grading, favoritism in the classroom, or abuse of power).

Defining "consent" is helpful for Title IX administrators in gaining clarity as they investigate and adjudicate cases of gender-based violence. And while this clarity in policy is essential, it does not address the larger need to educate students about the importance of sexually positive and healthy dialogue. What a consent policy does, whether in legislation or in our campus conduct codes, is provide a floor rather than a ceiling for the dialogue needed on campus.

Educating students about the institution's and state's definitions of "sexual assault" and how to obtain consent prior to sexual activity is a starting place. The aspirational goal for our education efforts should be engaging students in conversations about making thoughtful decisions about their sexual activities in a way that respects and honors individual agency and choice.

Challenges remain for administrators and educators as they wrestle with the gray area between policy and education. For example, including a term such as "enthusiastic consent" may be helpful in conversations with students who engage in sexual activity. In fact, one way to avoid a sexual assault allegation is to have not only a willing partner but also one who is enthusiastic and excited about the activity. This is certainly part of healthy, sex-positive dialogue that educators facilitate on campuses across the country.

The difficulty here, from a policy and enforcement standpoint, is how to actually measure enthusiasm. We are reminded of Robin Williams' character in *Dead Poet's Society* as he discussed the scoring of poetry on a numeric-based scale: "I like Byron. I give him a 42, but I can't dance to it." How would a conduct officer or Title IX investigator assess enthusiasm in sexual activity? It becomes almost a ridiculous concept when looking at writing policy or adjudicating cases. However, this example highlights the stark differences between establishing a consent policy in the student code of conduct and teaching consent practices to students in an orientation event or educational session. Simply stated, while what we teach students should be established in the policy, we must teach practical application issues that reach beyond the letter of the code.

HAVING THE SEX-POSITIVE TALK

Let's face it: sex isn't always easy for people to talk about. In fact, it could be argued that many religious and political ideologies are firmly built upon the foundations of controlling sexuality and, in particular, female impulse. Freud described women's sexuality as the "dark continent" and began his work attempting to calm the "hysterical" impulses of women.

While we would like to think that we have moved beyond the Victorian view of sexuality, the reality is that sexuality in American culture is saturated with negative and one-dimensional images, from Carl's Junior hamburger ads to the hot wings at Hooters. And while sexuality is in front of us every day, there remains a puritanical barrier to open discussion, like an elephant in the living room of American culture. In-depth conversations about healthy sexual desires and pleasure are uncommon. Rather, sex is seen as something forbidden, or at the very least, controlled; it is difficult to even imagine healthy sexuality between consenting adults being seen as a valid conversation topic for many adults.

So, our challenge as educators is to broach this topic with our students. One of the larger problems we have seen in the years following the Violence Against Women Act (VAWA) push on campus is the focus on the negative aspects of sex related to assault, rape, stalking, dating/domestic violence, harassment, and the creation of hostile environments. What we haven't seen to the same extent as policy clarification and training for those Title IX administrators and conduct officers charged with the investigations of gender-based violence has been a strong push for healthy and positive sex discussions with our students.

While there is certainly a need for the lawyers, law enforcement, and conduct officers in higher education to clarify and improve existing policy definitions and investigatory procedures, it is equally important to address the problem from a prevention framework. Educating students about affirmative consent before they engage in sexual activity is crucial.

Adopting a clear consent policy on campus and making it available to students is necessary, but not sufficient. Policy is needed because it informs our programming. We must be cautious, however, to not confuse our policy with education. As the Polish American philosopher Alfred Korzybski wrote, "The map is not the territory" (cited in Kendig 1990, p. 299). The code is not the same as what we teach.

For those students who choose to engage in sexual activity—and here we offer an essential and careful nod to those students who choose to not be sexually active due to religious or personal reasons—investing some of our university time and resources aimed at the prevention, rather than the intervention, of sexual assault and other forms of gender-based violence would be wise. By having active, healthy, and positive sex-focused discussions about consent and how consenting adults negotiate sexual activities and boundaries, we can better prepare our students to stay out of our campus conduct hearings, Title IX investigations, and off-campus criminal court proceedings.

LESSONS FROM DRINKING EDUCATION

College counseling centers, conduct officers, and orientation departments are not new to the work of teaching college students about high-risk drinking. This programming has evolved from punitive and overly simplistic abstinence-only–based efforts to a more refined discussion of moderation management, harm reduction, and careful decision making to better mitigate risk. We've come a long way from the days of "Just say no."

What we have learned in conversations with students about their alcohol choices is simple: the best programs are ones that treat students with respect and a sense of agency, and provide them with the information they need to make better informed risk-management choices. In the end, it is for students to decide if they choose to drink beyond their limits or put themselves in higher-risk situations. What we can do as prevention educators is help them to better understand how alcohol impacts the body (through a process called the biphasic curve), teach them skills to regulate their drinking and attend to their emotions when they begin drinking, and help them develop social skills to avoid drinking more when they have had enough.

With consent, the concept is similar. We should not dumb down our message to "No means no," or we fall prey to silly applications that progressively allow students to check off on their iPhones what they are comfortable doing as they are making out. What we need to do is help them understand that good sex, whether with the same person in a monogamous relationship, in a polyamorous pod, in a threesome, or in a one-night stand, is more difficult to obtain when the communication is bad, it is with someone they just met, or there is a lot of drinking involved. If they choose to move forward, they should do so better informed about the risks and realities.

One critical tool we have as prevention educators talking about consent is our own experience and wisdom. While caution is always recommended when sharing personal stories, there is a value in drawing on our own personal experiences and sharing some of our well-earned wisdom about how healthy (or unhealthy) sexual communication and relationships develop.

Take purchasing things like sex toys and contraceptives (stay with us). At 20 years of age, there is a natural embarrassment for most with these kinds of purchases. As people grow older, they become more comfortable with themselves and the embarrassment tends to fade, and more open communication and desires can be expressed. You become more comfortable in your skin, more confident in your wishes, and, typically, better in your communication about your needs and desires. There is a benefit to those who have positive experience discussing healthy sex and consent with their partners sharing some of these lessons with students who are attempting to navigate similar waters.

FROM THE FRONT LINES

Consent Culture

Consent is a concept often talked about but rarely understood. This is mostly because we have found a way to grossly overcomplicate a simple black and white issue. Social norms and misnomers have made us think otherwise.

Let's clarify.

Obtaining consent is the sole responsibility of the person who is initiating the sex act. It is not the other person's task to rebuff the aggressor. Consent is ongoing. You may not always engage in a multitude of sex acts with every person you connect with sexually—hence the need for partners to continue the consent conversation. This does not have to be clinical; it can be quite good (dare I say erotic?) for meeting the needs of your partner(s) but it does require a level of confidence and maturity. Shame and sex are a terrible combination. It is the plague of consent culture. Adults have been made to feel dirty and shameful for enjoying carnal pleasure. That is really too bad. This shame has made it nearly impossible for victims and survivors to be believed and even harder to come forward and report these heinous acts. It is perfectly acceptable for adults* to engage in and enjoy the sex they choose to have. The removal of shame fosters a consent culture so that victims and survivors feel they may come forward if they so choose. The link between shame and sex has also made it remarkably difficult for parents and caretakers to effectively educate youth on the issues related to consent. Simply put, you cannot teach what you do not understand.

Alcohol is so deeply linked to sex that their images are hard to separate from one another. It is linked to romance and dating in movies. While it is a tool employed in many (most) sexual assaults, it is not a rapist. Alcohol does not rape people. Rapists rape people. The distinction is important. Culturally we are addressing the wrong things. Banning alcohol? There is a reason that does not work. There will always be access and there has been nothing to help us identify the rapists or curtail the shame. No problems solved. Just Band-Aids. A better idea is to educate and empower your youth.

The reason many students do not discuss their plans to hook up (which does not imply sex, just some level of sexual activity) in advance with their peers when drinking is the shame associated with a normal biological activity. What if we stripped away the shame and then created a space where students could actively engage bystanders or their friends in advance? Make a plan that included what they wanted their night to look like. Maybe it includes a hookup. Maybe it includes a few drinks but is entered into with maturity, community, and confidence. These are cornerstones of a consent culture. Remove the shame, and replace it with tools.

College orientation is too late. Consent education should start much earlier. We need children to understand they have autonomy over their bodies. We should ask before we touch a child, even our own. It reinforces the message that no one has the right to violate them. There are opportunities to practice this each and every day.

A consent culture is one where shame and sex do not intersect. Where confidence and maturity are held in highest regard. Where our youth are given the benefit of the doubt. Consent is black and white. Everything else is just background noise.

*The legal age of consent.

Becca Tieder
Founder, One Student
www.onestudent.org

BURNING MAN, KINK, AND BDSM

What exactly does the hedonistic, seven-day party and rave of Burning Man have to teach us about sexual consent and healthy relationships? Quite a lot, actually. It's the same with the kink and BDSM communities (the not-safe-for-work website https://fetlife.com is a good starting place for those interested in learning more).

Let's start with Burning Man, a festival in Nevada that, on many levels, defies description. John Steinbeck's famous opening quote describing *Cannery Row* as "a poem, a stink, a grating noise, a quality of light, a tone, a habit, a nostalgia, a dream" is a good way to describe Burning Man. The gathering rises once a year out of the Black Rock Desert in the heat of August and early September on a dry lake bed about three hours north of Reno, Nevada. It's been going on for more than 20 years, with the earliest festival taking place on San Francisco's Baker Beach in 1986. It is an intentional community based on the concept of gifting. No money changes hands at Burning Man and nothing is sold or purchased. Around 70,000 people join the community each year. Once the week comes to a close, the 100-foot-plus wooden man is burned on Saturday night, followed by the burning of the wooden temple structure on Sunday. It's a leave-no-trace experience. The lakebed resumes its natural state as the participants leave to return to the "default world" until the following year.

People come searching for something—a break from everyday life, a chance to connect with other people, to interact with art, to party, to seek a higher spiritual connection, to get drunk, to consume illegal drugs, to run naked in the sunshine, to listen to music, to check an experience off a bucket list, or to ride on cars turned into pirate ships and giant sharks. There is no shortage of things to do at Burning Man. Everyone finds what they are looking for at Black Rock City. In the end, the playa provides.

A group of self-proclaimed sex-positive Burning Man participants formed the Bureau of Erotic Discourse (BED). Through this group, they share with those on the playa information about healthy sex and consent for the benefit of the community. In their published notes for a Clarity and Consent workshop in 2014, they shared some useful information for educators tasked with a similar challenge in working with college students. They suggested sex is a very good thing when it is mutually desired and values an individual's right to not have sex. Nothing matters more than communication and consent.

They (BED 2014) wrote,

Good sex needs to be negotiated between people. It doesn't happen magically like you might see on a TV commercial, where two strangers share a hot glance and everything works perfectly without any discussion. In real life, the couple races across the meadow only to have one of them sprain an ankle in a gopher hole and the other one have an allergic reaction to the wildflowers. If they had talked about it, they might have been happily making out at the movies. Good sex is not usually what you see in porn. Not only are the physical attributes misleading, but the attitudes, positions, and practices can be way outside the comfort zone for many people. If you both know your desires and they include some X-rated movies, then feel free. But don't assume that everyone wants to be a porn star.

(p. 2)

BED suggests that the heart of the problem is that verbal sexual communication is awkward. You make yourself vulnerable and there is a very real risk of rejection. To compound matters, there is very little education about how to talk about sex. We have all been conditioned by thousands of unrealistic images about sex, and it becomes difficult to suggest a more realistic or better alternative.

It would be easier, certainly, to simply rely on nonverbal communications. But there is a very real possibility of misinterpreting nonverbal cues. While a partner may be okay with sexual petting or fondling, this may be that person's limit, and penetration was never on the individual's list of options for the night. Others may see petting as foreplay to the main event. By relying on nonverbal communication around these expectations, the opportunities for miscommunication are quite large.

BED spells out several ideas about consent on page 6 of its manual that will hopefully seem very familiar to sex educators:

- Sexual consent is an agreement that requires people who are of legal age, are properly informed, are not under coercion, and are not incapacitated. The consent model holds that one person proposes an action and the other gives permission for it. Consent is the bare minimum required for legal and ethical sexual activity.
- Consent may be withdrawn at any time. If you have agreed to start something and find that it feels wrong to you, you have the right to stop it, and your partner has the obligation to honor your change of heart. Losing the ability to say "No" through intoxication also withdraws consent.
- BED emphasizes that consent is required, but we want more than mere consent. We believe in mutual enthusiasm! The best way to get to that enthusiasm is for the involved parties to talk about what they all really desire, and what they want to avoid. That requires open and honest communication and negotiation.

The BED Clarity and Consent document offers several exercises to improve verbal communication, explain the differences between sexual boundaries and desires, and learn how to set limits. This can be downloaded here: www.bureauoferoticdiscourse.org.

In addition to Burning Man, other communities that are on the fringe of sexuality offer guidance, expertise, and wisdom when it comes to sexual communication. The bondage and kink communities stress the importance of clear and direct communication, talking openly about various sexual desires, and respecting partners' boundaries. While there may be a temptation at first glance to see the kink and BDSM communities as heightened risk groups on a college campus, it is far more likely they are resources for healthy and sex-positive communication.

Recent media depictions of bondage and kink sex play in movies like *50 Shades of Grey* tend to be met with frustration and outright hostility by those involved in these groups in real life (Smith 2015). While the movie portrays sex acts similarly to real life, issues of consent and communication are portrayed as coercive at best, and as sexual assault at worst.

McGowan (2015) offers advice to those interested in kink and the BDSM lifestyle. This advice is useful for anyone as part of healthy sex. Suggestions include communicating, negotiating expectations beforehand, and establishing a check-in scale. It is important that both partners use a similar scale. McGowan shares thoughts from Miette Rouge, a kink-oriented contributor from San Francisco, on this scale.

Because people experience sensations differently from each other, Miette recommends establishing a check-in scale. She suggests having a standard one to 10 scale, with one representing "I don't feel much," five being something like "Very nice, I'm warmed up," seven as the sweet spot that's getting intense, and 10 being "Holy sh*t! Stop!"

(p. 4)

College educators would do well to look at the writing and wisdom shared in the Burning Man, kink, and BDSM communities as they look for ways to engage students in healthier, sex-positive communications.

FROM THE FRONT LINES

Permission Granted

I have been a university counseling center director for the more than a decade. During this time, I became a certified sex therapist through the American Association of Sex Educators, Counselors and Therapists (AASECT), the premier certifying body for sexual health professionals. AASECT (2013) "affirms as the fundamental value of sexuality as an inherent, essential, and beneficial dimension of being human." This statement proclaims a sex-positive view of human sexuality, which also espouses safe sex and the importance of consent.

As a director of counseling services and a sexual health professional, I've observed, with fascination, the politics around sex and sexuality education across the nation, both within the general discourse and within institutions of higher education (IHEs), in particular. It appears that the predominant view of sexuality is a negative one, where consequences and abstinence-only education are emphasized.

Within IHEs, it would appear they'd prefer that students not engage in sexual activity so as to ensure that no assaults occur and no negative publicity come upon the institution. Unfortunately, IHEs are seeing an influx of students from schools and states that provide only abstinence-only education. These programs rarely address sexual violence. They emphasize fear-based tactics to encourage students to put off sexual behaviors until marriage (as if marriage is a prophylactic to violence). More often, they describe premarital sex as shameful, immoral, and harmful. Ironically, these programs, according to the ACLU (n.d.), "depict boys as sexually uncontrollable and desiring sexual activity from any and all women." In addition, these programs portray women as provocateurs of sexuality. Could it be that many consent programs within IHEs unintentionally promote similar messages or worse? For example, IHE consent/Title IX programs may promote messages that women are fragile and require the protection of an authority. Might such programs reinforce sex-negative views about men and women that they must guard against their own sexuality?

Sex educators and sexual health professionals espouse a sex-positive view of sexuality:

> an attitude towards human sexuality that regards all consensual sexual activities as fundamentally healthy and pleasurable, and encourages sexual pleasure and experimentation. The sex-positive movement is a social and philosophical movement that advocates these attitudes. The sex-positive movement advocates sex education and safer sex as part of its campaign.
>
> (Gabosch 2014, p. 1)

How refreshing! Sex-positive approaches to consent acknowledge that sexual expression is a good thing. These approaches include messages about healthy, sex-positive communication throughout the sexual encounter as a means for increasing the pleasure of the sexual experience. For so many students, they see the "issue of consent" as an impediment to sexual spontaneity rather than an opportunity to mature into their sexual identity within a mutually satisfying and respectful relationship. For example, Yana Tallon-Hicks (2016) declares "consent makes you better at sex." Who doesn't want to be better at sex?!?

Again, if we hold the premise that we want to aid students in developing this "foundational value," we would promote consent as a tool to support sexual expression. Consent, as part of a component of sexual communication, enhances an experience in which individuals can make their preferences known for and against sexual requests. Consent also ensures that everyone is on board with what's about to ensue. Pleasure parties are way more fun when everyone wants to be there! Consent also helps people to remove the mind reading from the equation. Asking whether someone would find something pleasurable means that less time is spent doing something that no one enjoys!

The foregoing explores the implications of sex-negative education and policies that frame sex and sexuality within a fear-based mind-set in which the avoidance of consequences trumps the reality of what motivates people to have sex. Conversely, a sex-positive view of sex and sexuality reflects the reality of sex and sexuality: most people are motivated to have sex because it's fun and pleasurable. Moreover, the sex-positive view addresses the same concerns (i.e., promoting the use of consent strategies) while encouraging the use of consent as a tool for improving one's sexual experiences. Permission granted!

Thomas L. Murray, Jr., PhD, LMFT, LPCS
Director of Counseling Services
Student Affairs
University of North Carolina School of the Arts

TEACHING THE CORE IDEAS WELL

So, where does this leave educators, professors, counselors, and law enforcement when it comes to teaching consent to students? What are, if you will, the core ideas to be taught to our students, and how might we best ensure the seeds of these teachings find some fertile soil in their hearts and experiences? Think of the following list as a template to lay over your existing prevention efforts and consider areas where you may look to improve.

Prevention efforts, when done well, are always looking for ways to improve. Walt Disney introduced this concept at his parks with the process of "plussing." This meant looking at an existing ride or attraction to find ways to make it better. His Imagineers were never done with a project or ride. There was always the push to see how they could make it better.

1. **Think dialogue, not monologue.** We've seen the futility in programs where students are preached to or treated like

children unaware of the issues at hand. Successful consent education takes into account the type of audience and the developmental critical thinking and moral reasoning of those receiving the message. The days of Jon Houseman, the law professor in *The Paperchase*, are long gone. We cannot simply lecture students and expect them to come in as containers ready and excited to receive our information. The best consent programs engage the audience, answer questions, and work through scenarios the students can relate to on and off campus.

2. **Know your policy and code.** Each school has its own nuances to its policy and codes that are informed by state and federal law. It is helpful to provide these to students during programs by using handouts, links, and other resources. While we have made the point several times in this chapter that one should not mistake the language in the code for educational programing, it is essential to link educational programming discussions about consent with the student code of conduct.

3. **Use technology to help.** Whether it is the latest app summarizing consent-related issues or your favorite tea-based video on YouTube, technology has created a host of useful resources and talking points for educators looking to augment their programs and better engage their audiences. A word of caution, however: don't let the technology drive your content, but rather have the content highlighted by the technology. Given the ease of retrieving videos, slideshows, and handouts from the Web, there is a temptation to allow others' creative and entertaining work to supersede the point, helping students engage in open communication around their sexual activity and consent prior to finding themselves having to think fast on their feet in the middle of a situation.

4. **Good sex begins with good communication.** What are the qualities of a good relationship? So often, consent conversations become about what not to do, what not to ask, and what behaviors to avoid, rather than a discussion about what *to* do. As with Martin Seligman's (2006) work in positive psychology, we encourage consent educators to study and share the qualities of what makes up excellent, sex-positive communication, rather than focusing solely on the negative. How do people who have good, consensual sex go about making that happen? Talking to each other about their turn-ons, turnoffs, boundaries, and comfort zones. To quote Burning Man's Bureau of Erotic Discourse (BED), "Communication is the best lubrication."

5. **Thou shalt not . . .** Make sure to review those times where consent is just not possible. These include relationships with power differentials (e.g., therapists and clergy), as well interactions involving minors. The biggest teaching point here must be around incapacitation and alcohol. Help students understand the difference between intoxication and incapacity. Incapacity is an extreme form of intoxication, in which a person cannot make rational or reasonable decisions. Someone who is asleep or unconscious, has a mental/cognitive impairment, or has been seriously injured cannot consent. While there is not a specific blood alcohol level that correlates with incapacitation, it remains helpful to discuss the challenges that students may encounter when attempting to ascertain incapacity. For example, it may be easier to determine this if you know what someone has had to drink because the person has been with you all night. It may be more difficult to ascertain if someone was drinking apart from you. Similarly, if you are meeting someone for the first time, it is exponentially harder to know that person's tolerance for alcohol, what that person's baseline behavior is, and whether the individual can consent given a particular consumption level. In trainings, we suggest making the point that obtaining the low bar of "Well, I don't think I will get accused of rape" shouldn't be the goal. Imagine you are jumping from a plane with a parachute. Is checking the straps once sufficient, or does it make sense to check multiple times? Would it be safer if you were familiar with the parachute instead of just putting it on without further thought?

6. **Teach students about coercion and pressure.** Consent cannot be obtained freely if the person giving consent is under pressure or is being coerced. Repeatedly asking someone for sex until you hear a "yes" is not consent; it's coercion. The trouble here is that much of our popular media and culture extolls the virtues of pursuing someone, even to the point of absurdity, as a romantic virtue. We grew up watching Pepe Le Pew chase that poor cat in the Warner Bros. *Looney Tunes* and *Merrie Melodies* series. We watch Disney movies like *Beauty and the Beast*, where there is the unmistakable message, "I have taken your father and locked him in my dungeon until you consent to be with me." We see Lloyd Dobbler's pursuit of Diane Court in *Say Anything*, holding his boom box over his head playing, "In Your Eyes." Where is the line between romantic pursuit and coercion?

These scenarios present an excellent opportunity to raise this very question with the students you are teaching about consent. It becomes less important to have a clear line spelled out for them and more important to teach them how to think about this. In most cases, it is about how to think about their partners' agency and choice, how they feel being pursued. This issue frequently comes up for international students new to the United States' use of subtle social cues. Issues such as personal touch, flirting, dress, and expectations around buying meals and drinks create many opportunities for mis-understandings and miscommunications. In the end, good consent educators engage students around these issues prior to occurrence, allowing them to think more critically about their choices in a framework of harm reduction and risk management.

7. **Address the hookup culture.** In this fast-paced age, our students tend to move more quickly into sexually active relationships and hookups. While we refrain from making any judgments about the morality of this or opining about larger societal issues around this practice, there is the unmistakable problem of simply not knowing those with whom they are spending time. For students, we stress this point to encourage critical thinking and risk-management awareness. If you don't know the person you are with well, the risks of mis-reading that individual, doing something the person isn't necessarily okay with, and generally having less open communication are concerns. While these are all obstacles that can be overcome, when you add the lack of experiences of many younger students and start to mix in alcohol, most see why this becomes a perfect storm for miscommunication (and worse).

8. **Use scenario-based training.** One of the best training methods is the use of scenarios that allow students to consider situations (either read to them, acted out live at an orientation event, or viewed in a video). These role-plays allow students to think about the issues of alcohol consumption, consent, and sexual communication, while providing an opportunity to see how others approach similar challenges. Concrete examples help students consider various circumstances and the consequences of their choices while providing an opportunity to brainstorm solutions. A large-group setting makes it difficult to get genuine and direct answers, so we recommend the use of technology such as survey clickers or phone apps to gather information from the group. Alternatively, index cards

could be passed around the room before a talk as a way to gather questions that some students might be too shy to ask.

9. **Build from research and assess what you are doing.** It is important that education efforts be based on sound research to reduce the risk factors for gender-based sexual violence. Luckily, we have spent the heart of this book discussing the literature and research related to these risk factors. This should serve as a foundational framework for future educational programs and targeted prevention efforts. Additionally, it is important to spend some time assessing the effectiveness and efficacy of efforts made. This can be done more broadly through a climate survey (discussed in more detail in chapter 14) or through individual surveys given before or after events. The key to assessment is using the information gathered to directly improve future programming and educational efforts. It may be helpful to see assessment as being akin to the dashboard lights on a car. The utility of this process lies in the real-time feedback used to make decisions about future steps, in the same way a low gas gauge indicates the importance of stopping to fill up at the gas station.

10. **Embrace the prevention year, not the prevention month.** One temptation on college campuses is to view prevention efforts as a one and done thing. With so many competing needs, there is a temptation to complete one task (e.g., eating disorder awareness, a depression screening, or domestic violence walk) and then move onto the next thing. However, programs work best when they have the proper dosage of frequency. While it may be convenient for an institution to offer a consent-based orientation program during the week when new students arrive at school (and there are some valid reasons to do this, given the heightened risk for new students as they come to campus), this type of program should be seen as necessary, but not sufficient. Student may or may not digest the information during this program, and there are the larger concerns about whether a single program will change behavior and, if so, the length of time for which that behavioral change might last. The best approach to educational prevention efforts is to offer booster programs in various modalities (e.g., during orientation groups, with resident advisors, passive advertising campaigns in the dining hall and bathroom stalls, in first-year seminar classes) to reinforce the message.

FROM THE FRONT LINES

Get Permission, Not Just Penetration

"But she didn't say no!" said the young man, his voice raised beyond what was reasonable. His anger and desperation were apparent. This was the explosive reaction of a student discovering that the outcome of a campus hearing on sexual assault was not in his favor. His mother stared blankly and uncomprehendingly into space. He continued to rattle off in protest. "She didn't say no! She invited me over! We kissed!"

That is the end of a long story. The beginning is a familiar one. It starts like so many of the stories conduct officers hear: at a party, with drinks, and playing drinking games. It starts with flirtatious text messages and contact between two students through a variety of social media apps. Each person is flirting with more than one person that night, giving off the impression to those who will later be witnesses that the two in question were hoping to get lucky with somebody—anybody. The party extends beyond four hours, with extensive drinking happening the entire time. No one considers this to be strange—this is a normal Saturday night for this group, and a few of them go as far as to "boot and rally," meaning they force themselves to throw up when they feel sick so they can continue drinking. The witnesses will all have conflicting and fuzzy versions of the same party. The only clear distinction will be that each person's friends will support their version of the events.

The party slows; she gets escorted home by friends, and begins texting multiple guys. He, on the other hand, is pushing to come over to her place. Once she realizes that her options for having someone come over to her apartment have dwindled down to him, she focuses her attention. All of this will play out in the hearing through pages and pages of text messages. He asks her several times whether coming over "will be worth it." She either misses or ignores the questions. She tells him to hurry because she's getting sleepy. He responds that he has arrived.

Whatever happens next will be a question, one that those in charge of the conduct process will agonize over: Did it violate our code? As professionals and educators, we so often focus on that question, and on what happens after the two parties come together. But there is so much more that can be extrapolated from this all too common tableau. What education could have been made available to encourage the two individuals to have made different decisions that night? Why aren't we having frank conversations with our students about how good sex can be when you talk about it, and when you're sober? Why do we have to be afraid to encourage our students to have safe *and* good sex lives? Our challenge becomes that of making the ultimate goal that of consent, the pursuit of permission, not penetration.

Sex has become such a taboo subject. We have done ourselves and our students a disservice by limiting the conversation to "Be safe, get consent." The core ideas listed earlier encourage education of a much higher and more proactive caliber: "Be safe, get enthusiastic consent so that both of you are having a great time, and if you suspect the other person has had too much to drink, then it won't be good or safe for either of you." This approach encourages students to talk about sex with their partners, not drink to oblivion to ignore that they are violating repressive upbringings, or to just get over the fear of saying "Hello."

We cannot expect our students to talk to each other about sex if we will not talk to them. Open the conversation, and lead by example. Showing that it is okay to speak up and speak out may help our students know what to say when they need words the most: whether it is "No," or "Are you okay with this?" Those may be some of the most important words of all. In this way, we're not only helping our students become better equipped for adult life, but also helping them avoid conduct violations and even criminal acts that could derail their academic careers and, indeed, their entire lives.

Miranda Perry, MS
Associate Director of the Office of Student Conduct and Conflict Resolution
Northeastern University, +5 for dragon fire

DISCUSSION QUESTIONS

1. What are some of the barriers you have seen on campus to good consent conversations? How can these be addressed?

2. What religious, cultural, or political barriers might exist on your campus when talking about having sex-positive talks? What departments or groups on campus could contribute to these ideas?

3. How does alcohol complicate consent? Some teach a zero-tolerance policy when it comes to consent and alcohol (e.g., no consent if you have been drinking). What are some of the problems with this kind of policy?

4. Discuss some key factors you believe that are essential in healthy relationships. How do you go about teaching these ideas to college students based on the principles and theories discussed in chapter 3? Address the importance of developing programming that is not a "one and done" approach.

5. The authors make the point that teaching good consent and healthy relationships is a key ingredient in the recipe to reduce sexual assault on campus. What other ingredients would you add here?

Chapter 17

Campus Climate

A nation that destroys its soils destroys itself.
—Franklin D. Roosevelt

KEY TAKE-AWAYS

1. Monitoring the climate of a college or university requires more than administering a survey.

2. To remedy aspects of campus climate that support gender-based harassment and discrimination, an institution may have to challenge long-standing traditions.

3. Campus climate efforts require strategic planning and should be integrated with other climate initiatives on a campus.

The climate of a college or university is much like the soil that surrounds the roots of a tree. It is the environment where students grow and develop. It supports or hinders the emergence of new or repeated attitudes and behaviors. When the climates of our colleges and universities are cultivated with the objectification of women and misogynistic ideologies, sexual harassment breeds sexual violence and gender-based discrimination. Just as a tree's growing environment impacts how it matures and forms, campus climates can support or discourage the emergence of incidents of sexual violence.

Sexual violence is not only about a series of individual behaviors. It is also about a system that supports and even nurtures those behaviors. Campus climate efforts look for opportunities within the institution to address trends and issues of concern. So often, when we think about prevention efforts, our minds first think of what program will we implement. True prevention exists at multiple levels and scales across the institution via a diverse array of strategies, initiatives, and programs. Campus climate efforts are the constant environmental scan of the college or university for opportunities to engage directly to prevent future concerns.

DEFINING CLIMATE

In Chapter 1, we provided a brief synopsis of Title IX and the requirements for colleges and universities. Office of Civil Rights guidance and case law indicate that a school violates Title IX if it has notice of a sexually hostile environment and fails to take immediate and effective corrective action. Monitoring a school's campus climate is ultimately a form of compliance with Title IX. Several recent resolution agreements between institutions and the Office of Civil Rights related to Title IX violations have included agreements for the school related to campus climate requiring that institutions seek input from campus constituents to ensure the ongoing monitoring of the environment for concerns through surveys, polls, and forums. *The First Report of the White House Task Force to Protect Students From Sexual Assault* includes "1st action step: Identify the problem: Campus climate surveys. We urge schools to show they're serious about the problem by conducting the survey next year" (2014).

WHAT DO WE MEAN BY CAMPUS CLIMATE?

Campus climate has long been acknowledged as a factor in student retention and student success. When describing campus climate and the influence of the institutional environment on students, Prof. Leonard L. Baird wrote in *Reworking the Student Departure Puzzle* that "students' personal interpretations of their institutions' opportunities and challenges shape their decisions and behaviors" (2000, p. 65). Each decision is influenced by social norms and expectations, campus support systems, perceptions of accountability systems, institutional marketing, messages about campus resources, and the values of the campus. Climate is also perceived through students' individual lens based on their backgrounds and experiences.

A student who attends new student orientation and hears orientation leaders talking about how difficult it can be as a woman in the engineering program is influenced by those perceptions and may choose not to enroll in engineering, further decreasing the numbers of women in the field. The victim of sexual assault who searches online for how to report and get help from the campus only to find information about how she should watch her drinking and not go

243

out alone will probably not search further for reporting options and resources. The editorial in the student newspaper about the fraternity that was not held accountable for a party that resulted in several student injuries conveys to the campus that accountability systems will not remedy organizational concerns. Each of these examples could indicate a climate concern related to gender-based discrimination that would need to be addressed.

George Kuh and Elizabeth Whitt (1988) define institutional cultures as "persistent patterns of norms, values, practices, beliefs, and assumptions that shape the behavior of individuals and groups in a college or university and provide a frame of reference within which to interpret the meaning of events and actions on and off the campus" (p. iv). They go on to call it "the invisible tapestry that weaves together parts of an organization." The role of these dominant paradigms of thinking and knowing in an organization cannot be overlooked when creating strategies around the prevention of sexual violence in the campus community, particularly when you address group attitudes and behaviors.

Closed communities will often have their own distinctive culture or organizational climate because of their isolated and continuous interactions with one another. The lack of diverse interactions means they are less likely to take into account different perspectives. That lack of diversity also means a lack of conflict around ideas, so there is no challenge to the individual or group and that lack of challenge results in a lack of learning and development. The ethical development process begins with those times of disagreement and the opportunity to think about our choices. When thinking about culture and climate, the examination should include physical and visible signs of culture as well as activities, stories, rituals, terminology, and traditions.

WHAT ABOUT CAMPUS TRADITIONS?

Let's face it, colleges and universities love to espouse the history and tradition of their institutions. We encourage school spirit by asking alumni and students to wear the school colors and learn school songs. Virtually every campus has lore around a statue on campus that you rub for good luck or an administrator who exemplifies the founding spirit of the school. Campus activities are hosted annually to provide rites of passage and markers of completion for students. We want students to connect in multiple ways to our institutions because they are more likely to be retained and become supportive alumni. But what happens when our institutional histories and traditions are ripe with some of the same risk factors for sexual violence identified here?

The idea is that these subtle, and often not so subtle, messages and rituals represent an institutional approval for sexism and gender-based harassment. Sometimes it might show up in a traditional song, chant, or cheer. At the University of Virginia in 2014, the University Glee Club decided to retire a traditional song titled "Rugby Road" that contained the lyrics: "All you girls never let a Cavalier an inch above your knee / He'll take you to his fraternity house and fill you full of beer / And soon you'll be the mother of a bastard Cavalier!" (Hainbach 2014).

Student organizations and activities may also characterize negative attitudes around the roles of women and the treatment of others based on gender. Hazing traditions and new member rituals may include requirements related to sex or interactions with women. Stanford University's Full Moon on the Quad is an annual campus activity where freshman students are kissed at midnight by senior students. The activity has recently focused on a discussion of consent and receiving permission before kissing another student, but in the midst of that revelry, consent messages get mixed.

Sometimes organizations that were founded as single-sex organizations to support an aspect of campus involvement have not evolved their membership practices for inclusion. At Texas Tech University, an all-male organization is still the prominent mechanism for students to be involved in supporting men's athletic events. While these examples may appear isolated, they can serve to disempower women and send institutional messages that the campus is not inclusive of all students regardless of background and that the power belongs disproportionately to one group or another.

CAMPUS CLIMATE SURVEYS

The importance of climate efforts to better understand the problems on a college campus was reinvigorated with the release of recommendations in *Not Alone: The First Report of the White House Task Force to Protect Students From Sexual Assault* (2014), but campus climate monitoring is not a new idea, especially the idea of monitoring climates with regularly occurring campus climate surveys of students, faculty, and staff. Campus climate surveys are helpful because they provide transparency to the campus community about Title IX efforts and ways community members can help inform the system of prevention and response on a campus.

Climate surveys are part of a comprehensive prevention strategy that includes community-level or environmental strategies. Climate surveys inform a campus's educational challenges and opportunities and help to demonstrate change over a period of time in the community. This type of effort can also be a remedy when a hostile environment is found to exist or concerns are raised. Climate surveys can also help inform other areas of concern, such as alcohol and drug use, civility, violence prevention, diversity, and the perception of numerous campus resources and services.

Historically, campus climate surveys and similar efforts have been used to examine the experiences of marginalized communities in order to identify patterns of treatment and exclusion that may impact their opportunity to succeed. "It is important to conduct climate surveys not merely in reaction to challenging events, but also as part of proactive, ongoing assessments of the environment experienced by students and those who work at the institution" (Hurtado and Halualani 2014, p. 8). Climate surveys are one indicator to the institution that the topic of the survey—in this case, gender-based discrimination—is one of importance to campus leaders.

Climate surveys can assess the following:

- Community awareness, satisfaction, and perception of policies, procedures, resources, and campaigns
- Experiences of community members and reporting rates related to violence and other sexual misconduct
- Attitudes of community members related to sex, alcohol, and violence
- Climate concerns and impressions in specific departments, groups, and the campus community
- Opinions of the campus community on prevention efforts and their opportunities for involvement
- Effectiveness of efforts to address sexual violence on the campus
- Trends of incidents and changes in patterns of occurrence over time
- Other issues related to violence, safety, and wellness

When considering a campus climate survey, there are a number of institutional choices that should be made well in advance of survey administration in order to ensure a smooth implementation. So often, institutions run into obstacles that damage the credibility of climate survey results because of a lack of planning around survey implementation. Climate survey planning should address the following questions:

1. **What is the purpose or goal of the survey?** Some surveys will look broadly at insights around campus sexual violence, health and wellness, or diversity. Others will look more specifically at student attitudes related to rape myths or student behaviors along the continuum of sexual violence. Always be thinking about what data is needed at completion and how the data will be used.
2. **Who will be surveyed?** Surveys can be designed for students, faculty, and staff, but it can also be helpful to consider a more targeted effort to focus on specific departments, organizations, or subpopulations. Special population surveys for athletes or fraternities and sororities can also be considered.
3. **How will the survey be administered?** The most common administration options are pen/paper or online. If a campus has access to administer surveys in a diverse array of classrooms, paper options can result in a better response rate to the survey. Online surveys, on the other hand, can give the administrator more control over the survey administration and multiple opportunities to solicit responses.
4. **When and how often will the survey be administered?** Survey fatigue is real. Climate surveys should be scheduled with consideration of other campus survey efforts. Special population groups can help to determine the appropriate time frame for surveys. For example, fraternity and sorority life staff would tell you not to solicit online survey responses during a busy homecoming week for students, or faculty senate would indicate that surveys would not be well received during the summer, when many faculty are not on campus.
5. **Who will design the survey? Will the design occur in-house or will a third-party vendor be utilized?** There are a number of tools and resources available to assist institutions with survey design. The White House Task Force (2014) released a template survey design to assist institutions, and a number of associations and vendors have since designed other options (see list ahead under the section "Examples of Campus Climate Surveys"). Some campuses may have access to faculty well versed in research design with an interest in sexual violence who can also assist. The survey design process is often one of the more difficult steps as it involves negotiating answers to all of the questions in this list with a diverse array of stakeholders. Complications related to timing, bias, language selection,

limitation of self-report data, ethical standards, institutional review board approvals, and survey fatigue are likely to come up as areas of discussion in this process.

6. **What questions will be included in the survey?** Questions for consideration should assess student knowledge of campus resources related to sexual assault; perceptions of helpfulness and the accessibility of campus resources related to sexual assault; student experiences of behaviors that constitute sexual misconduct; and attitudes and behaviors related to sex. There should also be a discussion of how to handle the possibility that the survey triggers additional community member trauma and how to approach administration in a way that utilizes a trigger warning or cautionary note in the materials.

7. **What will the question format be? What response categories will be included?** The survey needs to reflect the experiences of a variety of groups on campus, even when numbers are small. Even with the difficulties of small sample sizes, excluding those groups can continue to underrepresent related problems (Hurtado and Halualani 2014).

8. **How will a representative sample be achieved?** In a perfect survey world, every survey administration would result in a high response rate from a sample that represents the diversity of the campus, but it is more likely that choices will have to be made about balancing the ease of administration, access to survey responses, and the quality of the sample. Criticism comes quickly when survey data is being used to encourage institutional change related to areas of concern, so survey planners should be ready to defend their choices related to survey design and sampling.

9. **Will incentives be offered to increase responses?** The survey design process should also consider if incentives should be offered in an effort to increase response rates. Just a cautionary note that while incentives might gain attention for your survey administration, they can also result in insincere responses just because the person wanted a free t-shirt or gift certificate.

10. **Who are the stakeholders related to a campus climate survey?** This question should really be one of the first that planners consider. It is important to engage with those areas at your institution with an interest in the climate survey administration and results. This builds support for the climate survey efforts and will help with the institutionalization of any final recommendations.

11. **How will the survey data be analyzed?** One of the more common failures of a climate survey effort is the one where the

results arrive in a spreadsheet, but no one ever takes the time to review and dissect the responses. Survey data is not meaningful without this critical step.

12. **How will results be disseminated?** The summary and organization of results into small, easy-to-understand components alongside a brief set of recommendations and future action items will help to ensure that the work related to campus climate continues well beyond the survey administration.

One other cautionary topic to discuss in advance is what information will be made publicly available related to survey results and what information will remain confidential. Will aggregate data be provided, or campus- or unit-specific data? It is common to be fearful about public and media response to negative climate survey information. Climate surveys tell stories, and more often than not, they are not flattering stories. To prepare for the results of a campus climate survey, teams should discuss in advance what the outcomes may be and how to prepare administrators for negative results. Results should always be shared with narratives about areas of improvement that have already occurred and future action items with timelines. The stakeholders engaged early in the process should be ready to share information about the importance of transparency with climate surveys and that a campus's willingness to consider carefully opportunities for improvement is a symbol of that campus's commitment to student success.

13. **How will the campus respond to concerns identified by the survey? How will improvement plans be designed and implemented?**

One of the worst things that can happen is to perform a climate survey but do nothing with the results. There should be a plan in place for how to initiate new strategies to address concerns identified in the survey. The results will guide the need for other climate assessment mechanisms, such as targeted focus groups on the reporting website or interviews with those involved in reporting incidents. There should also be a plan for what elements will be tracked longitudinally, from survey administration to survey administration.

EXAMPLES OF CAMPUS CLIMATE SURVEYS

- AAU Campus Climate Survey on Sexual Assault & Sexual Misconduct

- Association of Title IX Administrators (ATIXA) Gender-Based Violence Student Climate Survey
- EverFi Climate Survey
- #iSPEAK: Rutgers Campus Climate Survey pilot with the White House Task Force
- White House Task Force Climate Survey Toolkit and Example Survey
- MIT Community Attitudes on Sexual Assault
- Skyfactor Campus Climate, Safety, and Sexual Assault Assessment

OTHER CLIMATE MECHANISMS

There are several methods to consider when initiating campus climate efforts beyond the administration of a climate survey. While climate surveys are valuable, they are only one part of a comprehensive plan to address violence and discrimination on campus. Institutions should consider diversifying assessment strategies beyond surveys. No other campus programming or prevention effort relies solely on one method to measure effectiveness and efficacy.

- Supplementing survey data with focus groups, case studies, and interviews can address limitations of quantitative, survey-based research. Qualitative methodologies add deep and rich narratives to survey data, allowing students to dive deeper into their responses and provide more specific, complex information.
- Seek help from key campus partners who are skilled in related campus climate efforts. Take cues from other campus initiatives, recognizing that climate research has long been a strategy related to institutional diversity efforts. Chief diversity officers are typically well versed in understanding the influence of climate on underrepresented populations. Institutional research units are also engaged in such research. By reaching out to those units for historical information on institutional climate studies and opportunities for collaboration, these departments can help articulate an overall design and strategy for initiatives.
- Consider what campus data might exist that could help in your assessment efforts. For example, institutions that use online educational products may also receive data about their student populations' attitudes and behaviors related to sexual assault and alcohol. Surveys such as the CIRP Freshman Survey or the American College Health

Association/National College Health Association Survey can provide good student profile information to link to efforts. Faculty in various departments often have research agendas that are related to understanding gender, sex, communication, or violence on the campus as well. In addition, housing, Greek life, and athletics often administer their own surveys that may have individual questions that cross over with climate initiatives.

- Become involved in initiatives that track student outcomes. By using existing systems to track the retention, academic performance, and other success indicators of those involved in Title IX processes, it's possible to identify patterns and trends related to these students and shine a light on how well the school is remedying issues of violence, harassment, and discrimination to help students remain enrolled and succeed.

- Expand opportunities for reporting and tracking trends. Electronic databases for tracking and processing reports of sexual assault, harassment, stalking, and domestic/dating violence make it easier to look for and recognize trends in reporting. Doing that allows campuses to provide targeted prevention and educational efforts. Climate efforts should educate and guide those reporting incidents while also encouraging reporting of more general concerns. Offering multiple options for reporting, such as online forms and even old-school suggestion boxes, allows individuals to report in ways in which they are comfortable and encourages them to identify unspoken climate concerns that may be known in the campus community.

Last, select a method that is sustainable for the long-term. Isolated climate efforts are less effective because they are unable to assess for areas of improvements or patterns of concern.

An overall improvement in climate can manifest unevenly at the local scale, with microbursts of volatile activity. Just as falling atmospheric pressure suggests the likelihood of stormy weather, decreased pressure affecting the atmosphere for diversity in higher educator may not occur without significant storms.

(Campbell 2014, p. 4)

Climate research is best when it occurs in a collaborative and sustainable manner that appreciates the unique diversity of the institution and combines a variety of perspectives over time.

FROM THE FRONT LINES

Climate Surveys Provide Insight and Guide Institutional Action

There is a growing need for data about the scope and nature of campus sexual misconduct. Over the last few years, campus climate surveys have emerged as a key tool that colleges and universities can use to gather data, measure improvements, and design effective strategies that reduce instances of sexual misconduct over time.

Climate surveys provide an immediate snapshot of students' experiences, attitudes, behaviors, and perceptions about sexual misconduct. Long-standing research shows that students who experience sexual misconduct are unlikely to report their experiences to campus authorities or to law enforcement, making it difficult to know the actual prevalence of sexual misconduct. Climate surveys provide another forum for students to share their experiences, allowing the university to better understand the reality of the issue on campus and tailor future prevention and response strategies.

Moreover, conducting a climate survey signals to the campus community that there is an institutional commitment to understand and address the issue. In this way, climate surveys can serve as an educational tool to raise awareness and build trust in the institution's actions. The survey effort itself can educate students, faculty, and staff about the issue, reporting options, and campus and community resources.

Some institutions conduct advertising campaigns about their survey initiative, inviting students to participate and raising awareness about the issue on campus. Other institutions use the data release as an educational opportunity, encouraging students who have experienced some form of sexual misconduct to come forward and share their experiences and seek support and resources. For example, universities are including information about their survey's findings on their central webpage for sexual misconduct. This allows visitors to review the data alongside information about reporting options, resources, and planned campus action to address the problem.

When regularly administered and combined with other data sources, climate surveys can mark long-term changes in campus climate. Year-over-year findings can be used to measure progress on strategic goals and initiatives, such as reporting rates among students, increased knowledge and action as a bystander, and increased awareness of campus and community resources like counseling and advocacy services. For example, some institutions are comparing the number of formal reports with incidence data from climate surveys to measure changing reporting rates among students.

Finally, climate survey data can be used to drive decision making on campus. Survey findings can inform a campus action plan to address sexual misconduct, directing future investments of staff members and resources. For example, one institution used climate survey data to better target education and resources to specific student populations. They discovered from their climate survey data that incoming sophomores were experiencing high rates of sexual misconduct. To help curb this trend, the institution designed new prevention interventions that reach these students with education and resources prior to the start of their sophomore year.

Findings can also identify specific strengths and opportunities for improvement in institutional policies, awareness and education efforts, prevention programming, and campus resources. Some institutions are revisiting their institutional policy with climate survey data in mind to ensure that it reflects the breadth of students' experiences with campus sexual misconduct. Others are using data to craft targeted awareness messages for students. For example, one institution redesigned its awareness campaign about campus resources to address students' top barriers to reporting and accessing services. Some institutions are also updating prevention programming to take into account new, campus-specific data that clarifies perceptions and realities of campus bystander behaviors, like when students choose to intervene in a potentially risky situation or how likely students are to confront a friend about their behavior.

Reducing sexual misconduct on campus will continue to be an enduring challenge for colleges and universities. Without knowing the size and shape of the problem, institutions can't design solutions that work. Climate surveys illuminate the extent and effects of students' experiences, attitudes, behaviors, and perceptions and provide the information necessary to understand the scope and nature of the issue, measure institutional progress, and design effective prevention strategies. Colleges and universities are making great strides forward. In the near future, institutions will be able to compare their own climate survey data with other institutions and national research on the subject to identify evidence-based best practices. The rapid growth in climate survey use shows that institutions are learning how data is a powerful tool that can help safeguard students and reduce campus sexual misconduct.

Liz Brown, Research Consultant, EAB

Jane Alexander, Research Consultant, EAB

DISCUSSION QUESTIONS

1. What information currently exists on your campus related to the climate for gender-based harassment and discrimination? Who else on campus is collecting related information? Where are the gaps in information? What questions do you have about the campus community's perceptions, experiences, and awareness?

2. What do you anecdotally know about climate concerns on your campus? Are there departments, units, organizations, or settings that raise concerns and need to be evaluated further?

3. What do the reports of sexual violence on the campus indicate? Are there certain locations or time periods of concern? Where are reports most likely to be made? Are the reports resulting in formal conduct proceedings? Do sanctions appear consistent and appropriate?

4. Besides a climate survey, what other opportunities exist to collect climate information on the campus?

5. How would climate information be used on the campus? What are creative ways to analyze, share, and disseminate the information?

Chapter 18

Future Directions

> I took a walk in the woods and came out taller than the trees.
> —*Henry David Thoreau*

We have led you through the forest and come out the other side. This book describes for you and your campus community the primary root factors of sexual violence and gives you a framework for reducing the risk on your campus. If it feels like the root factors overlap, it is because they do. Just like roots on trees, these factors are interconnected and often difficult to untangle or distinguish. More so, they feed upon one another and grow together. With this, the work is just beginning. As a field we must continue to unearth the problematic attitudes and behaviors present in our communities in order to prevent sexual violence. This chapter shares with you our ideas about what the future holds and how to begin applying the risk factors in your work.

First, consider the various risk-reduction tips shared throughout the book and ways to incorporate the 12 root factors of sexual violence:

- Begin with strategic prevention planning (chapter 3)
- Teach concepts of nonobjectification (chapter 4)
- Link to moral development efforts (chapter 4)
- Incorporate sex education and sexual health (chapter 5)
- Design and utilize consistent sanctioning models (chapter 5)
- Integrate bystander intervention strategies (chapter 6)
- Use safety planning (chapter 6)
- Define healthy masculinity (chapter 7)
- Establish consistent organization accountability structures (chapter 7)
- Address microaggressions (chapter 7)
- Cultivate healthy relationships (chapter 8)

- Build confidence and self-esteem (chapter 8)
- Develop comprehensive and sound policies (chapter 9)
- Incorporate alcohol and drug prevention efforts (chapter 9)
- Monitor social event planning (chapter 9)
- Train faculty and staff to support reporting and victims (chapter 9)
- Encourage critical thinking and problem identification (chapter 10)
- Utilize values clarification with organizations (chapter 10)
- Identify baseline behaviors and attitudes early (chapter 11)
- Teach otherness and empathy (chapter 12)
- Consider strategies for rehabilitation (chapter 12)
- Use motivational interviewing strategies (chapter 13)
- Employ adult mentors and advisors (chapter 13)
- Employ change theory (chapter 14)
- Promote healthy college transitions (chapter 15)
- Train hearing officers and boards (chapter 15)
- Educate about consent (chapter 16)
- Monitor campus climates (chapter 17)

With college staff and faculty more aware of the 12 risk factors, there is the opportunity for early prevention education, more effective intervention, and more informed sanctioning and educational events for those groups or individuals involved in an assault. Next steps would involve creating a prevention curriculum based on two separate but important tasks. The first is increasing awareness and identification of these risk factors on campus. This would require the creation of an awareness education campaign to identify the risk factors in both individuals and groups. This approach would be most effective if it combined both an in-person training to student activity leaders, sports captains, fraternity and sorority governing councils, resident advisors, and orientation staff and a passive advertising campaign through printed materials and social media.

The second is educational effort related to these risk factors targeted to the populations of at-risk groups, such as fraternities and athletics teams and those who have been involved in Title IX–related incidents. In research-based evaluations of sexual violence prevention, findings indicate that, while universal interventions are helpful, targeted interventions for populations most at risk are critical (Morrison et al. 2004). Ahead we have identified some of the strategies that we believe are critical to prevention efforts moving forward as well as being relevant to the integration of the 12 risk factors for sexual violence.

EDUCATE AND ENGAGE STUDENTS IN PREVENTION

Prevention efforts are most effective (and some would argue only effective) with the buy-in, support, and involvement of students in the planning and implementation of initiatives. Students are able to inform program planners about how to engage other students through marketing and promotions, what language is appropriate, and what timing and locations should be selected for activities. The opportunities for students to be involved in prevention planning and initiatives will not only create a better program but also provide a beneficial learning opportunity for the students. Student participation in program planning creates a learning environment outside the classroom where students can be introduced to concepts in this book and apply them in different ways.

It is as critical to educate nonperpetrator groups as it is to rehabilitate those who are offenders. We are all exposed to the same messages and attitudes identified throughout the 12 factors. If victims do not recognize that what happened to them is problematic, they are less likely to report and perpetrators are less likely to be held accountable for behaviors. Peer education efforts have been identified as a valuable dissemination message for prevention concepts, but even those students willing and poised to be peer educators need the foundational knowledge of the root factors. Program quality will be enhanced by providing opportunities for peer educators to discuss their experiences and perceptions before being placed in front of an audience. Any trainers or facilitators can be unaware of their own biases and problematic perceptions and that can impact the entire prevention effort.

This learning must translate to the leaders in student organizations and campus ambassadors. Our treatment and support of students reporting sexual violence are a central part of prevention because the response can either reinforce rape myths and concepts that decrease reporting or provide support and assistance to the student impacted by trauma. There have also been a number of studies on how to specifically educate men and involve men in these issues. One of the aspects of the 12 factors is they can be adapted for an all-male, all-female, or coed audience. Just as with any specific population of students, our prevention efforts must consider the unique learning requirements of each group, how they are motivated, and where they are likely to be most involved. Future efforts could consider each factor and how they intersect with the various student populations.

Some student groups are also poised for activism related to sexual violence, victim's rights, and against systems that support gender discrimination. It is important to find ways to engage with these organizations and understand what goals and priorities they have. Campus administrators can easily misstep with activist groups because of adversarial relationships or concern about neutrality related to controversial efforts, but it is quite possible to partner with these organizations on common goals and priorities, such as prevention work. I had an opportunity recently to listen to a panel of college student activists. It is tough work that they do, and there are very few formal systems and resources to support their efforts. By finding ways to identify common projects, it supports student leadership and activism on the campus as well as involves students in prevention strategies.

With each of the suggested areas in this chapter, the risk factors can be integrated into the efforts. The risk factors can be effective in appealing to student involvement on a number of levels. They provide clear examples of behaviors on the sexual violence continuum beyond nonconsensual sexual intercourse, making it likely that students can relate to one or more of the factors, having experienced or observed them. It also provides an engaging way to think about sexual violence prevention in a student-led training session on the Dirty Dozen (DD-12) (Van Brunt et al. 2015), highlighting both individual and group behaviors with attention-grabbing yet realistic scenarios.

DEVELOP BYSTANDER INTERVENTION EFFORTS

VAWA identifies bystander intervention as "safe and positive options that may be carried out by an individual or individuals to prevent harm or intervene when there is a risk of dating violence, domestic violence, sexual assault, or stalking." The 12 risk factors can be particularly effective when paired with bystander intervention. Some bystander initiatives jump straight to skills training on how to intervene in problematic situations and a call to action. This will not work. Bystander intervention strategies should be specifically tailored for each audience and each context and address for each setting the obstacles to intervention.

Bystander intervention trainings must first include efforts to help students have an awareness for and ability to identify problematic behavior and believe it will result in harm. Gentry McCreary writes on this topic regularly (2015), and he indicates that it becomes pertinent to help students see the harm caused by behaviors in order for them to see them as emergencies that are worthy of intervention. For more of Dr. McCreary's thoughts on the topic, he joins us in an afterword following this chapter to give additional thoughts on group behaviors.

Consider for a moment the group examples throughout the book. Why are unhealthy behaviors so problematic in the group setting? Because of the pressure to conform and the perception that is often held by members of the group about what is the established social norm in the organization. Organization members believe that their fellow members think that a committed relationship with a woman is uncool and that in order to be more accepted, they need to have similar attitudes and behaviors about women. Bystander intervention cannot work without addressing these specific concerns and creating options for intervention that take conformity and social norms into account.

By recognizing the 12 factors as red flag indicators for sexual violence and understanding the influence of groups on conforming to false norms, bystanders are more likely to recognize problems and utilize the skills developed to intervene and prevent sexual violence.

TEACH OTHERNESS AND EMPATHY

The 12 factors can also be paired with initiatives to teach community members otherness and empathy. Lack of empathy is outlined in chapter 12 as a root factor; clearly, teaching the concept must be embedded in prevention efforts. In fact, empathy skills are related to all of the other concepts listed in this chapter impacting a student's willingness to be engaged in prevention efforts, influencing the recognition of microaggressions, and affecting the ability to train bystander intervention effectively because it impacts the individual's perspective of problematic behavior and the harm caused.

Developing empathy related to sexual violence means giving a face to the often faceless victim. Strategies cannot just focus on feeling bad for the victim who is sexually violated, but they should include information to combat rape myths and to illustrate the impact of trauma. Here are some of the common rape myths from the Illinois Rape Myth Acceptance Scale:

- *If a woman is raped while she is drunk, she is at least somewhat responsible for letting things get out of control.*
- *Many so-called rape victims are actually women who had sex and "changed their minds" afterwards.*
- *Although most women wouldn't admit it, they generally find being physically forced into sex a real "turn-on."*
- *A rape probably didn't happen if the woman has no bruises or marks.*
- *Being raped isn't as bad as being mugged and beaten.*

These are just a few common rape myths. Skill development related to empathy, just like bystander intervention, should be context-specific and should address rape myths.

In a similar manner, strategies related to empathy development and sexual violence need to include information on the impact of trauma on victims in order to help participants understand what actions and behaviors they might observe. If these elements are not addressed and misperceptions of how victims should behave remain prominent, then empathy building is less likely to be effective because of how victimization is recognized is skewed. Addressing concepts related to the diverse emotional responses that victims may display, the reluctance to report and delays in reporting, the erratic memory gaps, and the behaviors that may be displayed can help confirm what may be observed in the future.

Training faculty, staff, administrators, and even alumni (especially those working with student organizations or interacting regularly in campus environments) is important in order to reinforce positive behaviors and attitudes about sexual violence. If students observe a faculty member being insensitive to a victim or if an administrator makes an objectifying comment, these behaviors are magnified by the student, who is already questioning what is being taught. If the alumni advisor of a student organization does not believe that an organization hosting a party with an objectifying theme is a form of sexual harassment, then the students in that organization will certainly not take educational or accountability efforts seriously.

ADDRESS MICROAGGRESSIONS

The central challenge in addressing microaggression is found in the understanding that these slights are often unintentional. This may involve a student who sees his stalking behavior as positive attention he is offering an object of his affection or sexist catcalling as a way to give positive compliments to a woman who is well dressed. This creates the dual problems of a blind spot for the person unaware that the comment or action is offensive to the person receiving it and the common reaction of defensiveness when confronted about the behavior ("Well, that certainly wasn't what I meant. Why do they have to be so sensitive?")

Sue (2010) used the images of thumbtacks and raindrops on his books to illustrate the power of these small, unintentional, everyday microaggressions and to help the reader connect to the larger concept of how the volume and continual nature of these experiences are cumulative for the individual experiencing them. In other words, what matters is not only what an individual just experienced from you but also what the individual had already experienced on the same day or within a short period. The cumulative effect of microaggressions is considerable over time.

Educational programs should discuss the unintentional impact of rape jokes, objectification of individuals, and slurs against someone's race, gender, or sexual orientation. A key facet of this training should be the impact of such statements separate from the intent. It is not enough that those making the jokes did not mean to cause harm with their comments. Few men see themselves as potential rapists or perpetrators (Scheel et al. 2001), and so the challenge of this programming is to increase empathy and understanding that even unintended jokes or comments can lead to harm.

FROM THE FRONT LINES

Yo Mama So Ugly: Cultural Perspectives on the DD-12

The 12 risk factors for sexual violence on college campuses, otherwise known as the dirty dozen or DD-12, are valuable indicators that may assist in identifying those prone to violent behavior before they can inflict physical harm. While it is important to recognize warning signals, to intercede when they are noticed, and to use information like this as a basis for developing effective education and intervention programming, it is also important to place the DD-12 in a variety of cultural contexts. Doing so enables us to consider how different populations may be impacted by mainstream cultural shifts and how we might develop educational programming that provides group-specific messages that are often more effective than the "one size fits all" approaches for changing behaviors.

A specific example of how certain aspects of the DD-12 may be viewed as appropriate rather than as violence-predicting behaviors can be seen through the lens of African American culture. One hallmark of American black culture, particularly among males, is the verbal banter known as playing the dozens or simply "the dozens," which was formally recognized in the 1920s and popularized through the writings of Harlem Renaissance literary figures, such as Zora Neale Hurston and Richard Wright. Most recognizable today as "yo mama" jokes, the dozens continues to provide an arena for demonstrating quick thinking and verbal prowess.

While forms of verbal sparring have been traced back to Africa and have appeared on other continents in various forms, there is a recognizably African American element to the dozens, which may have developed as an outlet for black men unable to display their authority or ability under slavery and racial oppression. The often misogynistic nature of the dozens clearly evokes factors 1 and 4 of the DD-12: objectification and deperson-alization, and misogynistic ideology. This aspect of the dozens, particularly cracks on yo mama, may speak to a verbal revolt against African American matriarchal culture in which absent father figures loom as a specter of his-torical objectification and depersonalization of black bodies and families.

Grounded in a history of violent oppression, the dozens is one example of a cultural aspect that may be considered out of the "norm" of main-stream American culture, even if emulated by white suburban "thug" wannabes. The dozens positions black men as part of the problem with a misogynistic society that is shifting as women and their allies demand and receive greater equity.

When viewed through this culturally specific perspective, one can see how aspects of the DD-12 get attributed to black men, particularly ath-letes and especially football players. (And if we have any doubt that football teams are being "trained" for predation, the Comedy Central video "Inside Amy Schumer: Football Town Nights" presents a hilari-ous correlation between rape and successful football play/outcomes that extends to implicate all of American society.)

This is but one of many examples of cultural traditions that complicate a linear application of the DD-12. As we welcome more international stu-dents to our college campuses, we must be aware of the diverse cultural lenses through which to view sexual behaviors and relationships, ranging from the expected subservience of women to female sexual activity as an acceptable cause for homicide. To say that such perspectives jeopardize our efforts to eliminate any acceptability of sexual violence seems like an understatement, but we need to be cautious of how we impose our own cultural expectation on those with different traditions. The collision of mul-tiple cultures deserves much more investigation—not to explain away the DD-12 but to guard against disparate impact through a more nuanced understanding of community behaviors and their basis. We can explore cul-turally specific frameworks of the DD-12 that can inform our efforts. By providing ourselves with information about cultural beliefs, practices, and their histories, we arm ourselves with the means through which to develop multiple tools/approaches to address and extinguish violent behavior.

Georgina Dodge, PhD
Chief Diversity Officer and Associate Vice President
Title IX Coordinator
University of Iowa

CAMPUS CLIMATES: A FINAL WORD

The previous chapter outlines what climate is and how to approach the monitoring of climate on campus. However, it is not possible to outline what future efforts should include without a final mention because before a campus can engage its community in any education or intervention programming, it must first have an accurate understanding of the issues related to sexual assault, stalking, and IPV as they occur contextually within its campus community. This means examining the campus environments for the root factors of sexual violence outlined in this book.

An understanding of the existing climate helps a college or university stay out ahead of the "streetlight effect" (Freedman 2010). The streetlight effect is an observational bias where people look for what they are searching for only where it is easiest. Freedman (2010, p. 1) tells it this way:

The fundamental error here is summed up in an old joke scientists love to tell. Late at night, a police officer finds a drunk man crawling around on his hands and knees under a streetlight. The drunk man tells the officer he's looking for his wallet. When the officer asks if he's sure this is where he dropped the wallet, the man replies that he thinks he more likely dropped it across the street. "Then why are you looking over here?" the befuddled officer asks. "Because the light's better here," explains the drunk man.

The risk here is colleges and universities programing and educating around the issues that make up the low-hanging fruit to be picked first. The problems here are the deeper issues contributing to violence against women on campus and they often have complicated and difficult-to-understand motivations. By developing a better understanding of these issues on campus, a college has the opportunity to get out in front of the problem and offer solutions and interventions that are tied more directly to the specific, contextual factors on their campus.

FROM THE FRONT LINES

The Case That Haunts Me

When I think back on my experiences as a student affairs administrator responding to incidents of sexual violence on campus, there are many cases that come to mind, but probably like many of you, there is "that one" that haunts me. One case remains prominent in my memory after more than 15 years, not because of the nature of the incident, who was involved, or any elaborate fact pattern. In fact, it was the type of report that occurs too often on college campuses of a student reporting that she was intoxicated and taken back to her residence hall and assaulted by a "friend." I think of the case often because I feel like I failed the students involved.

I had the best intentions. I did not go to work that day with a plan to not help a student or to deprive students of their rights. I was not lazy or unmotivated about my response. If anything, I tried to get it right. There was just so much that I did not understand.

I did not understand the impact of trauma on a student who had just been assaulted and the resulting irrational thought, intense anger, and distrust of anyone seeking to help. I kept attempting to give the student more information about processes and options. I should have just stopped and listened.

I did not understand why the remedies offered to the student were not enough. Why, when I scheduled appointments with medical providers and counselors for her, did she become more irate? Why, when we talked about residence options, did she focus only on what would happen to the accused?

I did not understand why she kept talking about how the system would not work for her. She kept mentioning the relationships within a student organization that were against her, the connections to alumni, the turmoil of participating in a conduct process, and the pervasive culture in which her assault occurred. At times, she was so irrational that I became frustrated and in the back of my mind even questioned what the student was reporting.

This was prior to 2011 and the renewed focus on colleges' and universities' roles in preventing sexual violence. My graduate program in student affairs did not include the complexities associated with these incidents. My own experiences with gender roles, sex, and relationships had not prepared me. My colleagues, while committed to helping students and tremendous professionals, had not prepared me. Like on many campuses, reporting of assaults was low and infrequent, so I just was not ready.

Ultimately, the student in this case withdrew from her courses and left the institution. I do not know if she enrolled elsewhere to complete her degree or what happened to her.

I know this case is not unique, and I know similar situations occur on campuses every day. I also know that students are not always going to agree with our procedures and resources, and sometimes we just are not going to say the right thing. This case haunts me because it represents for me the intersection of all that I have learned over the past five years about sexual violence, how I could have acted differently, and mainly how I could have been more prepared. This book, *Uprooting Sexual Violence*, is important to me and I hope important to the field because it challenges each of us to think not just about the roots of sexual violence but about our own roots as well.

Dr. Amy Murphy
Assistant Professor, Curriculum and Instruction
Angelo State University

FINAL THOUGHTS

While the sheer volume of research citations necessary to establish the risk factors that contribute to sexual violence in the higher education arena is daunting, it is essential to undergird the front-line public health model of teaching awareness, prevention, and intervention on campus. Without a solid research base, our education and intervention efforts fall short in reaching their goals. This book provides the reader with an initial investigation into how the research from criminology, forensic psychology, community mental health, domestic and dating violence, and stalking blends to create a useful foundation to better target these risk factors for reduction and mitigation.

We encourage those interested in prevention to look more closely at the literature in the field and adopt an inclusive philosophy when developing year-long education and prevention curriculum on college campuses. The issue is too important to be relegated to conversations about "what not to do" or single-orientation programs on consent and healthy relationships. What we need here is a continuous dialogue that weaves its way into our everyday conversations and the academic mission of our colleges and universities.

Afterword
Group-Level Risk Factors in Fraternities and Sororities

Gentry McCreary[1]

> The line between good and evil is permeable and almost anyone
> can be induced to cross it when pressured by situational forces.
> —*Phil Zimbardo*

In no other college subpopulation is the problem of sexual violence more prevalent than it is in fraternities and sororities. Sorority members are two to three times more likely than nonmembers to be sexually assaulted, and fraternity members are three times more likely to rape than nonmembers (Foubert et al. 2007). Fraternities have made themselves an easy and popular target for victims' advocates—they've been labeled "rape factories" not only because of the statistics cited earlier but also because of their very public embrace of rape culture. From the "No means yes, yes means anal" chants of the Delta Kappa Epsilons at Yale aimed at Take Back the Night participants to the "Freshman Daughter Drop-off" signs flung from fraternity house balconies across America during move-in weekend, fraternities frequently exhibit a complete lack of understanding and regard for issues related to rape culture and sexual violence. Sororities, too, have not been immune from criticism on these issues. In 2015, the leaders of the National Panhellenic Conference (NPC)— the governing body of the 26 traditionally white sororities—were publicly called to the mat by U.S. senator Claire McCaskill (D-Mo) for their support of the Safe Campus Act. This legislation would have required, among other things, that sexual assault survivors report incidents of sexual violence to the police before campus officials would be permitted to take any action. The bill was strongly opposed by hundreds of victims' advocacy groups, demonstrating a certain level of tone-deafness on the part of the NPC leaders who backed the legislation. Campus administrators working to prevent sexual violence and support survivors of sexual violence would be wise to pay special attention to fraternity and sorority communities, and this chapter is devoted to helping those administrators better understand the unique culture of those groups, paying particular attention to the culture of sexual violence in fraternities and how it can best be addressed.

RAPE CULTURE IN COLLEGE FRATERNITIES

All of the risk factors discussed in this book become magnified within the context of an all-male group, especially all-male groups whose history is one of social elitism, sexual entitlement, and solidarity. Groupthink, moral disengagement, cognitive dissonance, and unethical pro-organizational behavior are all magnified within the modern-day college fraternity. This assemblage of psychological mechanisms, combined with the neurological maturity of 18–22-year-old men and the historical context of fraternities and sex, can lead to incredibly problematic cultures related to sexual violence.

Despite this dangerous combination of factors, we see many fraternity communities on many college campuses taking significant positive steps related to addressing rape culture. This has been seen on a number of campuses, where fraternities have taken swift action to address allegations of sexual violence involving their members. This is perhaps best demonstrated in the case of Sarah Butters, a James Madison University student who reported being sexually assaulted by three members of Sigma Chi fraternity in a hotel bathroom on spring break. In that case, according to court records, the local fraternity chapter immediately expelled the three members accused of the assault, while the institution was later sued by Butters for allowing her alleged attackers to remain on campus until their graduation. Fraternities are not only responding to sexual violence reports but also becoming actively involved in campus awareness and prevention efforts. Progress is being made.

This progress notwithstanding, rape culture in fraternities remains problematic. A number of risk factors come into play, and administrators working to prevent sexual violence in fraternities need to be cognizant of and responsive to these factors in the fraternities on their campuses.

THE SOLIDARITY PROBLEM

In their research into fraternal brotherhood, McCreary and Schutts (2015) explained the four ways that fraternity members define and conceptualize brotherhood. The most salient schema of brotherhood, brotherhood based on solidarity, is one in which fraternity members describe brotherhood as "having one another's back," "being there for one another, no matter what," "keeping your brothers' secrets," and "always looking out for your brothers." While this schema of brotherhood can manifest in positive ways (e.g., supporting a brother who has lost a family member), it often manifests in ways more resembling a gang mentality (I would have my brother's back if we were out and he got into a fight). This notion of looking out for one another is often reinforced not only symbolically but also directly through organizational rituals. As many fraternity rituals are derived from Masonic ritual, it is safe to assume that keeping one another's secrets and supporting one another in times of trial are not only symbolic gestures of brotherhood but also something that many fraternity members have taken an oath to do. Taking punitive action against a brother who has been accused of sexual assault, then, may be particularly problematic for many fraternity chapters, particularly if the allegation is vague or disputed, or represents behavior that may not be considered violent.

These notions of solidarity are not only an implied or explicit part of fraternity ritual but also often reinforced in the fraternity new member education process. Cimino (2011) examined hazing through the lens of evolutionary psychology and identified solidarity as one of the primary outcomes of newcomer induction activities in groups. Many fraternity leaders readily and quickly identify "the bonding and unity of the pledge class" as one of the primary objectives of their new member education programs, and hazing is often used as the means to that end. Fraternity members are often indoctrinated by their peers to maintain those notions of solidarity and loyalty toward one another.

This heightened sense of solidarity inevitably leads to victim blaming in cases where a fraternity member is accused of sexual assault. McCreary and Schutts (2016) found a strong correlation between solidarity and victim blaming in a national sample of fraternity members. In other words, as feelings of solidarity in a fraternity chapter increase, so does the likelihood that members of that fraternity will circle the wagons, support their brother, and blame the victim of his alleged violence (in the form of calling her a liar or in the form of minimizing the impact of her allegations). Understanding attitudes related to solidarity, then, can be a powerful predictor of understanding and addressing attitudes related to victim blaming/support among fraternity members.

SOCIAL STATUS, ALCOHOL, AND THE
DRUNK HOOKUP CULTURE

Some members see their fraternity experience as a purely social experience, and join explicitly for the purpose of having increased exposure to alcohol and opportunities for sex. These members see brotherhood as a bond between men who share social experiences together—the relationships that arise out of these experiences form the basis of their brotherhood.

Fraternity men who view brotherhood in this way are also much more likely to seek out and join fraternity chapters that will enhance their own social status, presumably for the sexual opportunities that social status will provide them. In addition, these members are more frequent binge drinkers and report a higher frequency of sexual encounters involving alcohol. As studies have shown that more than 90% of assaults on college campuses involve alcohol, fraternity members and chapters who conceptualize brotherhood in this way are especially at risk for perpetration.

The drunken hookup culture prevalent in these chapters is particularly problematic because of the skewed reality it creates. Koss and her colleagues (1987) demonstrated that while 1 in 12 men engaged in activity that meets the technical definition of sexual assault, less than 20% of the men who engage in those activities consider what they did to be sexual assault. There is a tremendous disconnect between what most fraternity members define as a sexual assault and what actually constitutes a sexual assault. Many men engage in behavior that is, by definition, sexual assault, but do not consider themselves rapists.

This phenomenon can be attributed to the drunken hookup culture in many college fraternities. Through their experiences with consensual drunken sex, many fraternity members become numb to the possibility of drunk sex being sexual assault. They may have frequent experiences of consensual, drunken sex (or at least sex that is not defined by the other party as assault). If this happens on multiple occasions, and on every occasion the behavior is positively reinforced, the lines between acceptable sexual behavior and rape become less and less discernable. Then, at some point, the line between a drunk hookup and rape is crossed, and a victim who is beyond just drunk—someone who is truly incapacitated—defines the experience differently than previous partners. As a result, two lives are forever changed, in large part because we failed to help fraternity members understand the difference between sexual assault and drunk sex.

ADDRESSING THESE RISK FACTORS
IN FRATERNITIES

Professionals seeking to address sexual violence in fraternities should invest resources in three specific areas. First, we must help fraternity members overcome their misconception of harm as it relates to nonstranger sexual assault. Secondly, we must adjust our approach in bystander training as it relates to fraternity members. Lastly, we need to confront the drunk hookup culture and help students understand the difference between drunk sex and sexual assault.

Misconceptions of Harm

Most fraternity members demonstrate a lack of understanding related to the emotional trauma that can be caused by sexual assault. Some have described this as a lack of empathy, but we prefer to describe this as a misconception of harm. Thinking of sex using traditional gender roles, many fraternity men are unable to understand the emotional harm and trauma that can come about as a result of nonstranger sexual assault. Our prevention efforts must involve first helping fraternity members understand that harm. A great tool for this is the Police Rape Training Video, in which a police officer describes the forcible sexual assault of a male officer. The video invites male participants to put themselves in the shoes of a victim, helping them better understand the shame, humiliation, self-blame, and regret that can come from having your body violated. Regardless of the tool used, it is important to help fraternity members move from an attitude of "it's just sex—what's the big deal" to one of "I understand how being violated, even by someone you know and trust, can be traumatic."

Reconceptualize Bystander Training

If you read the literature on bystander behavior, you will find that there are a number of things an individual must do in order to intervene in a dangerous situation (i.e., not be a bystander). The first and arguably most important thing on that list is that the person must interpret the situation as an emergency worthy of intervention. People fail to correctly interpret situations as problematic for one of two reasons: ambiguity or conformity. In ambiguous situations, it isn't clear whether a situation is an emergency. An example of this is the Kitty Genovese murder—one of the things that often gets lost in the Kitty Genovese story is that many people who heard the attack incorrectly interpreted it as a lover's quarrel, and not a situation that required any sort of intervention (in fact, they were often surprised to learn that a murder had taken place). Much has been written of conformity—most famously the Asch study, in which individuals discuss the lengths of lines and conform to the answers of those around them. A lesser-known study applies directly to bystander behavior—the Latane and Darley "Smoke-Filled Room" study. In this study, individuals were placed in a waiting room in one of two conditions—alone or with confederates. After a few minutes waiting, smoke began entering the room through a vent. Those in the "alone" condition immediately got up and said something to someone or left the room 75% of the time. But in the "with others" condition, the confederates would sit silently and pay no attention to the smoke. The research subject would notice the smoke, but then notice that everyone else seemed to be paying the smoke no mind. In such conditions, less than 10% of research subjects said or did anything related to the smoke. The reason they did not say or do anything is often mistakenly attributed to diffusion of responsibility (I assumed someone else would do something), but the inaction was actually due to conformity. They looked around to see how everyone else interpreted the situation. When they surmised that they were the only person interpreting the smoke as a problem, they conformed to the norms around them and decided that the smoke was not a problem after all.

Many campuses have turned to bystander training as a means of combating sexual violence. These programs show promise, but the research cited earlier illustrates an important concept that is often overlooked in these trainings. In order for bystander training to be effective, we must first help students correctly interpret situations involving potential sexual violence as emergencies worthy of their intervention. That is, we must address the misunderstanding of harm before we can expect students to intervene. As we think about our prevention programming, building understanding comes first, and bystander training comes second. Before we teach students *how* to intervene in potential sexual assaults, we must first help them understand *why* they should intervene.

Confront the Drunk Hookup Culture

The drunk hookup culture has become normalized by fraternity members. And when they are told that someone who is under the influence of alcohol cannot consent to sexual activity, it goes against everything they have learned and personally experienced, thereby diminishing the credibility of the message they are receiving. Educational programs that fail to acknowledge this fact are sure to fall short in their impact.

Unfortunately, many well-intentioned prevention programs feature statements like "someone who has had even one drink cannot consent to sexual activity." In addition to alienating students who may regularly mix alcohol and sex, these statements are not technically or legally accurate. "Incapacitated" is the law regarding sexual consent, and "incapacitated" is a different threshold than "drunk." While one does not need to be passed out or completely unconscious in order to be incapacitated, the person does need to be more than just "drunk" or "under the influence" (Sokolow 2005). It is important that we begin helping students understand the difference between drunk sex and incapacitated assault, because helping students understand and navigate the fine line between those two things may be the most important thing we can do in preventing sexual assaults on college campuses. Frankly, our prevention conversations with students need to be more sophisticated than "drunk people cannot consent to sexual activity." In order to really reach fraternity members on this topic in a way that will prevent incapacitated assaults, we have to be comfortable acknowledging that sometimes drunk sex is okay, and begin helping students understand the line at which it becomes problematic, while at the same time confronting the drunk hookup culture and the overall campus alcohol culture. Rape culture and alcohol culture are intricately intertwined on college campuses, and any attempts to address one without addressing the other would best be described as halfhearted.

NOTE

1 Dr. Gentry McCreary, PhD, is an affiliated consultant with the NCHERM Group and his unique experiences as both a scholar and practitioner allow him to serve as a valuable resource for campuses and inter/national fraternal organizations grappling with hazing, risk management, and substance abuse problems.

References

AASECT (American Association of Sex Educators, Counselors and Therapists) Board of Directors. (2013). Visions of sexual health. Retrieved on May 25, 2016, from https://www.aasect.org/vision-sexual-health

Abbey, A., Zawacki, M.A., Buck, P.O., Clinton, M., & McAuslan, P. (2001). Alcohol and sexual assault. *Alcohol Research and Health.* 25(1), 43–51.

ACHA (American College Health Association). (2008). Shifting the paradigm: Primary prevention of sexual violence [Internet]. Linthicum (MD): The Centers for Disease Control and Prevention and the American College Health Association. Retrieved on May 25, 2015, from http://www.acha.org/SexualViolence/

ACLU. (n.d.). Abstinence-only education and sexual violence. Retrieved on May 25, 2016, from https://www.aclupa.org/download_file/view_inline/416/351

Allen, M., Emmers, T., Gebhardt, L., & Giery, M. (2006). Exposure to pornography and acceptance of rape myths. *Journal of Communication.* 45(1), 5–26.

APA (American Psychiatric Association). (2013). *Diagnostic and statistical manual of mental disorders* (5th ed.). (American Psychiatric Publishing, Arlington, VA).

Armstrong, E., Hamilton, L., & Sweeny, B. (2006). Sexual assault on campus: A multilevel, integrative approach to party rape. *Society for the Study of Social Problems.* 53(4), 483–499.

Aronowitz, T., Lambert, C., & Davidoff, S. (2012). The role of rape myth acceptance in the social norms regarding sexual behavior among college students. *Journal of Community Health Nursing.* 29, 173–182.

ASIS (ASIS International and the Society for Human Resource Management). (2011). Workplace violence prevention and intervention: American national standard. Retrieved from www.asisonline.org/guidelines/published.htm

Association of Threat Assessment Professionals (ATAP). (2006). *Risk assessment guideline elements for violence (RAGE-V): Considerations for assessing the risk of future violent behavior.* (ATAP, Los Angeles, CA).

AVN director's roundtable. (2003, January). *Adult Video News.* 45–68.

Baird, L.L. (2000). College climate and the Tinto model. In *Reworking the student departure puzzle.* John M. Braxton, ed. (Vanderbilt University Press, Nashville, TN), pp. 62–80.

Bandura, A. (1999). Moral disengagement in the perpetration of inhumanities. *Personality and Social Psychology Review.* [Special issue on evil and violence] 3, 193–209.

Barnett, N.D., & DiSabato, M. (2000). Training camp: Lessons in masculinity. In *Just sex: Students rewrite the rules on sex, violence, activism and equality.* J. Gold & S. Villari, eds. (Rowman & Littlefield, Lanham, MD), pp. 197–210.

Belfrage, H., & Strand, S. (2008). Validation of the stalking assessment and management checklist (SAM) in law enforcement: A retrospective study of 153 cases of stalking in two Swedish police counties. *International Journal of Police Science and Management.* 11(1), 67–76.

Bendixena, M., Henriksenb, M., & Kvitvik, Nøstdahl R. (2014). Attitudes toward rape and attribution of responsibility to rape victims in a Norwegian community sample. *Nordic Psychology.* 66(3), 168–186.

Berkowitz, A. (1992). College men as perpetrators of acquaintance rape and sexual assault: A review of recent research. *Journal of American College Health.* 40(4), 175–181.

Berkowitz, A.D. (2004). An overview of the social norms approach. In *Changing the culture of college drinking: A socially situated prevention campaign.* L. Lederman, L. Stewart, F. Goodhart, & L. Laitman, eds. (Hampton Press, Creskill, NJ), pp. 187–208.

Bieneck, S., & Krahe, B. (2011). Blaming the victim and exonerating the perpetrator in cases of rape and robbery: Is there a double standard? *Journal of Interpersonal Violence.* 26, 1785–1797.

Bleeker, E.T., & Murnen, S.K. (2005). Fraternity membership, the display of degrading images and rape myth acceptance. *Sex Roles: A Journal of Research.* 53(7/8), 487–496.

Bloom, B.S., ed. (1956). *Taxonomy of educational objectives. The classification of educational goals. Handbook I: Cognitive domain.* (David McKay, New York, NY).

Boeringer, S. (1999). Associations of rape-supportive attitudes with fraternal and athletic participation. *Violence Against Women.* 5, 81–90.

Boswell, A., & Spade, J. (1996). Fraternities and collegiate rape culture: Why are some fraternities more dangerous places for women? *Gender and Society.* 10(2), 133–147.

Boysen, G. (2012). Teacher and student perceptions of microaggressions in college classrooms. *Journal of College Teaching*. 60, 122–129.

Brownmiller, S. (1975). *Against our will: Men, women, and rape*. (Simon & Schuster, New York, NY).

The Bureau of Erotic Discourse (BED). (2014). Clarity and consent: B.E.D. workshop notes for 2014. Retrieved on February 14, 2016, from www.bureauoferoticdiscourse.org

Calhoun, F., & Weston, S. (2009). *Threat assessment and management strategies: Identifying the howlers and hunters*. (CRC Press, Boca Raton, FL).

Campbell, K. (2014). Climates for diversity: Checking the barometer. *Diversity & Democracy*. 4(17), 3.

Caputo, A.A., Frick, P.J., & Brodsky, S.L. (1999). Family violence and juvenile sex offending: The potential mediating role of psychopathic traits and negative attitudes toward women. *Criminal Justice and Behavior*. 26, 338–356.

Carr, J., & VanDeusen, K. (2004). Risk factors for male sexual aggression on college campuses. *Journal of Family Violence*. 19(5), 279–289.

Carrera, M., Williams K.J., & Philiber, S. (2000). Knowledge about reproduction, contraception, and sexually transmitted infections among young adolescents in American cities. *Social Policy*. 30, 41–50.

Centers for Disease Control. (2016a). The public health approach to violence prevention. Retrieved on February 22, 2016, from www.cdc.gov/ViolencePrevention/overview/publichealthapproach.html

Centers for Disease Control. (2016b). The social-ecological model: A framework for prevention. Retrieved on February 22, 2016, from http://www.cdc.gov/ViolencePrevention/overview/social-ecological model.html

Chickering, A.W., & Reisser, L. (1993). *Education and identity* (2nd ed.). (Jossey-Bass, San Francisco).

Cimino, A. (2011). The evolution of hazing: Motivational mechanisms and the abuse of newcomers. *Journal of Cognition and Culture*. 11, 241–267.

Clarke, R.V., & Felson, M. (1993). Introduction: Criminology, routine activity, and rational choice. In *Routine activity and rational choice*. R.V. Clarke and M. Felson, eds. (Transaction, New Brunswick, NJ), pp. 1–14.

Covey, S. (1990). *Seven habits of highly effective people*. (Free Press, New York, NY).

Cowan, G. (2000). Women's hostility toward women and rape and sexual harassment myths. *Violence Against Women*. 6(3), 238–246.

Crain, W. (1985). *Theories of development*. (Prentice-Hall, New York, NY).

Craissati, J., McClurg, G., & Browne, K. (2002). Characteristics of perpetrators of child sexual abuse who have been sexually victimized as children. *Sexual Abuse: A Journal of Research and Treatment*. 14, 225–239.

Dahlberg, L., & Krug, E. (2002). Violence—a global public health problem. In *World report on violence and health*. E. Krug, L. Dahlberg, J. Mercy, A. Zwi, & R. Lozano, eds. (World Health Organization, Geneva, Switzerland), pp. 1–56.

Davis, R., Parks, L.F., & Cohen, L. (2006). *Sexual violence and the spectrum of prevention: Towards a community solution*. (National Sexual Violence Resource Center, Enola, PA).

Deisinger, G., Randazzo, M., O'Neill, D., & Savage, J. (2008). *The handbook for campus threat assessment and management teams*. (Applied Risk Management, Boston, MA).

Department of Defense. (2015). *Report to the president of the* United States *on sexual assault prevention and response*. (DOD, Washington, DC).

Ehrensaft, M.K., Cohen, P., Brown, J., Smailes, E., Chen, H., & Johnson, J. (2003). Intergenerational transmission of partner violence: A 20-year prospective study. *Journal of Consulting and Clinical Psychology*. 71, 741–753.

Ellis, A. (2007). *The practice of rational emotive behavior therapy*. (W.W Norton & Company, New York, NY).

EverFi. (2013). *The relationship between alcohol and sexual assault on the college campus*. Insight Report, August 2013. (EverFi, Washington, DC).

Fein, R.A., & Vossekuil, B. (1998). *Protective intelligence and threat assessment investigations: A guide for state and local law enforcement officials*. (National Institute of Justice, Washington, DC).

Forbes, G.B., Adams-Curtis, L.E., Pakalka, A.H., & White, K. (2006). Dating aggression, sexual coercion, and aggression-supporting attitudes among college men as a function of participation in aggressive high school sports. *Violence Against Women*. 12, 441–455.

Foubert, J.D. (2000). The longitudinal effects of a rape prevention program on fraternity men's attitudes, behavioral intent, and behavior. *Journal of American College Health*. 48, 158–163.

Foubert, J.D., Newberry, J.T., & Tatum, J.L. (2007). Behavior differences seven months later: Effects of a rape prevention program on first-year men who join fraternities. *NASPA Journal*. 44, 728–749.

Foubert, J.D., & Perry, B.C. (2007). Creating lasting attitude and behavior change in fraternity members and male student athletes: The qualitative impact of an empathy-based rape prevention program. *Violence Against Women*. 13, 70–86.

Franklin, K. (2000). Inside the mind of people who hate gays. *Frontline*. Retrieved on February 16, 2015, from http://www.pbs.org/wgbh/pages/frontline/shows/assault/roots/franklin.html

Freedman, D. (2010). Why scientific studies are so often wrong: The streetlight effect. *Discover Magazine*. Retrieved on February 25, 2015, from http://discovermagazine.com/2010/jul-aug/29-why-scientific-studies-often-wrong-streetlight-effect

Gabosch, A. (2014). A sex positive renaissance. Retrieved on February 21, 2016, from https://allenagabosch.wordpress.com/2014/12/08/a-sex-positive-renaissance/

Gailey, J.A., & Prohaska, A. (2006). "Knocking off a fat girl": An exploration of hogging, male sexuality, and neutralizations. *Deviant Behavior*. 27, 31–49.

Gattuso, R. (2016). What I would have said to you last night had you not cum and then fallen asleep. Retrieved on February 14, 2016, from http://feministing.com/2016/01/19/what-i-would-have-said-to-you-last-night-had-you-not-cum-and-then-fallen-asleep/

Glasl, F. (1999). *Confronting conflict: A first-aid kit for handling conflict*. (Hawthorn Press, A. Stroud, UK).

Glasser, A. (1975). *Reality therapy: A new approach to psychiatry*. (Colophon Books, New York, NY).

Glasser, A. (2001). *Counseling with choice theory: The new reality therapy*. (Harper Perennial, New York, NY).

Godenzi, A., Schwartz, M.D., & DeKesedery, W.S. (2001). Toward a gendered social bond/male peer support theory of university woman abuse. *Critical Criminology*. 10(1), 1–16.

Gordon, R. (1963). An operational classification of disease prevention. *Public Health Reports*. 96(2), 107–109.

Gordon, W. (2002). Sexual obsessions and OCD. *Journal of Sexual and Relationship Therapy*. 17(4), 343–354.

Grant, J., Pinto, A., Gunnip, M., Mancebo, M., Eisen, J., & Rasmussen, S. (2006). Sexual obsessions and clinical correlates in adults with obsessive-compulsive disorder. *Comprehensive Psychiatry*. 47, 325–329.

Grimmett, J., Lewis, W.S., Schuster, S.K., Sokolow, B.A., Swinton, D.C., & Van Brunt, B. (2015). *The challenge of Title IX responses to campus relationship and intimate partner violence. The 2015 whitepaper*. (ATIXA, Philadelphia, PA).

Grossman, D. (1996). *On killing: The psychological cost of learning to kill in war and society*. (Little, Brown, and Company Back Bay Books, Lebanon, IN).

Hainbach, S. (2014, November 24). University glee club temporarily retires "Rugby Road": Gilliam says song does not promote "bad behavior." *The Cavalier Daily*. Retrieved February 15, 2015, from www.cavalierdaily.com

Hamilton, M., & Yee, J. (1990). Rape knowledge and propensity to rape. *Journal of Research in Personality*. 24, 111–122.

Hare, R. (1999). *Without conscience: The disturbing world of psychopaths among us.* (Guilford, New York, NY).

Hare, R.D. (1985). Checklist for the assessment of psychopathy in criminal populations. In *Clinical criminology MH Ben-Aron.* S.J. Hucker & C.D. Webster, eds. (Clarke Institute of Psychiatry, University of Toronto, ON), pp. 157–167.

Hare, R.D. (1991). *The Hare psychopathy checklist—revised.* (Multi-Health Systems, Toronto, ON).

Hare, R.D. (2003). *The psychopathy checklist—revised technical manual* (2nd ed.). (Multi-Health Systems, Toronto, ON).

Harper, S.R., & Harris III, F. (2010). *College men and masculinities: Theory, research, and implications for practice.* (Jossey-Bass, San Francisco, CA).

Harris, A., Phenix, A., Hanson, K., & Thornton, D. (2003). STATIC-99 coding rules revised—2003. Retrieved on January 11, 2015, from http://www.static99.org/pdfdocs/static-99-coding-rules_e.pdf

Helmus, L., & Hanson, R. (2007). Predictive validity of the Static-99 and Static-2002 for sex offenders on community supervision. *Sexual Offender Treatment.* 2(2), 1–14.

Henry, M., Lewis, W., Morris, L., Schuster, S., Sokolow, B., Swinton, D., & Van Brunt, B. (2016). The 7 deadly sins of Title IX investigation. *The Association of Title IX Administrators.* 1–18.

Hines, D.A. (2007). Posttraumatic stress symptoms among men who sustain partner violence: An international multisite study of university students. *Psychology of Men & Masculinity.* 8, 225–239.

Humphrey, S., & Kahn, A. (2000). Fraternities, athletic teams, and rape: Importance of identification with a risky group. *Journal of Interpersonal Violence.* 15, 1313–1322.

Hurtado, S., & Halualani, R. (2014). Diversity assessment, accountability, and action: Going beyond the numbers. *Diversity & Democracy.* 17(4), 8–11.

Iconis, R. (2006). Rape myth acceptance in college students: A literature review. *Contemporary Issues in Education Research.* 1(2), 47–52.

Jackson, A. (2015). A prominent college feminist was strangled to death—and her friends say the campus is a hostile place. Retrieved on May 17, 2015, from http://www.businessinsider.com/grace-rebecca-mann-strangled-to-death-2015-5

Jensen, R. (2004). *Pornography and sexual violence.* (VAWnet, Harrisburg, PA), a project of the national resource center on domestic violence/Pennsylvania coalition against domestic violence. Retrieved on May 18, 2015, from http://www.vawnet.org

Jewkes, R., Sen, P., & Garcia-Moreno, C. (2002). Sexual violence. In *World report on violence and health.* E.G. Krug, L.L. Dahlberg, J.A. Mercy, A. Zwi, & R. Lozano, eds. (World Health Organization, Geneva, Switzerland), pp. 147–181.

Jhally, S. (1999). *Tough guise: Violence, media & the crisis in masculinity.* (Media Education Foundation, Northampton, MA).

Kafka, M. (2010). Hypersexual disorder: A proposed diagnosis for the DSM-V. *Archives of Sexual Behavior.* 39, 377–400.

Kalish, R. (2013). Masculinities and hooking up: Sexual decision-making at college. *Culture, Society & Masculinities.* 5(2), 147–165.

Kanin, E. (1985). Date rapists: Differential sexual socialization and relative deprivation. *Archives of Sexual Behavior.* 14, 219–230.

Katz, J. (1995). Reconstructing masculinity in the locker room: The mentors in violence prevention project. *Harvard Educational Review.* 65(2), 163–174.

Kaufman, K.L., ed. (2010). *The prevention of sexual violence: A practitioner's sourcebook.* (NEARI Press, Holyoke, MA).

Kendig, M. (1990). *Alfred Korzybskli: Collected writings: 1920–1950.* (Institute of General Semantics, Englewood, NJ).

Kilmartin, C. (2000). *Sexual assault in context: Teaching college men about gender.* (Learning Publications, Homes Beach, FL).

Kilpatrick, D., Best, C., Veronen, L., Amick, A., Villeponteaux, L., & Ruff, G. (1985). Mental health correlates of victimization: A random community survey. *Journal of Consulting and Clinical Psychology,* 53, 866–873.

Kimmel, M.S. (2008). *Guyland: The perilous world where boys become men.* (Harper, New York, NY).

Kingkade, T. (2014). Texas Tech investigating frat for "no means yes, yes means anal" sign. *The Huffington Post.* Retrieved on February 15, 2015, from www.huffingtonpost.com

Kingston, D.A., Malamuth, N.M., Fedoroff, P., & Marshall, W. (2009). The importance of individual differences in pornography use: Theoretical perspectives and implications for treating sexual offenders. *Journal of Sex Research.* 46, 216–232.

Knight, R., & Sims-Knight, J. (2009). *Using rapist risk factors to set an agenda for rape prevention.* (VAWnet, Harrisburg, PA), a project of the national resource center on domestic violence/Pennsylvania coalition against domestic violence. Retrieved on January 11, 2015, from http://www.vawnet.org

Kohlberg, L. (1973). The claim to moral adequacy of a highest stage of moral judgment. *Journal of Philosophy.* 70(18), 630–646.

Koss, M., & Gaines, J. (1993). The prediction of sexual aggression by alcohol use, athletic participation, and fraternity affiliation. *Journal of Interpersonal Violence.* 8, 104–108.

Koss, M., Gidycz, C., & Wisniewski, N. (1987). The scope of rape: Incidence and prevalence of sexual aggression and victimization in a national sample of higher education students. *Journal of Counseling and Clinical Psychology.* 35 (2), 162–170.

Krahe, B., Temkin, J., & Bieneck, S. (2007). Schema-driven information processing in judgments about rape. *Applied Cognitive Psychology*. 21, 601–619.

Krebs, C.P., Lindquist, C.H., & Warner, T.D. (2007). *The campus sexual assault (CSA) study: Final report.* (National Institute of Justice, Washington, DC).

Kropp, P., Hart, S., & Lyon, D. (2002). Risk assessment of stalkers: Some problems and possible solutions. *Criminal Justice and Behavior*. 29(5), 590–616.

Kropp, P., Hart, S., & Lyon, D. (2008). *Guidelines for stalking assessment and management (SAM) user manual.* (Proactive Resolutions, Sydney, NSW, Australia).

Kropp, P.R., Hart, S.D., Webster, C.W., & Eaves, D. (1994). *Manual for the spousal assault risk assessment guide.* (British Columbia Institute on Family Violence, Vancouver, BC).

Kropp, P.R., Hart, S.D., Webster, C.W., & Eaves, D. (1995). *Manual for the spousal assault risk assessment guide* (2nd ed.). (British Columbia Institute on Family Violence, Vancouver, BC).

Kropp, P.R., Hart, S.D., Webster, C.W, & Eaves, D. (1998). *Spousal assault risk assessment: User's guide.* (Multi-Health Systems, Toronto, ON).

Kuh, G.D, & Whitt, E.J. (1988). *The invisible tapestry: Culture in American colleges and universities.* ASHE-ERIC Higher Education, 1. (Office of Educational Research and Improvement, Washington, DC).

Langman, P. (2014). Elliot Rodger: An analysis. *Journal of Campus Behavioral Intervention*. 2, 4–18.

Larimer, M., Lydum, A., Anderson, B., & Turner, A. (1999). Male and female recipients of unwanted sexual contact in a college student sample: Prevalence rates, alcohol use, and depression symptoms. *Sex Roles*. 40, 295–308.

LaViolette, A., & Barnett, O. (2000). *It could happen to anyone: Why battered women stay.* (SAGE, Newbury Park, CA).

Lazarus, M., Wunderlich, R., Stallone, P., & Vitagliano, J. (1979). *Killing us softly: Advertising's image of women.* (Cambridge Documentary Films, Santa Barbara, CA).

Lisak, D., & Miller, P. (2002). Repeat rape and multiple offending among undetected rapists. *Journal of Violence and Victims*. 17(1), 73–84.

Loh, C., Gidycz, C.A., Lobo, T.R., & Luthra, R. (2005). A prospective analysis of sexual assault perpetration: Risk factors related to perpetrator characteristics. *Journal of Interpersonal Violence*. 20, 1325–1348.

Malamuth, N.M., Addison, T., & Koss, M. (2000). Pornography and sexual aggression: Are there reliable effects and can we understand them? *Annual Review of Sex Research*. 11, 26–91.

McCreary, G., & Schutts, J. (2015). Towards a broader understanding of fraternity: Developing and validating a measure of fraternal brotherhood. *Oracle: The Research Journal of the Association of Fraternity/Sorority Advisors.* 10(1), 31–50.

McCreary, G., & Schutts, J. (2016). *Brotherhood, sisterhood, and sexual assault attitudes.* Manuscript in preparation.

McGowan, E. (2015). 7 tips for your first BDSM or kink experience. Retrieved on February 14, 2016, from http://www.bustle.com/articles/131373-7-tips-for-your-first-bdsm-or-kink-experience

McMahon, S. (2011, October). *Changing perceptions of sexual violence over time.* (VAWnet, Harrisburg, PA). Retrieved on May 25, 2016, from http://www.vawnet.org.

Meloy, J., & Fisher, H. (2005). Some thoughts on the neurobiology of stalking. *Journal of Forensic Science.* 50(6), 1–9.

Meloy, J., Hoffmann, J., Guldimann, A., & James, D. (2012). The role of warning behaviors in threat assessment: An exploration and suggested typology. *Behavioral Sciences and the Law.* 30, 256–279.

Mendelson, S. (2012). Blaming the victim: The 'problem' with beauty and the beast isn't Belle, but the Beast. Retrieved on May 25, 2016, from http://www.moviefone.com/2012/01/18/beauty-and-the-beast-3d/

Miller, W.R., & Rollnick, S. (1991). *Motivational interviewing: Preparing people to change addictive behavior.* (Guilford Press, New York, NY).

Morrison, S., Hardison, J., Mathew, A., & O'Neil, J. (2004). *An evidence-based review of sexual preventive intervention programs.* (U.S. DOJ Publication No. 207262). (National Institute of Justice, Washington, DC).

Mouilso, E., Calhoun, K., & Rosenbloom, T. (2013). Impulsivity and sexual assault in college men. *Journal of Violence & Victims.* 28(3), 429.

Multi-Health Systems. (2011). *Emotional quotient inventory 2.0 (EQ-I 2.0) user's handbook.* (Multi-Health Systems, Toronto, ON).

Murnen, S., & Kohlman, M. (2007). Athletic participation, fraternity membership, and sexual aggression among college men: A meta-analytic review. *Sex Roles.* 57(1/2), 145–157.

Murnen, S.K., Wright, C., & Kaluzny, G. (2002). If "boys will be boys," then girls will be victims? A meta-analytic review of the research that relates masculine ideology to sexual aggression. *Sex Roles.* 46, 359–375.

National Center for Campus Public Safety. (2014). Climate surveys: Useful tools to help colleges and universities in their efforts to reduce and prevent sexual assault. Retrieved on February 25, 2015, from http://www.nccpsafety.org/resources/library/climate-surveys-useful-tools-to-help-colleges-and-universities-in-their-eff/

Nay, R. (2004). *Taking charge of anger.* (Guilford Press, New York, NY).

Niehoff, D. (1999). *The biology of violence.* (The Free Press, New York, NY).

North, A. (2015). Is college sexual assault a fraternity problem? *New York Times*. Retrieved on February 16, 2015, from http://op-talk. blogs.nytimes.com/2015/01/29/is-college-sexual-assault-a-fraternity-problem/?_r=0

Oddone-Paolucci, E., Genius, M., & Violato, C. (2000). A meta-analysis of published research on the effects of pornography. In *The changing family and child development*. C. Violato, E. Oddone-Paolucci, & M. Genius, eds. (Ashgate, Aldershot, UK), pp. 48–59.

O'Hearn, H.G., & Margolin, G. (2000). Men's attitudes condoning marital aggression: A moderator between family of origin abuse and aggression against female partners. *Cognitive Therapy and Research*. 24(2), 159–174.

Orlich, D., Harder, R., Callahan, R., Trevisan, M., & Brown, A. (2004). *Teaching strategies: A guide to effective instruction* (7th ed.). (Houghton Mifflin, Boston, MA).

Osland, J., Fitch, M., & Willis, E. (1996). Likelihood to rape in college males. *Sex Roles*. 35, 171–183.

O'Toole, M.E. (2000). *The school shooter: A threat assessment perspective*. (National Center for the Analysis of Violent Crime, FBI, Quantico, VA).

O'Toole, M.E., & Bowman, A. (2011). *Dangerous instincts: How gut feelings betray*. (Hudson Street Press, New York, NY).

Peterson, Z., & Muehlenhard, C. (2004). Was it rape? The function of women's rape myth acceptance and definitions of sex in labeling their own experiences. *Sex Roles: A Journal of Research*. 51, 129–144.

Prochaska, J., Norcross, J., & DiClemente, C. (1994). *Changing for good*. (Harper Collins, New York, NY).

Randazzo, M., & Plummer, E. (2009). *Implementing behavioral threat assessment on campus: A Virginia tech demonstration project*. (Virginia Polytechnic Institute and State University, Blacksburg, VA).

Ravenscroft, K. (2011). 16 impacts of sexual assault. Retrieved on February 9, 2016, from https://16 impacts.wordpress.com/16-ways-to-fight-sexual-violence/

Reid, R.C. (2013). Personal perspectives on hypersexual disorder. *Sexual Addiction & Compulsivity*. 20, 4–18.

Reitzel-Jaffe, D., & Wolfe, D.A. (2001). Predictors of relationship abuse among young men. *Journal of Interpersonal Violence*. 16, 99–115.

Resnick, M., Ireland, M., & Borowsky, I. (2004). Youth violence perpetration: What protects? What predicts? Findings from the national longitudinal student of adolescent health. *Journal of Adolescent Health*. 35(5), 421–410.

Robinson, M. (2013). Chickering's seven vectors of identity development. Retrieved on February 22, 2016, from https://student developmenttheory.wordpress.com/chickerings-seven-vectors/

Rodger, E. (2014). My twisted world. Retrieved from www.schoolshoot ers.info

Rogers, C. (1961). *On becoming a person: A therapist's view of psychotherapy.* (Boston, MA, Houghton Mifflin).

Rogers, C. (1980). *A way of being.* (Houghton Mifflin, Boston, MA).

Rozee, P.D., & Koss, M.P. (2001). Rape: A century of resistance. *Psychology of Women.* 25, 295–311.

Runk, D. (2009, April 10). 2 killed in Henry Ford Community College shooting. *The Huffington Post.* Retrived on June 27, 2016, from http://6abc.com/archive/6754909/

Russell, D.H. (1998). *Dangerous relationships: Pornography, misogyny, and rape.* (SAGE, Thousand Oaks, CA).

Sanday, P.R. (2007). *Gang rape: Sex, brotherhood, and privilege on campus* (2nd ed.). (New York University Press, New York).

Sanford, N. (1966). *Self and society.* (Atherton Press, New York, NY).

Santich, K. (2014). Catcalling becomes issue on campuses. *Orlando Sentinel.* Retrieved on February 16, 2015, from http://www.orlandosentinel.com/features/education/os-catcalling-on-campus-20141108-story.html

Scheel, E.D., Johnson, E.J., Schneider, M., & Smith, B. (2001). Making rape education meaningful for men: The case for eliminating the emphasis on men as perpetrators, protectors, or victims. *Sociological Practice: A Journal of Clinical and Applied Sociology.* 3, 257–278.

Schewe, P.A., & O'Donohue, W.T. (1993). Rape prevention: Methodological problems and new directions. *Clinical Psychology Review.* 13, 667–682.

Schwartz, M.D., & DeKeseredy, W.S. (1997). *Sexual assault on the college campus: The role of male peer support.* (SAGE, Thousand Oaks, CA).

Seegers, J. (2010). The prevalence of sexual addiction symptoms on the college campus. *Sexual Addiction and Compulsivity: The Journal of Treatment and Prevention.* 10(4), 247–258.

Seligman, M.E. (2006). *Learned optimism: How to change your mind and your life.* (Vintage, New York, NY).

Seto, M., & Barbaree, H. (1997). Sexual aggression as antisocial behavior: A developmental model. In *Handbook of antisocial behavior.* D.M. Stoff, J. Breiling, & J.D. Maser, eds. (Wiley, New York, NY), pp. 524–533.

Seto, M., Maric, A., & Barbaree, H. (2001). The role of pornography in the etiology of sexual aggression. *Journal of Aggression and Sexual Behavior.* 6(1), 35–53.

Shastry, A. (2014). Sexual assaults are not centered around fraternities, university members say. *The Diamondback.* Retrieved on February 16, 2015, from http://www.diamondbackonline.com/news/article_318237fa-025a-11e4-807f-001a4bcf6878.html

Sinkovic, M., Stulhofer, A., & Bozie, J. (2013). Revisiting the association between pornography use and risky sexual behaviors: The role of early exposure to pornography and sexual sensation seeking. *Journal of Sex Research*. 50, 633–641.

Smith, E. (2015). Fifty shades of grey: What BDSM enthusiasts think. Retrieved on February 14, 2015, from http://www.theguardian.com/film/2015/feb/15/fifty-shades-of-grey-bdsm-enthusiasts

Sokolow, B. (2001). *Comprehensive sexual misconduct judicial procedures*. (The NCHERM Group, Malvern, PA), 1–34.

Sokolow, B. (2005). The typology of campus sexual misconduct complaints. *National Center for Higher Education Risk Management 2005 Whitepaper*. Retrieved from https://www.ncherm.org/pdfs/2005NC3.pdf

Sokolow, B., & Lewis, S. (2009). *2nd generation behavioral intervention best practices*. (The NCHERM Group, Malvern, PA).

Sokolow, B.A., Lewis, W.S., Schuster, S.K., & Swinton, D.C. (2015). *ATIXA sex/gender-based harassment, discrimination and sexual misconduct model policy*. (The NCHERM Group/ATIXA, Berwyn, PA).

Sokolow, B., Lewis, W., Schuster, S., Swinton, D., & Van Brunt, B. (2014). *Threat assessment in a campus setting*. (The NCHERM Group, Malvern, PA).

Sokolow, B., Lewis, W., Van Brunt, B., Shuster, S., & Swinton, D. (2014). *Book on BIT*. (The NCHERM Group, Malvern, PA).

Sokolow, B., Swinton, D., Morris, L, Price, M., & Isadore, M. (2015). *Investigation in a box: A toolkit from the association of Title IX administrators*. (ATIXA, Berwyn, PA).

Somani, S. (2014). OSI disbands phi kappa tau for continual violations. *Technique*. Retrieved on February 15, 2015, from http://nique.net

Speer, R. (2014). A selfie-era killer: Social media and Elliot Rodger. *The New York Post*. Retrieved on May 28, 2014, from http://nypost.com/2014/05/28/a-selfie-era-killer-social-media-and-elliot-rodger/

Stein, S., Book, H., & Kanoy, K. (2013). *The student EQ edge: Emotional intelligence and your academic & personal success*. (Wiley, San Francisco).

Strippers said to be commonplace at football-recruit parties. (2004). *Associated Press*. Retrieved on May 18, 2015, from http://www.foxnews.com/story/2004/02/10/strippers-said-to-be-commonplace-at-football-recruit-parties/

Sue, D. (2010). *Microaggressions in everyday life: Race, gender, and sexual orientation*. (John Wiley & Sons, Hoboken, NJ).

Sue, D., Bucceri, J., Kin, A., Nadal, K. & Torino, G. (2007a). Racial microaggressions and the Asian American experience. *Cultural Diversity and Ethnic Minority Psychology*. 13, 72–81.

Sue, D., Capodilupo, C., Torino, G., Bucceri, J., Holder, A., Nadal, K., & Esquilin, M. (2007b). Racial microaggressions in everyday life: Implications for clinical practice. *American Psychologist*. 62, 271–286.

Sue, D., Lin, A., Torino, G., Capodilupo, C., & Rivera, D. (2009). Racial microaggressions and difficult dialogs on race in the classroom. *Cultural Diversity and Ethnic Minority Psychology*. 15, 183–190.

Sussman, S., Lisha, N., & Griffiths, M. (2011). Prevalence of the addictions: A problem of the majority or the minority? *Evaluation & the Health Professions*. 34, 3–56.

Tallon-Hicks, Y. (2016). Consent makes you better at sex. Retrieved on February 21, 2016, from http://mashable.com/2016/01/20/consent-good-sex/#jP1P7wQACSqU

Teranishi-Martinez, C. (2014). Engendered expressions of aggression: The role of gender, proprietary behaviors, and jealousy in intimate partner violence. *Violence and Gender*. 2(2), 112–188.

Turner, J., & Gelles, M. (2003). *Threat assessment: A risk management approach*. (Routledge, New York, NY).

Van Brunt, B. (2012). *Ending campus violence: New approaches to prevention*. (Routledge, New York, NY).

Van Brunt, B. (2014). *Harm to others: The assessment and treatment of dangerousness*. (Routledge, New York, NY).

Van Brunt, B., Murphy, A., & O'Toole, M. (2015). The dirty dozen: Twelve risk factors for sexual violence on college campuses (DD-12). *The Journal of Violence and Gender*. 2(3), 1–16.

Violence Against Women Reauthorization Act (VAWA) 34 CFR § 668.46(j) (2)(v), 2013.

Warren, L., Mullen, P., & McEwan, T. (2014). Explicit threats of violence. In *The international handbook of threat assessment*. J.R. Meloy & J. Hoffmann, eds. (Oxford University Press, New York, NY), pp. 18–38.

White, J.W., & Smith, P.H. (2004). *A longitudinal perspective on physical and sexual intimate partner violence against women*. (National Institute of Justice, NCJ 199708, Washington, DC).

White, M., & Epston, D. (1990). *Narrative means to therapeutic ends*. (W.W Norton & Company, New York, NY).

White House Task Force to Protect Students From Sexual Assault. (2014). *Not alone: The first report of the White House Task Force to Protect Students From Sexual Assault*. Retrieved from https://www.notalone.gov/assets/report.pdf

Willingham, A. (2013). Frat chapter suspended over "rapebait" email. HLN? Retrieved on May 24, 2015, from www.hlntv.com

Zapp, D. (2014). *What have we learned about sexual assault from over half a million incoming college students?* (EverFi Coalition, Washington, DC).

Zuckerman, M. (1994). *Behavioral expressions and biosocial bases of sensation seeking*. (Cambridge University Press, Cambridge, UK).

Zuckerman, M. (2007). *Sensation seeking and risky behavior*. (American Psychological Association, Washington, DC).

Index

Delta Kappa Epsilon, rape chants 266
denigrating messages, sending 90
depersonalization 47; factor, defining 48–9; group, addressing 50–2; individual, addressing 49–50; risk reduction 58; support 183; target 49; thoughts/behaviors 16
depression, experience 92
de Saint-Exupéry, Antoine 47
desensitization, obsessive pornography (impact) 63
desperation, feelings 57
destructive decisions 173
developmental sanctions, placement 72–3
development (promotion), social experiences (impact) 33
deviant fantasies, suffering requirement 195
Diagnostic and Statistical Manual of Mental Disorders (addiction definition) 67
direct assaults 96
direct threat, absence 110
Dirty Dozen (DD-12) 14, 217; cultural perspectives 261–2
Dirty Dozen (DD-12) risk factors: multidisciplinary approach 18–20; overview 17
discrepancy, development 190
disease, sexually transmitted disease (comparison) 70–1
Disney, Walt 234
dissemination mechanisms, increase 37
diversity, embracing 92
domestic violence: definitions, impact 6; grooming behaviors, subtlety 106; incidents, reporting requirements (increase) 4; institution prohibition statement 6; sexual violence form, recognition (rarity) 15; situations, male abuse 93–4;

student/employee report 85–6; term, usage 8; threats, form 78; threats/ultimatums, occurrence 77
dominant liaison, biological imperative 97
double-down 138
double penetration (d.p.), viewing 66
DQ30 172
drinking: education, lessons 227–8; problem, example 162
drunk hookup culture 269; confrontation 271–2
duty of care 38

early childhood addictive/impulsive behaviors, history 195
early childhood messages 88–9
early prevention education 256
early problem behaviors 19
educational activities/learning, domains 29
educational efforts 35
educational sanctions, placement 72–3
educational training module 158
education efforts: combination 14–15; improvement 13
ejaculation 111
Ellis, Albert 171–2
Emergency Medical Service (EMS), arrival 165
emergency planning 86
emotional isolation 57
emotional stress, creation 85–6
emotions: management 30; up-and-down quality 182
empathizing, assistance 187
empathy 116–17; challenge 164; development, strategies 260; expression 188; initiation 166–7; loss, words/ideas (impact) 53; sympathy, difference 158–9; teaching 166–8, 259–60

problem 267–8; stakeholders, presence (recognition) 99
Fraternity Gang Rape 81
fraternity members: conduct, treatment 100; isolation 81–2
fraternity membership: communications, prompting 101–2; control 81; requirements, demands 112
Freud, Sigmund 208
Friends (TV show) 64
friendships, vector 31
friends, isolation 108, 109
Frost, Robert 88
Full Moon on the Quad (Stanford University campus activity) 245
future behaviors (prediction), past behaviors (usage) 210, 211

Gaiman, Neil 106
gangbang, viewing 66
gang rape, result 81–2
Gattuso, Reina 91, 97
Gay Lesbian Bisexual Transsexual (GLBT) support meeting, example 156
gender-based sexual violence, risk factors (reduction) 238
gender-based stereotypes 97
gender-based violence 16; bystander intervention/empowerment, usage 212; mitigation 223–4; nice guys/bad boys, relationship 95; prevention 24; problems, gender contribution 139; reduction 48; risk 127, 149; risk, increase 209
gender bias 103–4
gendered violence: impact 95; naming 96; problems 94–5
gender group, rejection 52
gender hierarchies, reinforcement 89
gender representation, diversity (embracing) 92
gender roles 16

genders, mix (inequality) 111
genogram: creation 173; sample *174*
Genovese, Kitty (murder) 270–1
genuineness, sense (conveying) 166
Georgia Tech fraternity, "7Es of Hooking Up" 111
Girls Gone Wild 49
gonzo market 66
"Good Boy" orientation 33
"Good Girl" orientation 33
Gordon, Robert Jr. 26; typology, usage 27
Gordon's Operational Classification 26–7, 38
governing example 79–80
grading, bias (role) 224
Greek Life staff, interaction 28
Green Dot, The 86
Green, Laci 70
green ladies 52
grooming behaviors 106; addressing 114; application 107; coercion, combination 78; environments 153; factor, defining 107–9; group, addressing 111–12; impact 111; individual, addressing 109; risk reduction 115–20; stalking, relationship 106; usage 107, 123–4
groups: behavior, problems 98; choices, reduction 109; creation 138; culture, sex focus 68; events, elements 72; group-level risk factors (fraternities/sororities) 266; indicators 68; isolation 108; negative group behaviors, impact 211–12; objectification 108–9; online interaction 93; risk factors, presence 20; settings, responsibility diffusion 60; sex, focus 71; sexualization 93
group theory 50; indications 182–3

Lesbian, Gay, Bisexual, Transgender and Queer Student Association 27
lesbian sexual experiences 97–8
liaisons, establishment 36–7
life changes 171
Lincoln, Abraham 24
Lisak, David 217
listening ability, demonstration 167
loss, feelings 57
Lower, Steve 68

maintenance (change theory) 175, 206–7
male abuse 93–4
male-dominated society, impact 48
male friends, impact 21
male-on-male rape scenario 160
male peer-support model (DeKeseredy) 20
male perspective 89
males: internal inhibitions, undermining 66; social inhibitions, undermining 66–7
male sexual scripts, peer group effect 91–2
Mann, Grace Rebecca 139
marginalized group, harm 137
masculine attitudes, problems 88
masculine ideology, sexual aggression (association) 90–1
masculinity: defining, aggression/ dominance (relationship) 96–7; philosophy, perspective 97; strengthening 98
masculinity, achievement 92
masturbation 151
McCaskill, Claire 266
McCreary, Gentry 214, 266
men: empathy, increase 160; favoritism 91; natural aggression, belief 144
menstruation, occurrence 66
mental health history 18

microaggressions 90; addressing 104, 260–1; examples 103; response 102–4
microinsults 102–3
microinvalidations 102; example 103
military organizations, threat cultures 82
millennials, empathy absence (accusation) 166
mindfulness 167
minor conduct infractions 68
misandry 139
misogynistic attitudes 88, 91–2; understanding 218
misogynistic behaviors 88
misogynistic ideology 65, 88, 136, 138; factor, defining 89–92; group, addressing 93–4; individual, addressing 92–3; risk reduction 96–8; support 125
misogyny, definition 88–9
MIT Community Attitudes on Sexual Assault 250
molestation: example 214–16; secrecy 215
monster, identity 57
mood-altering events 194
moral development, theory (Kohlberg) 32–4
moral disengagement: examination 59–61; initiatives 60–1
morality, levels 33
moral justification, usage 59
morals, exploration 50–1
motivation, absence 189
motivational enhancement therapy (MET), development 188
motivational interviewing (MI) 179, 187–90
movement, concept 150
movies, degrading/offensive comments 72

off-campus party, problems 52
off-campus police, involvement 206
offenses, reoccurrence 36
Office Hoes, women objectification 52
Office of Civil Rights guidance 243
on-campus police, involvement 206
on-campus treatment 177
one-track mind, example 141–2
on guard, perpetual state 83
online educational module, Title IX coordinator review 30, 37
open communication 118
open-ended questions, usage 189
Operational Classification (Gordon) 26–7, 38
opinion, diversity 137
oppression, root factor 16
oral sex: pornography, relationship 199; videos, collection 197
organization: accountability 98–102; grooming behavior 111; risk factors, presence 20
organizational accountability efforts, reward 99
organizational behaviors, impact 52
organizational change, initiation 146
organizational climate concerns, remedy 100
organizational conduct, sanctioning 100
organizational leadership, information (gathering) 101–2
orientation events 166
otherness, teaching 166–8, 259–60
O'Toole, Mary Ellen 113, 154

Paperchase, The 235
paraphilias, defining 195
paraphilic behaviors, consideration 195
paraphilic sexual behaviors 193
partialism 195

partners: behaviors, control 138; idea, perpetrator property 138; interaction 119; needs/wants, empathetic understanding 117; violent degradation 64
partygoers, communication 52
party themes 52
past experiences 208; culture, impact 214–16; example 212; factor, defining 210; group, addressing 211–14; individual, addressing 211; risk reduction 216
patience, sense (requirement) 58
patriarchy: examination 91; impact 88; understanding, importance 91
peer group: effect 91–2; expectations 22
peer pressure, impact 22
permission, getting 239–40
perpetration: repetition 217; risk, increase 210
perpetrators: men, majority 16; outing 215; portrayal 14; rehabilitation 168; term, usage 8–9; women, flirting (absence) 54
Perry, Miranda 240
personal goals, achievement 48
personal information, sharing 79
personality: diminishment/trivialization 48; trait, pattern (absence) 56; types, conflict (relationship) 177
personal vulnerability, denial 162
person movements/location, stalking/tracking 107
petting, foreplay perspective 231
Phi Kappa Tau Fraternity (Georgia Tech), suspension 94
physical presence, impact 108
physiological survival mechanism 47
pictures, sharing 68

reporting requirements (increase)
4; institution prohibition
statement 6; risk factors,
understanding (importance)
7; term, usage 8
Static-99 score, usage 18–19
Steinbeck, John 229
Step Up! 86
story, belief (balance approach)
218–19
"stranger in the bushes" trope
94–5
stranger rape 89
strategic curriculum, design
process 36
strategic prevention efforts 27
straw men 94–6
streetlight effect 263
strippers, commonness 68
student conduct officers: involvement
201; police report examination
142; training 14
students: communities, vector 31;
conduct, system 72; cultural
experiences 92; development
programs/services, vector
31; faculty, relationship
31, 82; imagery, impact
129–30; in-depth treatment
203; intervention plan 155;
organizations, training 208;
outcomes, tracking initiatives
251; point of view, respect
188; prevention education/
engagement 257–8; prevention
programming 4; protection,
failure (example) 214–16;
refund demand 92; role-plays,
usage 237–8; self-expression,
right 212–13; staff,
distancing 189
subservient liaison, biological
imperative 97
substance abuse 18; addictive
sexual behaviors, relationship

209; relationships 172–3;
screening measure 172
substance use 123, 127
suicidal ideation 18, 57
suicidal intent 57
superficial emotional
responsiveness 19
support, challenge (balance) 32
support networks, establishment
168
surprise, absence 67–8
survivors: men, empathy (increase)
160; party/complainant,
term (usage) 8; recollections
199–201; support 13
Swinton, Daniel 25
sympathy, empathy (difference)
158–9
synergism 170
synthesis, involvement 30

tagging 101, 102
Take Back the Night rally 40
Tallon-Hicks, Yana 233
"tea and consent" video, usage
(example) 212
teaching vector 31
technology, usage 235
teenage sexually addictive/
impulsive behaviors,
history 195
Texas Tech University, all-male
organization (prominence)
245
theory, limitations 24
theory of identity development
(Chickering) 30–2
theory of moral development
(Kohlberg) 32–4
therapy, usefulness 177
third-party establishments,
participation 128–9
third-party vendors, organizational
usage 133
Thoreau, Henry David 255

threat assessment 155, 213; factors 20
"Threat Assessment in a Campus Setting" (Sokolow et al.) 138
threat escalation, pattern 149; case study 153–4; factor, defining 150–1; group, addressing 152–3; individual, addressing 151–2; risk reduction 154–7
threats 76; cultures 82; determinations, continuation 216–17; direct threat, absence 110; escalation 77–8; example 79–80; factor, defining 77–8; group, addressing 81–3; implied threats 78; individual, addressing 79–81; occurrence, written form 77; overt threats 84, 86; risk reduction 84; sexual violence form 76–7; strategies, escalation risk 154; subtle threats 84, 86; usage 76; weapons, usage 18
Tieder, Becca 229
Title IX: cases, complainant 55; challenge 9–11; conduct, impact 11; efforts, reemergence 99; guidance 38; impact 40; investigations 20, 226; mandate 11; overview 9–10, 243; requirements 3; staff, training 217–19; threats 213
Title IX coordinator: alert 134; case review, example 25; Human Resources interaction 28–9; incidents, sexual misconduct (relationship) 32; liaison contact 27, 36–7; offenses consideration 34; online educational module review 30; prevention strategy 35; RA reports examination

32; residence hall incidents examination 28–9
Title IX incidents: conduct officer/hearing board review 122; specialized investigators, hiring 15
Title IX investigators 126; training 14, 128
tolerance level, knowledge 114
torture pornography, possession 203
Tough Guise 97
tracking 107
train-the-trainer-type programs, engagement 93
transportation options, safety plan outline 86
trashcan punch 127
trauma: histories 199; negative past experiences 219–20
trigger events, occurrence 171

ultimatums 76; escalation 77–8; factor, defining 77–8; group, addressing 81–3; individual, addressing 79–81; occurrence, written form 77; overt ultimatums 84, 86; risk reduction 84; sexual violence form 76–7; subtle ultimatums 84, 86; usage 76
underage students, alcohol (serving) 127
unhealthy relationships, dangers 115
United States Institute of Medicine, Gordon typology usage 27
universal prevention 26
universities: hostile environment prevention/elimination, Title IX requirements 3; VAWA prevention programming requirements 5–7